MYTHS
Shattered and Restored

Proceedings of the Association
for the Study of Women and Mythology

Volume 1

Edited by
Marion Dumont and Gayatri Devi

Printed in the United States of America
ISBN: 978-0-9969617-2-1

Published by

Women and Myth Press
www.womenandmyth.org
An imprint of Goddess Ink

Interior and cover designed by Rebekkah Dreskin
www.blameitonrebekkah.com
Front cover art "Bee Goddess Rhodes Banner" by Lydia Ruyle
Bee Goddess logo by Sid Reger
Line drawing of Our Lady of Aparecida by Loona Houck (pg. 174)
Photo of bust of Persephone, Getty Villa at the Sanctuaries of Demeter and Persephone
Morgantina Exhibit, 2012 by Alexis Martin Faaberg (pg. 273)
Photo of Spring Fresco, National Archaeological Museum of Athens, Greece, 2012
by Alexis Martin Faaberg (pg. 267)

To Patricia Monaghan

Across time and space, we place this book in your hands today. Without you it would still be just a shared dream. We honor your tireless dedication to goddess scholarship in all its forms and remember you in so many ways: as researcher, author, editor, poet, mentor, advisor, co-conspirator—but most of all, as our friend.

CONTENTS

FOREWORD

W hy, in a time when there are many women's studies and gender studies departments, are these articles from Association for the Study of Women and Mythology(ASWM) events worthy of presentation in a separate volume under the general topic of goddess studies?

Goddess spirituality is the most radical expression of women's studies. The inclusion of the feminine divine is more necessary than ever, because the patriarchal, competitive, warlike masculine divine in most religions has been overemphasized. Our received heritage of warrior gods has nothing to do with the human necessities of love, connection, healing and reframing our relationship with our planet, whereas the goddess archetype is associated with life-affirming spiritual beliefs, connection with the human family, and the nurturance of others and our planet. These beliefs can run very deep in the psyches of modern women and men.

It is necessary to re-integrate study with belief.

Our studies are not only about equal pay or status but also about the deepest sources of inspiration for new and restorative ideas and actions that support those ideas.

For some women, it is important to work within traditional religions and to bring about change from that perspective. But it is also important to carve out space to inspire new perspectives and scholarship. Goddess studies foster the creative impulse of all people who are hungry for a new paradigm, one that integrates experience and belief with scholarly pursuits.

Such scholarship does not belong only to the academy. There are independent scholars, artists and performers who contribute to research and to our understanding of the importance of goddess- and woman-oriented scholarship. ASWM events and publications exist to nourish this broad community of scholars.

It is not possible to introduce this volume or series without acknowledging the immeasurable contributions of ASWM co-founder Patricia Monaghan. Through decades of social change, she never lost the vision of a community that would foster new types of scholarship that reflect women's experiences. When she discovered in Sid Reger another scholar who held the same vision, she insisted that they create an organization that would both recognize foremothers and assist emerging scholars, and thus ASWM was born.

Patricia was a great teacher, inside and outside of the academy. Her intelligence and energy were brought to bear in all of her many projects. She was always generous with her time, and she encouraged students everywhere. She also encouraged colleagues, remembering in her brilliant mind and huge heart what was important to them, from their largest dreams to small details about their lives. Patricia also presented me with the 2012 Sarasvati Book Award for *Sacred Display*, co-authored with Victor Mair. As if the award were not enough, Patricia presented me with a box of Fannie May chocolates – a favorite of my family throughout my childhood, as Patricia knew. The memory of her kindness is as sweet as the chocolates.

Those of us who continue to support goddess scholarship believe that this volume will please Patricia, if she is looking over our shoulders today.

Miriam Robbins Dexter, Ph.D.
Los Angeles, CA

INTRODUCTION

Today's history becomes tomorrow's myths. This exceptional collection of essays is a valued contribution toward contemporary feminist and womanist efforts to re-cover the *herstory* of mythology and to ensure that today's herstory is not forsaken in tomorrow's myths. This anthology reflects the mission of the Association for the Study of Women and Mythology (ASWM) to elucidate aspects of the sacred feminine through scholarly and creative explorations in the fields of women's spirituality, goddess studies and women-centered mythology. The writings presented in this volume serve to strengthen and support the circle of women and men who share a scholarly passion for sacred myths by and about women.

Mythology is the branch of knowledge or field of study of the important stories we tell ourselves that enable us to gather meaning in our daily lives. Imaginative analogues to our lived experience, myths are cultural and spiritual stories that arise out of humanity's experience of life on earth. Myths speak to a deep and real desire in us to understand our context here on earth while yearning to comprehend our connection to our ancestors and our roots, to share experiences that transcend binaries and boundaries, and to envision the future from a liminal present. Myths allow us to see ourselves as both timeless and historical beings. Through awakening belief, mythic stories afford us an opportunity to participate in a non-material realm, a realm of sacred, creative power, whose intimations we experience in our encounters with ourselves and with the world around us through a multitude of modalities, such as ritual, art, storytelling and dance. They are the threads that link our present with our past and serve to shape our future.

The twelve essays in this collection explore various facets of myths that specifically address the cosmic as well as the immanent arrangement and situatedness of the sacred feminine, from historical to contemporary times, and its implications for women's lives everywhere. They range from discussions of archaeomythology and its methodological contributions to understand and interpret the sacred feminine from their cultural matrices to detailed explorations of specific foundational women-centered myths such as those of Demeter and Persephone, Ariadne and the Labyrinth, the black Madonna, Artemis and Sakti/Devi. These essays also explore the power and capacity of myths to directly institute change in our personal lives, by means such as reconceptualizing healthcare through curanderismo or grounding a feminist and spiritual model of power sharing and sacred sisterhood through the stories of collective female deities.

Our opening essay, "Archaeomythology as Academic Field and Methodology: Bridging Science and Religion, Empiricism and Spirituality," by Mara Lynn Keller provides an overview of Marija Gimbutas and the field of archaeomythology as it relates to goddess studies and feminist mythology. The work of Marija Gimbutas has been instrumental in providing support for a contemporary, feminist interpretation of myths that allows for the inclusion of women and women's worldview. Keller provides an overview of Gimbutas's archaeomythology methodology and its impact on practitioners of feminist spirituality and mythology studies: "As the next generations of researchers apply similar epistemological approaches and practical methodologies to infer sacred symbols and mythic narratives from the material artifacts of ancient peoples, we will benefit from clarifying our understanding of this relatively new academic field and its distinctive methodology."

Joan Cichon, in her essay "Archaeomythology from Neolithic Malta to Modern Poland: Apprehending the Material and Spiritual Realities of Ancient and Present-Day Cultures," elaborates on the methodology of archaeomythology as it applies to three different cultural matrices. In discussing goddess-related historical and current phenomena in Malta, Turkey and Poland, Cichon demonstrates, in particular, archaeomythology's ability to create a "gestalt that makes sense of a variety of data" as opposed to proving or disproving individual details.

In "Honoring the Web: Indigenous Wisdom and the Power of Place," Arieahn Matamonasa-Bennett discusses the "cocreative" influence of geography on the "metaphoric mind" or "nature mind" of indigenous and earth-based communities to heal "soul wounds" that result from a damaged relationship to one's place in the world. Matamonasa-Bennet discusses productive ways to incorporate the wisdom of the metaphoric mind of the indigenous people in mythology studies: "A value that indigenous people around the world share is that they must preserve their stories, languages, customs, songs and philosophies, because these sustain life—the life of individuals, the life of families, the life of communities and the life of our planet. Stories are particularly important, because they integrate ancestral wisdom and hold the essence of people's spiritual being through time and place." Matamonasa-Bennett argues that, insofar as myths speak to certain fundamental human experiences accessible through rituals, ceremony and artistic expressions, particularly story-telling or "medicine," they sustain life and have the capacity to redress the spiritual wounds brought by our disconnection from place and nature.

In imaginative forms, through narratives and poems, myths often contain historical, cultural and spiritual truths that have survived the passage of time. Today, women are re-evaluating and re-presenting myths in order to reclaim aspects of truths that have been suppressed by a predominantly male-populated field of study. In "Ariadne, Mistress of the Labyrinth: Reclaiming Ariadnian Crete," Alexandra K. Cichon retells and reinterprets the myth of Ariadne's labyrinth from a Jungian mythological perspective, in the process debunking the patriarchal narratives of Ariadne as Minos's daughter and Theseus's lover. Cichon's analysis contextualizes the Ariadne myth that was meshed with the myths of a Dionysian great mother or moon goddess prevalent in the Mediterranean and Asia Minor regions, drawing attention to the transboundary formulations of key goddess myths.

Likewise, Mary Beth Moser in "Wild Women of the Waters: Remembering the Anguane of the Italian Alps" leads us through an entire folk and myth cycle pertaining to these water deities of the Italian Alps and their immanent presence in the lives of villagers from antiquity to modern times. In Moser's treatment of the myth, we see the applied meaning and value of mythic deities to influence the full life cycle of a woman from birth to death and spiritual regeneration.

The work to reclaim female deities intentionally for women is continued in Denise Saint Arnault's "Artemis as Protectress of Female Mysteries: Modern Worship in the Dianic Tradition in America," in which she discusses the relationship between Artemis myths and mysteries and the feminist goddess religious practitioners of the Dianic tradition. Artemis, although identified with wilderness in mainstream mythology, is specifically a deity of girls and women, as exemplified in the accounts of her temples, extant literature, symbols and rituals. Arnault describes how the specific female mythic energy associated with Artemis is indispensible to Dianic followers because it allows women to celebrate the unique body and biology of women as a complete gender that transcends the male-female binary.

The cultural cross-pollination of myths is explored in April Heaslip's "Securely Attached: Brazilians and their Black Madonnas," which discusses the syncretic worship of Yemanja and Nossa Senhora Aparecida in Brazil to chart the complex give-and-take that occurs when myths and meanings fuse across cultures and evolve with time and material, historical changes. Heaslip's discussion posits the Black Madonna of Brazil as a female protectress in the goddess tradition through the hybrid identity of the Yemanja/Madonna.

The cross-cultural scope and power of myth to effect deep soul healing and psychic integration is discussed in Natasha Redina's "Weaving Cross-cultural Narratives: Curanderismo and Psychotherapy." After providing a succinct overview of the complex practices of curanderismo, Redina argues that the ritual praxis embodied in curanderismo helps those suffering from psychic wounds to heal themselves by helping them to connect with archetypal processes and emotions in the manner in which we understand the benefits of psychotherapy in the Western world.

Continuing the cross-cultural approach to goddess and mythology studies, in "The Goddess and the Myth of Citizen Rights," Gayatri Devi and Savithri Shanker de Tourreil demonstrate the timeless power of myths to reframe, re-energize and re-interrogate established and hegemonic narratives about the status of women within mainstream patriarchal Indian ethos. The authors discuss Indian tribal activist Mahasweta Devi's retelling of the myth of Draupadi in her short story "Draupadi" from the Indian national epic *Mahabharata* to challenge the mythic grounds of women's abjection through the counterpoint of a goddess myth.

The archaeomythological investigation into goddess myths is continued in Joan M. Cichon's "Demeter and the Eleusinian Mysteries: Ancient Origins and Modern Impact," in which the Eleusinian mysteries are read as an amalgamation of goddess cults of ancient Crete and the patriarchal religion of Mycenae and the Greek mainland. Drawing upon a rich trove of mythological and linguistic sources, Cichon's analysis demonstrates the enduring significance of the Demeter-Persephone myth for women to access the great solidarity of daughter-mother, soul and its home dyad across all cultures and all times. As Cichon's inspired reading of the myth affirms, most women, unlike Persephone, live the myth backwards: They live in the world of fathers and Hades most of their lives and have to travel back to reunite with their mothers.

Our experiences and the forces that shape our lives evolve into the myths that inform future generations. In Alexis Martin Faaberg's "The Three Faces of Persephone: Cup, Demoted Sproutling and Disembodied Psychosis," the original representations and later appropriations and interpretations of the Persephone figure are viewed through a feminist lens. Faaberg argues that the Persephone myth is one of the earliest examples of a myth of female community and that the abduction and rape of Persephone is a downgrading of this female community in preference for the patriarchal order of marriage. Faaberg cautions that contemporary interpretations of Persephone's return to Demeter from Hades see it as rebirth, with perhaps intentional or unintentional sanctioning of violence against women as intrinsic to their self-discovery. Myths help us to maintain our connection between the material and the spiritual; they are important in helping us to celebrate the mundane and the sacred. Faaberg writes, "Women's spirituality is the lens by which women experience religion. Most often, these experiences are rooted in the daily rituals in which family, maternal bonds, food, dance and song coalesce into a spiritual life."

The mythos of a sacred female collective fittingly bookends this collection of essays. The myth of a sacred female collective and the personal, social and spiritual implications of conceiving self and a deity as composed of an integrated yet well-defined sisterhood as opposed to a monolithic divinity is explored in Dawn E. Work-Makinne's "Deity in Sisterhood: The Collective Sacred Female in Germanic Europe." Discussing the European tradition's sacred goddess collectives, such as Deae Matronae, the Norns, the Dísir, Drei Heiligen Jungfrauen, et al., Work-Makinne points out that collective divinities appear to belong selectively to the domain of goddesses and that male god collectives are a rarity. Work-Makinne's analysis posits interesting connections among the values of cooperation, consensus and power sharing as opposed to domination, oppression and submission.

These essays highlight the importance of women's scholarly contributions to mythology, which allow for a more holistic representation of humanity's experience and the meaning found in our myths. Myths from Malta, Crete, India, Brazil, Italy, Poland, North America, Mexico and Germany are highlighted in this anthology. And, although we cannot claim a wider cultural

5

representation, we are grateful for these insightful conceptual and pragmatic analyses that will prove to be a valuable resource for scholars of women's spirituality and goddess studies.

We also note with distinct pleasure that all of these essays speak to the profound personal experience and intentional, conscious valorization of these myths by the authors in their personal lives. Thus, these essays are not merely intellectual exercises. They model transformative scholarship at its personal and intellectual best. Through the authors' commitment to academic excellence and authentic analyses and their willingness to engage with the personal, we are given to understand the power of myth to heal and restore both communal and personal peace and psychic balance. It is not surprising that in these essays we find important implications for the empowerment and celebration of contemporary women and their worlds. As Joan M. Cichon asserts in her remarkable essay, "Demeter and the Eleusinian Mysteries: Ancient Origins and Modern Impact," "Writing this article has been a great blessing for me. I was able to uncover evidence linking Demeter to Bronze Age Crete, which was very satisfying to the archaeomythologist part of me, and I finally was able to deeply relate to the myth. I believe these two events are connected. . . . Confirming through my own research the myth's ancient roots was immediately healing."

The essays in this collection affirm the central role of feminist spirituality in women accepting and acknowledging our sacred origins and ongoing divine guidance in everyday life.

Gayatri Devi
Lock Haven, Pennsylvania

Marion Dumont
Seattle, Washington

ARCHAEOMYTHOLOGY AS ACADEMIC FIELD AND METHODOLOGY: BRIDGING SCIENCE AND RELIGION, EMPIRICISM AND SPIRITUALITY

Mara Lynn Keller

The archaeologist Marija Gimbutas investigated the material culture of Neolithic Europe and discovered a mythic spiritual culture created by the indigenous peoples of Neolithic Europe. Gimbutas identified settlement patterns, household goods, burials and ritual equipment of the place and time she named Old Europe, which developed from ca. 7,500 to 3,500 BCE. From this empirical base in archaeology, she was able to decipher symbols used for spiritual communication. She interpreted the patterns of symbols in Old Europe as a goddess-centered mythology that represented powers of nature and the cosmos. Gimbutas named the research work she was doing *archaeomythology,* designating both a field of academic inquiry and a methodological approach, connecting scientific archaeology with the humanistic study of mythology. For further support for her mythological interpretations, she drew upon knowledge gleaned from the fields of linguistics, the history of religion and folklore.

As the next generations of researchers employ complex epistemological approaches and practical methodologies to infer sacred symbols and mythic narratives from the material artifacts of ancient peoples, we will benefit from clarifying our understanding of this relatively new academic field and its distinctive methodology. I first provide an introduction to Gimbutas's archaeomythology as academic field and methodology. Second, I discuss the underlying assumptions of archaeomythology as articulated by the archaeomythology scholar Joan Marler, and I survey the growth of archaeomythology since Gimbutas's death in 1994. Third, I provide an elaboration of the methodology of archaeomythology, noting its overlap with spiritual feminist hermeneutics. I close with some comments on the usefulness of archaeomythology for scholars of goddess studies, women's spirituality, and religious studies, which are my primary areas of research.[1]

I. Gimbutas and the Creation of Archaeomythology

Marija Gimbutas founded the academic field of archaeomythology in the latter part of the 20th century with a series of books published between 1974 and 1999: *The Goddesses and Gods of Old Europe, The Language of the Goddess, The Civilization of the Goddess: The World of Old Europe*, and *The Living Goddesses*. Her discoveries continue to inspire the work of many scholars today.[2] After completing extensive work on the Bronze Age cultures of the Baltic region, Gimbutas began to excavate the cultural remains of Neolithic Europe.

To her surprise, and in sharp contrast to her earlier study of Eastern European Bronze Age societies with their proliferation of bronze weapons and warfare, Gimbutas found in the Neolithic settlements of southeastern Europe a lack of weapons used for war and a preponderance of female figures decorated with enigmatic markings. Once the more scientific labors of archaeological survey, excavation, restoration, dating and assemblage had been completed, she turned to the task of deciphering the symbolic signs carved, painted or incised on the archaeological artifacts.

Gimbutas's publication in 1974 of *The Gods and Goddesses of Old Europe: 7000–3500 BC: Myths and Cult Images*[3] broke new ground for post-World War II archaeology, inferring from the archaeological record the mythologies and cosmological orientations of Old European and early Indo-European societies. Marler, a colleague, friend and biographer of Gimbutas, noted that Gimbutas first "began to develop a multidisciplinary approach to the study of prehistory during her student years in Lithuania" for her Master's thesis on Baltic prehistory (written 1940–1942) and that Gimbutas drew upon "archaeology, linguistics, mythology, ethnography, and the study of historical sources."[4] At that time, and into the 1980s, combining the sciences and humanities was largely shunned by elite academics as not being serious.

Gimbutas's next book meticulously analyzed the signs and symbols on the figurines, pottery, house models and grave goods of Old European peoples, symbols that were repeated over and again through generations and across millennia, in patterns related to their usage. From her careful analysis of these signs and symbols, Gimbutas argued that she had discovered a proto-language of symbolic communication that she called "the language of the Goddess."

Given the disciplinary limitations of archaeology in the United States and England at that time, Gimbutas decided to name her multidisciplinary approach *archaeomythology*. In the introduction to *The Language of the Goddess*, published in 1989, she asserted, "This volume is a study in archaeomythology, a field that includes archaeology, comparative mythology and folklore."[5]

In *The Language of the Goddess*, Gimbutas summarized her process for understanding the Neolithic symbolism as a complex system of meaning. The symbols "constitute a complex system in which every unit is interlocked with every other in what appear to be specific categories. No symbol can be treated in isolation; understanding the parts leads to understanding the whole, which in turn leads to identifying more of the parts."[6] The symbols are hieroglyphic or abstract (shaped, for example, like M, V, X, Y, tri-lines, triangles and meanders) or representational (for example, stylized breasts, pregnant bellies, vulvas, phalluses, water birds, snakes and bears).

As she studied the symbolic imagery of Old Europe, Gimbutas came to understand that these markings were connected to nature and to the people's sense of the divine within nature. "Symbols are seldom abstract in any genuine sense," she explained. "Their ties with nature persist, to be discovered through the study of context and association. In this way we can hope to decipher the mythical thought which is the *raison d'être* of this art and basis of its form."[7]

Gimbutas proposed that the Old European symbols represented the forces and functions of nature embedded in the lives of women and men, in plants and animals and insects, in mountain, forest, sea, sun, moon, stars and all the myriad elements of nature and the cosmos. She interpreted the religious symbolism of Neolithic Old Europe as implying spiritual beliefs in a goddess or goddesses of birth and nurture, death and regeneration, and in a god or gods as consort and life-giving stimulus to the life-giving powers of the goddess(es).

About the connections of Old European symbols to the term *Goddess*, the ecofeminist philosopher, cultural historian and women's spirituality scholar Charlene Spretnak explained:

> After decades of study of the ritually placed art and artifacts and the symbol system of the pre-Indo-European cultures of southeastern Neolithic Europe, Gimbutas used the term *Goddess* to refer to the diverse visual and folkloric imagery of metaphor and symbol behind which lies a complex of concepts expressing an awareness of embeddedness, participatory consciousness, and the immanence of the sacred. . . . Encompassing the cosmological drama of the changing seasons, the bounty of the land, and the cycles of endless regeneration, "The Goddess in all her manifestations, [Gimbutas concluded], was a symbol of the unity of all life in Nature."[8, 9]

Gimbutas did not restrict her focus to a single geographical region but kept expanding the scope of her studies. She discovered that the symbols she was studying had "systematic associations in the Near East, southeastern Europe, the Mediterranean area, and in central, western, and northern Europe." Furthermore, through these cross-regional studies, Gimbutas concluded that the symbols and their associations demonstrated "the extension of the same Goddess religion to all of these regions as a cohesive and persistent ideological system."[11]

In her magnum opus, *The Civilization of the Goddess: The World of Old Europe*, published in 1991 and edited by Marler, Gimbutas noted again that the econometric focus of archaeologists caused them to ignore and miss the significance of the religious dimensions of ancient cultures.

> Previous books on Neolithic Europe have focused on habitat, tool kits, pottery, trade, and environmental problems, treating religions as "irrelevant." This is an incomprehensible omission since secular and sacred life in those days were one and indivisible. By ignoring the religious aspects of Neolithic life, we neglect the totality of culture.

> Archaeologists cannot remain scientific materialists for-
> ever, neglecting a multidisciplinary approach. . . . Neolithic
> social structure and religion were intertwined and were
> reflections of each other.[12]

Again, Gimbutas insisted that a multidisciplinary approach to the religious aspects of ancient culture is indispensable if one hopes to understand an ancient people's patterns of belief. "A combination of fields—archaeology, mythology, linguistics, and historical data—provides the possibility for apprehending both the material and spiritual realities of prehistoric cultures."[13]

But even more controversial than her use of multiple disciplines to study religion implied by the archaeological record was Gimbutas's claim to have discovered a goddess-centered civilization in old Europe. Moreover, she claimed this civilization was peaceful, egalitarian, artistic and prosperous.

> Archaeologists and historians have assumed that civ-
> ilization implies a hierarchical political and religious
> organization, warfare, a class stratification, and a com-
> plex division of labor. . . . I reject the assumption that
> civilization refers only to androcratic warrior societies.
> The generative basis of any civilization lies in its degree
> of artistic creation, aesthetic achievements, nonmaterial
> values, and freedom which make life meaningful and
> enjoyable for all its citizens, as well as a balance of pow-
> ers between the sexes. Neolithic Europe was not a time
> "before civilization.". . . It was, instead, a true civilization
> in the best meaning of the word.[14]

This was a metanarrative that many of Gimbutas's colleagues found too extraordinary to accept.[15] The idea of a goddess-revering civilization at the root of European culture seemed preposterous to many, and it was mocked by some archaeologists and some religious scholars. Why is unclear. The challenge of the evidence for a peaceful, artistic, matristic and goddess-centered civilization in early Europe—which counters the long-prevailing assumption that universal male dominance, primary male gods, warfare and empire-building have always been the dominant ways of life—was too much for some to acknowledge even as a possibility.

While some of us welcomed Gimbutas's work enthusiastically, others made a concerted effort to distort and dismiss her work, as argued convincingly by Charlene Spretnak in "Anatomy of a Backlash: Concerning the Work of Marija Gimbutas."[16] Perhaps those who feel in harmony with Gimbutas's theory have internalized more of a pre-Indo-European cultural inheritance while those with an opposing view have internalized more of the Indo-European cultural inheritance. For whatever reasons, this conflict has been surprisingly deep and sharp, echoing what Gimbutas referred to as a "clash between these two ideologies and social and economic structures of cultures."[17]

In *The Civilization of the Goddess*, Gimbutas presented voluminous evidence that supported her claims.

> Old Europeans had towns with a considerable concentration of population, temples several stories high, a sacred script, spacious houses of four or five rooms, professional ceramicists, weavers, copper and gold metallurgists, and other artisans producing a range of sophisticated goods. A flourishing network of trade routes existed that circulated items such as obsidian, shells, marble, copper, and salt over hundreds of kilometers.[18]

This monumental work was illustrated with hundreds of images depicting dynamic symbols and mostly female and animal figures. Many figurines artfully merge the human female form with animal forms, and therefore are considered supernatural and divine.

Using comparative mythology, Gimbutas discerned contrasting symbolic, ideological and social systems for Neolithic Old Europe and Bronze Age Europe. Her conclusions remain controversial.

> The clash between these two ideologies and social and economic structures led to the drastic transformation of Old Europe. These changes were expressed as the transition from matrilineal to patrilineal order, from a learned theacracy to a militant patriarchy, from a sexually balanced society to a male-dominated hierarchy, and from a chthonic goddess religion to the Indo-European sky-oriented pantheon of gods.[19]

Archaeomythology was again the methodology for Gimbutas's last work about Old Europe and its cultural survivals, *The Living Goddesses*. This book discussed links between Old European religion and folkloric survivals in present-day European cultures. Gimbutas died on February 2, 1994. *The Living Goddesses* was published posthumously in 1999, edited and supplemented by her student and colleague, the linguist Miriam Robbins Dexter, also of the University of California at Los Angeles, where Gimbutas was a professor of archaeology from 1963 until her retirement in 1989. Dexter acknowledged that Gimbutas's work was controversial, "for she was an original thinker and strong in asserting her hypotheses. . . . She realized that the interpretation and interconnection of data are what lead to understanding and to a deep scientific contribution."[20]

Gimbutas's final four books founded the multidisciplinary academic field and methodology of archaeomythology. Although she used the scientific archaeological methods of her day, and whenever possible the most technologically advanced methods for dating artifacts, Gimbutas clearly acknowledged that her methodology was not strictly empiricist but also required interpretation, using intuition and artistic sensibilities. Gimbutas's research on the Goddess civilization of Neolithic Old Europe documented the "cohesive and persistent" symbol system of a "goddess religion" that stretched from Anatolia to the British Isles. She traced its transformation by the invasions of nomadic Indo-Europeans from northeastern Europe, which resulted in the mixture of these disparate cultures into the hybridized historical societies of Europe.

II. Archaeomythology and Its Working Assumptions

Marler conceptualized several of the "working assumptions" of the growing field of archaeomythology in her "Introduction to Archaeomythology," published in 2000. Each of these statements is significant, for they elucidate presuppositions that inform the process of archaeomythology.

- Sacred cosmologies are central to the cultural fabric of all early societies.

- Beliefs and rituals expressing sacred worldviews are conservative and are not easily changed.

- Many archaic cultural patterns have survived into the historical period as folk motifs and as mythic elements within oral, visual and ritual traditions.

- Symbols, preserved in cultural artifacts, "represent the grammar and syntax of a kind of meta-language by which an entire constellation of meanings is transmitted."[22, 23]

Together, these working assumptions provide a doorway and framework for the exploration of the spiritual beliefs and practices of ancient peoples.

In postmodern cultures of today that focus so intently on human constructs and language, it can be difficult for us to comprehend the embeddedness of ancient peoples in nature and their curiosity about the cosmos. But when approaching prehistorical cultures, it is plausible to assume that "sacred cosmologies are central to the cultural fabric of all early societies," as Marler stated in her first point above. Living as an integral part of the fabric of nature, Neolithic peoples were much more in tune with the elements, plants, animals, seasons and celestial sources of light than are urbanized and modernized people today.

Regarding Marler's second working assumption for the field of archaeomythology, that "beliefs and rituals expressing sacred worldviews are conservative and are not easily changed," we can provide several significant reasons for this. Beliefs and rituals were often created to secure survival. As Jane Ellen Harrison wrote in her 1913 work, *Ancient Art and Ritual*, "other things may be added to enrich and beautify human life, but, unless these [survival] wants are first satisfied, humanity itself must cease to exist. These two things, therefore, food and children, were what men [*sic*] chiefly sought to procure by the performance of magical rites."[24] Today we realize that rituals also serve the crucial need of creating group bonding, and therefore, again, have staying power. Rituals and beliefs that advance human survival become religious imperatives and are passed from one generation to the next.

This is one of the major reasons why religious conflicts are often so intransigent—they are tied to the differently perceived survival needs of different peoples. People come to explain the world to themselves in ways that become traditions, and then these traditions are sometimes held as if they were absolutely necessary to personal and group identity, to well-being as well as survival, as defined by one's own family or clan. Scholars of mythology argue, however, that these are not the only reasons why humans have created religious beliefs and practices.

Some religious beliefs and rituals have been created to respond to and engage with a felt sense of the sacredness and awesomeness of life, the powers of nature and all that is. People tell sacred stories or myths to explain life itself and their place in creation. They invent rituals to make manifest the mythos of divinity within material experience.

Marler's third point is that "many archaic cultural patterns have survived into the historical period as folk motifs and as mythic elements within oral, visual, and ritual traditions." This is affirmed by folklorists and historians of religion. We know that archaic cultural patterns persist in popular customs such as Christmas and Halloween, in fairy tales and even astronomy, as well as in the popularity of antiquities internationally. To state this point another way, folk motifs and mythic elements provide us with clues regarding earlier beliefs that have remained alive for long periods of time in popular culture, because of their survival value and also because of their connection to sacred cosmologies and traditions that express and renew people's spiritual feelings—including intense feelings of love, wonder, fear of the unknown, desires for healing, approaching and reconciling with death, and more.

What of Marler's fourth working assumption? Archaeomythology holds that "symbols, preserved in cultural artifacts, 'represent the grammar and syntax of a kind of meta-language by which an entire constellation of meanings is transmitted' (Gimbutas 1989, xxv)"? This claim is plausible, again, because religious symbols presuppose a spiritual realm of reference and values. The invisible dimension beyond the material realm, for most of human history has been deemed essential to people's survival, well-being, identity and connection with others, with nature and with the divine. This view was corroborated by the cultural anthropologist Clifford Geertz in his *Interpretation of Cultures*. Geertz saw the sacred stories and rituals of religion as infused with a set of cultural symbols and that "sacred symbols function to synthesize a people's ethos—the tone, character, and quality of their life, its moral and aesthetic style and mood—and their world view—the picture they have of the way things in sheer actuality are, their most comprehensive ideas of order."

These four working assumptions of Gimbutas's archaeomythology, as articulated by Marler, generate a framework that allows for both material and spiritual aspects of an ancient culture to be perceived and (to some extent) understood. It opens possibilities for the researcher to trace both material and spiritual changes from one era to another, from one place to another.

Eventually, Gimbutas's work was embraced by the Women's Spirituality Movement that emerged from the popular uprisings of the 1960s and 1970s during the era of the Vietnam War. Starr Goode, a feminist activist in Los Angeles, described the larger cultural context of the time: The year 1968 was a "tumultuous year, with the assassinations of Martin Luther King and Bobby Kennedy, the ongoing slaughter in Vietnam, [and] the military draft of students."[27]

> [In 1969] the [UCLA] campus became a combat zone of demonstrations over the War, People's Park, the near daily tear gas, the National Guard on street corners, curfews, mass arrests, a student shot to death. . . . We wanted the opportunity to learn how to protect ourselves from male violence. What passion we had, what a totality of commitment to our vision of a better world![28]

The LA Goddess Project that Goode initiated with friends produced special events for the publication of *The Language of the Goddess* in 1989 and *The Civilization of the Goddess* in 1991, which was documented on video as "Voice of the Goddess: Marija Gimbutas."[29] Another documentary of Gimbutas lecturing, this time at the California Institute of Integral Studies in San Francisco in 1990, was produced by psychologist and cultural historian Ralph Metzner: *Marija Gimbutas: World of the Goddess.*[30] Metzner is also the author of *The Well of Remembrance: Rediscovering the Earth Wisdom Myths of Northern Europe.* He drew upon Gimbutas's theory of Old European societies and their hybridization with Indo-European tribes to construct his fascinating discussion of the mythology of northern Europe.

Religious scholar and goddess theologian Carol P. Christ and religious scholar Naomi Goldenberg gathered several colleagues together and edited a collection of articles celebrating and defending Gimbutas and her work.

A special section titled "The Legacy of the Goddess: The Work of Marija Gimbutas" was published in 1996 in the leading feminist journal for religious studies, the *Journal of Feminist Studies in Religion*.[31]

In order to honor Gimbutas's breadth of scholarship and advance the development of the field of archaeomythology, Marler edited *From the Realm of the Ancestors: An Anthology in Honor of Marija Gimbutas*, a Festschrift published in 1997 and to which 56 colleagues, representing a wide range of disciplines, contributed. To welcome the publication of this book, Marler and I produced the international conference, "From the Realm of the Ancestors, Language of the Goddess," also sponsored by the California Institute of Integral Studies, where I was serving as director of the women's spirituality, philosophy and religion graduate program. Other events celebrating the life and work of Gimbutas and this Festschrift took place, most notably at the Smithsonian Institution in Washington, DC.

In 1998, Marler launched the Institute of Archaeomythology (IAM). It has "sponsored numerous international exhibitions, symposia, and other events on archaeomythological themes in collaboration with universities, academies, national museums, and other institutions located in the geographical area of Old Europe and beyond."[32] Marler, Dexter, the linguist and cultural scientist Harald Haarmann and other colleagues of Gimbutas have continued to grow the field of archaeomythology through international conferences, books, articles, courses in colleges and universities, and the open-access, online *Journal of Archaeomythology*.[33] Marler and Haarmann have written many articles and produced several books. Haarmann's most recent work, published in 2014, is titled *Roots of Ancient Greek Civilization: The Influence of Old Europe*.

The documentary *Signs Out of Time: The Life and Work of Marija Gimbutas*, created by filmmakers Donna Read and Starhawk, premiered in 2004. It projected the view that "determined and courageous, Marija Gimbutas stayed true to what she saw, amidst ridicule, criticism, and controversy. If her theories are correct, then reverence for the Earth, peace, and cooperation are the very underpinnings of European civilization."[34] Since 2004, the video has been distributed to colleges, universities and libraries in 48 states plus the District of Columbia in the United States and to countries on all of the habitable continents of the world. This is a testimony to the widespread appeal of Gimbutas's work around the world.

III. Archaeomythology Methodology and Goddess Studies

In this third section, I discuss the methodology of archaeomythology and how it overlaps with the women's spirituality methodology of spiritual feminist hermeneutics. Although I am a serious student of archaeology, I am not an archaeologist. My academic training has been in philosophy and religion, and I am primarily a women's spirituality and goddess studies scholar. I discuss the methodology of archaeomythology with a view toward its use in tandem with women's spirituality, goddess studies and religious studies more generally.

In 1999, Joan Marler hosted a conference on the beautiful western Greek island of Madouri about Archaeomythology: Taking the Disciplines Deeper. We were a gathering of archaeologists, linguists, religious scholars, folklorists, anthropologists, philosophers, artists, poets and others who were interested in creating new ways of bringing archaeomythology as methodology into our own disciplines.

As a woman of European heritage, I am interested in using archaeomythology research for deepening my knowledge of our goddess- and god-revering ancestors. When conducting field research about ancient myth and religion in Greece and Crete, I visit archaeological sites and museums repeatedly. I study the pertinent archaeological site reports and other archaeology texts written by the primary excavators, take relevant courses in archaeology, and talk with archaeologists in my areas of interest. I combine this archaeological knowledge with studies of mythology, with attention to linguistics, folklore and history of religions. I study the Bronze Age Linear A script of Crete and the Creto-Mycenaean Linear B script, and also Homeric and Attic Greek. I use the multiple disciplines that archaeomythology draws upon, for example, for my studies of the prepatriarchal, pre-Mycenaean cultures of ancient Crete, as well as my studies of the Eleusinian Mysteries of Demeter and Persephone. I also teach the methodology of archaeomythology to my students at the California Institute of Integral Studies when teaching my courses on "The Goddesses of Prehistory: An Archaeomythology" and "The Goddess and God Civilization of Ancient Crete."

I have learned much from the archaeomythology research of Gimbutas, Marler, Dexter, Haarmann and several doctoral students whose dissertation committees I have chaired. A primary example is the dissertation written by Joan Cichon, who applied an archaeomythology methodology in the research for her study, "Matriarchy in Ancient Crete: A Perspective from Archaeomythology and Modern Matriarchal Studies." She documented that the primary deity in ancient Crete was a mother goddess of nature; argued that ancient Crete was a woman-centered society; and correlated her archaeological findings with the definition of matriarchy provided by philosopher Heidi Goettner-Abendroth, the founder of modern matriarchal studies, on the economic, social, political and cultural levels.[35] Cichon concluded that Bronze Age Crete was a matriarchy.[36]

Haarmann's *Interacting with Figurines: Seven Dimensions in the Study of Imagery* (2009) is another significant application of archaeomythology methodology to the empirical and mythological study of prehistoric imagery. "Figurines serve as a *lingua franca* in social interactions that enhance the sustainability of communal life and as an expression of a matrix of established values and beliefs by which people with a similarly tuned mindset are interconnected."[37] Haarmann is intrigued by the social and symbolic significance of figurines as visual metaphors in cultures past and present. The earliest figurine yet discovered is the "Venus of Hohle Fels" in southwest Germany; it is 35,000 years old.

In light of this breadth and depth of research, I have elaborated the following methods for conducting archaeomythology research in tandem with women's spirituality and goddess studies. As a methodology, archaeomythology does the following:

1. Starts with archaeological survey and discovery of material artifacts, their scientific measurements, material analysis and determination of dates and chronological sequences.

2. Analyzes artifacts with respect to stature, stance, size, placement, sex and gender, class, race, age, costume, gesture, attributes, symbols and relationships of persons, animals, plants, deities and/or environments to determine specific characteristics as markers for the probable identity, status and role of each.

3. Identifies ritual equipment and practices in local contexts, using specific criteria to identify findspots as primarily religious or nonreligious in function; associations with place; cosmological conjunctions; regional religious customs; and cross-cultural comparisons of religious practices in neighboring regions or countries.

4. Distinguishes women, men and other genders, priestesses and priests, goddesses and gods, mythical creatures, and rituals for birthing, sacred marriage, healing, death and burial, and planting and harvesting.

5. Uses linguistics to discover contemporaneous and/or later language terms, inscriptions, and/or literary texts that imply plausible and probable meanings of the artifacts, noting linguistic similarities, survivals or reversals of meaning from earlier eras and cultures to later ones.

6. Compares archaeological data with later historical data, mythologies and folklore, looking for continuities, discontinuities, parallels and differences in ritual practices and spiritual beliefs from one time and place to another.

7. Interprets symbols as part of a complex system of meanings and as keys for inferring sacred stories and spiritual meaning, using steps such as those specified by Gimbutas: analysis of the archaeological data, association, seeing the parts and the whole, and engaging intuition and artistic sensibilities to infer symbolic and mythological significance.

8. Turns preliminary hypotheses, with sufficient warrant, into theories that interconnect both material culture and spiritual culture.

9. Distinguishes different truth claims regarding empirical material data, on the one hand, and mythological, spiritual or religious truth claims, on the other, recognizing that distinct epistemologies are at work in science or religion and in empirical quantitative research or qualitative humanistic research.

10. Renders compelling interpretations of the material data that are consistent with the empirical data and are strengthened by the convergence of archaeology and mythology and related disciplines, drawing inferences that are more plausible and probable than competing interpretations that may be more narrowly scientific or more narrowly religious/mythological.

These ten methods within an archaeomythology methodology serve to bridge the epistemological gulf between scientific archaeology and religious mythology. They respect deeply the material evidence provided by scientific methods, and at the same time these methods engage intuition, aesthetics and perhaps also a spiritual sensibility in the process of arriving at an interpretation of the empirical data.

The archaeomythology researcher acknowledges her or his own agency in the interpretation of the data. He or she may admit that knowledge is a social construct with political implications in the present.[38] And so, she or he will provide, at the outset and along the way, the researcher's socially situated standpoint, research interests, religious or spiritual biases and other influences on one's perceptions of the scientific data. They may consider that interpretations of the archaeological evidence could be enriched by the researcher cultivating a sense of interrelatedness among humans, nature, the cosmos and the source of all life (however that might be understood), especially when dealing with other cultures that seem to express a sense of the interrelatedness of all beings, such as those with more animistic, immanent and transcendent spiritualities.

Here is where we find a bridge to another methodology, that is, the one I most often use in doing research in religious studies. Goddess studies and women's spirituality are emergent fields of academic study that overlap with religious studies, women's studies, ethnic studies and ecofeminist philosophy and activism. Women's spirituality seeks a sense of the sacred in ancient and contemporary cultures, especially as created by women, for women, for children and men, for the larger society and for the larger environment.

IV. Women's Spirituality, Goddess Studies and Spiritual Feminist Hermeneutics

As a professor of philosophy, religion and women's spirituality, I consider what is contributed to the study of a prehistorical era or ancient historical era when it is explored from a primarily spiritual and religious orientation. What if I or others in goddess studies and women's spirituality use prayers and meditations, dreams and rituals, arts and divination, or the guidance of ancestors or other spirit guides or divinities to engage with the religious practices and spiritual experiences of ancient peoples? Can this more subjective approach be included in the methodology of archaeomythology? I am not sure. Maybe. Probably not. But then, even Einstein acknowledged kinesthetic feelings and dream images that suggested to him ideas for relativity and quantum physics.

I propose that women's spiritual practices and ways of knowing engage us in a *spiritual feminist hermeneutics*—a spiritual and political mode of interpretation. It is spiritual because it seeks to connect with a sense of the sacred and the divine. It is spiritual also because it looks to the dimensions of life that can be experienced but not adequately named, dimensions that are mysterious and ineffable but nonetheless offer wellsprings of providence, grace, healing, love and life itself. It is feminist because of its explicit interest in the lives and contributions of women in a more complete and truthful way, in personal and historical perspectives. It seeks to understand gender and gendered relations in societies past and present; it employs standpoint theory; and it seeks to transform social relations to become more equitable and just. Standpoint theory holds that a more complete understanding of an intended reality is possible if the standpoint of the researcher and of the subjects of research are acknowledged. And it is a hermeneutics because it sees the act of interpretation as a dialectic between text or artifact and the researcher. Although hermeneutics seeks to understand the text in its own context (with the help of language studies and historical studies), it also seeks to find its value for the present day.

Women's spirituality and goddess studies generally foreground the dimension of the researcher's self. Because in the past women were so often excluded from the creation or focus of research, we emphasize the importance of including oneself explicitly in one's research. This approach overlaps with the approach called *participatory research*, a practice developed in women's studies since its inception in the late 1960s and early 1970s; it is recently becoming more widely adopted in academia,[39] including archaeology. A spiritual feminist hermeneutics is participatory, because the researcher includes herself or himself as an active, self-reflexive agent in the search for knowledge. In participatory research, it is understood that both the researcher and the co-researchers (the subjects of the research) will be influenced and possibly benefited (or perhaps harmed) emotionally, politically and/or spiritually.

Women's spirituality and goddess studies research is usually also *transdisciplinary*, because these fields draw upon multiple disciplines, the researcher is a pivotal agent in the process of discovery; the researcher's standpoint becomes part of the unfolding research process; and these studies intend that the research may be transformative of self, others and the larger culture.[40] Finally, instead of being intraparadigmatic, transdisciplinary research is meta-paradigmatic, which is to say that, instead of staying within a single discipline of knowledge, it draws upon several disciplines and so must consider how the different disciplines can work together.[41]

What happens when the women's spirituality and goddess studies or religious studies researcher includes herself or himself explicitly in the design of the research project and the interpretation of its findings? What if the research is undertaken because of the interests of the researcher in the social, political and religious problems of the researcher's culture? Or with the researcher's express desire for discovering something that will be inspiring, empowering, enlightening, healing and/or transformative of self and culture? Here we move beyond the useful constraints of science that work to minimize or exclude researcher bias. Instead, we desire to honor the passion and compassion that connect us to our subject and guides our work. It is research for humanistic, socially just and spiritually illuminating purposes.

A transdisciplinary, participatory, spiritual feminist hermeneutic provides us with a methodology to develop a larger and more accurate picture of past cultures' religious practices and their spiritual significance. It seeks to understand what knowledge and insight they can impart to our lives today. It draws upon multiple disciplines, depending on the topic of inquiry, and can include one's own spiritual beliefs, practices and nonempirical modes of knowing, such as empathy, intuition and body wisdom.

A transdisciplinary, participatory, spiritual feminist hermeneutics overlaps with archaeomythology. Both seek to understand the subject of the research within its own context. But in addition, a transdisciplinary, participatory, spiritual feminist hermeneutics seeks to understand the research data as filtered through the persona of the interpreter, using reflexive self-awareness. Women's spirituality and goddess studies are informed and shaped by various liberatory movements not only for women and men around the world but also for indigenous, postcolonial, queer, working class, ecological and other movements for social justice at work today. They also intend the possible spiritual and social transformation of the researcher, co-researchers and readers.

All of this methodological complexity comes to bear for me professionally and personally in my study of the religious myth of Demeter and Persephone at Eleusis in Greece. I am primarily interested in the role that the myth and religious rites of the Mother and Daughter Goddesses played in the spiritual awakening, integration and transformation of individuals within the larger community. Here, my study of ancient Greek literary works, artworks, religion and politics is complemented by the use of archaeomythology. Yet it would not feel accurate to say that my methodology is archaeomythology alone, because my primary focus and my beginning point is not archaeology.

I begin with the myth of Demeter and Persephone as recorded in the *Homeric Hymn to Demeter* of archaic Greece, and I move from there to an exploration of temples, shrines, other archaeological artifacts, epigrapha (texts engraved in stone), linguistics, literature, cultural history and art history to discover how the mythos of the Mother and Daughter Goddesses, their separation and reunion, was re-enacted at Eleusis. Finally, I re-enact the nine-day rite of initiation into the Eleusinian Mysteries. As Joseph Campbell stated, "A ritual is the enactment of a myth. By participating in a ritual, you are participating in a myth."[42] My feeling for the myth is generated primarily by its resonance with my own life story and how it brings insight and healing. This has been my guiding thread and my inspiration—along with the love I experienced in my relationship with my mother, whom I choose to honor with this work. I hope my interpretations will have both material and spiritual value for other women and men and for our world today and the future. My research into goddess religions of the past converges with the rituals I co-create with others in my own time and place, to invite us to open more fully to the mysteries of birth, sexuality, death and rebirth.

Mine is a personal and communal spiritual approach, an embodied spiritual feminist approach that is transdisciplinary, participatory and interpretive. It engages the sciences and social sciences to assist my religious studies. I want my research to *find as much relatively objective scientific data as possible*, and I want to *interpret the empirical data in a way that honors the integrity of the past and that also speaks to me deeply, in ways that are relatively subjective*. My epistemology addresses the challenge of interfacing science and religion by seeing objectivity and subjectivity along an epistemological continuum, with some knowledge being *relatively objective* (like counting fingers and measuring rainfall) and some knowledge being *relatively subjective* (like dreaming, remembering and loving), with the purely material/objective pole and the purely energy/subjective (nonmaterial, ideational or ideal) pole of the spectrum as vanishing boundary points in human knowledge. A spiritual feminist hermeneutic can bridge the gulf between science and religion, empiricism and spirituality.

I embrace archaeomythology as both field and methodology as an invaluable dimension of my work in women's spirituality and goddess studies. It is part of my spiritual feminist hermeneutics methodology.

One of the reasons Gimbutas's work has such power for me and others today is that her analysis provides a window into a prepatriarchal egalitarian goddess and god civilization that I can honor. And it explains what happened when indigenous Old Europeans were colonized by Indo-Europeans, resulting in the hybridization of the Old European culture and the Indo-European culture during the Neolithic and early Bronze Ages in Europe. It also proffers an important perspective on the cultural dynamics of our own era.

Today we see ongoing struggles between the value systems of a more egalitarian, matristic, partnership ethos and a more hierarchical, patriarchal, dominator ethos; between the goals of sexual egalitarianism and sexual hierarchy; between earth-honoring religions and sky- or heaven-oriented religions; between peaceable cultures and militaristic cultures. In many ways, the political struggles within the world today reflect the desire among diverse populations for decolonization from the dominator values of many of the Indo-European and other colonizers of the globe, with their traditional cultural constructs of male dominance, monotheistic male gods and militarism. Many of us hope and work for a genuinely postcolonial, postpatriarchal world.

References

Moyers, Bill. *Joseph Campbell and the Power of Myth.* Video series, ep. 3: *The First Storytellers.* 1988. Accessed January 4, 2016. Moyers & Company: Public Square Media Inc.: 2017. http://billmoyers.com/content/

Christ, Carol P. "A Different World: The Challenge of the Work of Marija Gimbutas to the Dominant World-View of Western Culture." *Journal of Feminist Studies in Religion* 12, no. 2 (Fall 1966): 53–66.

Cichon, Joan Marie. "Matriarchy in Minoan Crete: A Perspective from Archaeomythology and Modern Matriarchal Studies." PhD diss., California Institute of Integral Studies, 2013. www.pqdtopen.proquest.com/results.html?QryTxt=3606922&fromyear=&toyear=&author=&Title=&pubnum=&school=&advisor=&keywords=

Connelly, Joan Bretton. *Portrait of a Priestess: Women and Ritual in Ancient Greece*. Princeton and Oxford: Princeton University Press, 2007.

D'Agata, Anna Lucia, M. B. Richardson and Aleydis van de Moortel. *Archaeologies of Cult: Essays of Ritual and Cult in Crete (Hesperia Supplement)*. Athens: American School of Classical Studies at Athens, 2007.

Dexter, Miriam Robbins. 1999. Editor's introduction to *The Living Goddesses*, by Marija Gimbutas, edited and supplemented by Miriam Robbins Dexter. Berkeley and Los Angeles: University of California Press, xv–xx.

———. *Whence the Goddesses: A Source Book*. New York: Teachers College Press, 1990.

Eisler, Riane. *The Chalice and the Blade: Our History, Our Future*. San Francisco: Harper and Row, 1987.

———. *Sacred Pleasure, Sex, Myth, and the Politics of the Body: New Paths to Power and Love*. San Francisco: Harper and Row, 1995.

———. The Real Wealth of Nations: Creating a Caring Economics. San Francisco: Barrett-Koehler Publishers, 2007.

Ferguson, Marianne. *Women and Religion*. Upper Saddle River, NJ: Prentice Hall, 1994.

Ferrer, Jorge N., and Jacob H. Sherman. *The Participatory Turn: Spirituality, Mysticism, Religious Studies*. Albany: State University of New York, 2008.

Geertz, Clifford. *The Interpretation of Cultures*. New York: Basic Books, 1973.

Gesell, Geraldine C. "The Place of the Goddess in Minoan Society." In *Minoan Society: Proceedings of the Cambridge Colloquium, 1981*. Edited by O. Krzyszkowska and L. Nixon. Bristol, England: Bristol Classical Press, 1983.

————. *Town, Palace and House Cult in Minoan Crete*. Gothenborg, Sweden: Paul Astroms Forlag, 1985.

Gimbutas, Marija. *The Civilization of the Goddess*. Edited by Joan Marler. San Francisco: HarperSanFrancisco, 1991.

————. *The Goddesses and Gods of Old Europe, 6500–3500 BC: Myths and Cult Images*. Reprint, Berkeley: University of California Press, 1982.

————. *The Language of the Goddess*. San Francisco: Harper and Row, 1989.

————. *The Living Goddesses*. Edited and supplemented by Miriam Robbins Dexter. Berkeley and Los Angeles: University of California Press, 1999.

————. *The World of the Goddess*, with Ralph Metzner, video. Green Earth Foundation: 1993. www.youtube.com/watch?v=GMutw5CNiRQ.

Goettner-Abendroth, Heide. "The Deep Structure of Matriarchal Society." In *Societies of Peace,* edited by Heide Goettner-Abendroth. Toronto: Inanna Publications and Education, 2009.

Goldenberg, Naomi. "Marija Gimbutas and the King's Archaeologist." In *From the Realm of the Ancestors: An Anthology in Honor of Marija Gimbutas*. Edited by Joan Marler, 41–46. Manchester, CT: Knowledge, Ideas and Trends, 1997.

Goodison, Lucy, and Christine Morris, eds. *Ancient Goddesses: The Myths and the Evidence*. London: British Museum Press, 1998.

Guba, E. G., and Y. S. Lincoln. "Competing Paradigms in Qualitative Research." In *The SAGE Handbook of Qualitative Research*, edited by N. K. Denzin and Y. S. Lincoln, 105–117. Thousand Oaks, CA: Sage Publications, 1994.

Haarmann, Harald. *Interacting with Figurines: Seven Dimensions in the Study of Imagery*. West Hartford, VT: Full Circle Press, 2009.

Hamilton, S. "Lost in Translation? A Comment on the Excavation Report." Forum in *Papers from the Institute of Archaeology* 10 (1999): 1–8.

Harrison, Jane Ellen. *Ancient Art and Ritual*. New York: Henry Holt, 1913.

Heron, John, and Peter Reason. "A Participatory Inquiry Paradigm." *Qualitative Inquiry Journal* 3, no. 3 (1997): 274–294.

Hershman, Debbie. "In the Beginning: Prehistory and the Origins of Myth." In *The Israel Museum at 40: Masterworks of Beauty and Sanctity*. Edited by Yigel Salmona. Jerusalem: The Israel Museum, 2005.

Hodder, Ian. *The Archaeological Process*. Oxford: Blackwell, 1999.

————. "Introduction: A Review of Contemporary Theoretical Debates in Archaeology." In *Archaeological Theory Today*. Edited by Ian Hodder, 1–13. Cambridge: Polity Press, 2008.

Hodder, Ian, ed. *Archaeological Theory Today*. Cambridge: Polity Press, 2008

Hodder, Ian, and Scott Hutson. *Reading the Past: Current Approaches to Interpretation in Archaeology*. 3rd ed. Cambridge: Cambridge University Press, 2003.

Insoll, Timothy. *Archaeology, Ritual, Religion: Themes in Archaeology*. London: Routledge, 2004.

Keller, Mara Lynn. "Crete of the Mother Goddess: Communal Rituals and Sacred Art," *ReVision: A Journal of Consciousness and Transformation* 20, no. 3 (Winter 1988): 12–16. Accessed January 3, 2016. www.ciis.edu/Documents/mlKeller%20CreteMotherGoddess.pdf.

————. "The Eleusinian Mysteries of Demeter and Persephone: Fertility, Sexuality and Rebirth." *Journal of Feminist Studies in Religion* 4, no. 1 (Spring 1988): 27–54. Accessed January 3, 2016. www.ciis.edu/Documents/Keller%20Eleusinian%20Mysteries%201988%20part1_1.pdf. www.ciis.edu/Documents/Keller%20Eleusinian%20Mysteries%201988%20part2_1.pdf.

————. 1996. "Gimbutas's Theory of Early European Origins and the Cultural Transformation of Western Civilization," Special Section on "The Legacy of the Goddess: The Work of Marija Gimbutas." Edited by Carol P. Christ and Naomi Goldenberg. *Journal of Feminist Studies in Religion* 12, no. 2 (Fall 1966): 73–90.

————. "The Interface of Archaeology and Mythology: A Philosophical Evaluation of the Gimbutas Paradigm." In *From the Realm of the*

Ancestors: Essays in Honor of Marija Gimbutas. Edited by Joan Marler, 381–398. Manchester, CT: Knowledge, Ideas & Trends, 1997.

———. "The Ritual Path of Initiation into the Eleusinian Mysteries." Special issue on Eleusis, *The Rosicrucian Digest* 87, no. 2 (2009): 28–42.

Kyriakidis, Evangelos, ed. *The Archaeology of Ritual.* Los Angeles: The Cotsen Institute of Archaeology, University of California, 2007.

Lincoln, Bruce. *Theorizing Myth: Narrative, Ideology, Scholarship.* Chicago and London: University of Chicago Press, 1999.

Longino, Helen. *Science as Social Knowledge: Values and Objectivity in Scientific Inquiry.* Princeton: Princeton University Press, 1990.

Marinatos, Nanno. *Art and Religion in Thera: Reconstructing a Bronze Age Society.* Athens: D. and I. Mathioulakis, 1984.

———. *Minoan Religion: Ritual, Image and Symbol.* Columbia, SC: University of South Carolina Press, 1993.

Marler, Joan. "Archaeomythology." In *From the Realm of the Ancestors: An Anthology in Honor of Marija Gimbutas.* Edited by Joan Marler, 140-144. Manchester, CT: Knowledge, Ideas & Trends, 1997.

———, ed. *From the Realm of the Ancestors: An Anthology in Honor of Marija Gimbutas,* Manchester, CT: Knowledge, Ideas & Trends, 1997.

———. "Introduction to Archaeomythology." *ReVision: A Journal of Consciousness and Transformation* 23, no. 1 (Summer 2000): 2.

———. "The Beginnings of Patriarchy in Europe: Reflections on the Kurgan Theory of Marija Gimbutas." In *The Rule of Mars: Readings on the Origins, History and Impact of Patriarchy.* Edited by Cristina Biaggi, 53–75. Manchester, CT: Knowledge, Ideas & Trends, 2005.

———, ed. *Journal of Archaeomythology,* 2005–2015. Accessed January 3, 2016. www.archaeomythology.org.

———. "Interview with Ian Hodder." *Journal of Archaeomythology* 3 (2007): 14–24.

———. "Cultivating Sacred Ground." In *Foremothers of Women's Spirituality: Elders and Visionaries.* Edited by Miriam Robbins Dexter and Vicki Noble, 93–102. Amherst and New York, NY: Teneo Press, 2015.

Meskell, Lynn. "Goddesses, Gimbutas, and New Age Archaeology." In *Feminisms in the Academy*. Edited by Domna C. Stanton and Abigail J. Steward, 199–247. Ann Arbor: University of Michigan Press, 1995.

———. "The Interpretive Framework," In *Private Life in New Kingdom Egypt*. Princeton and Oxford: Princeton University Press, 2002.

———. "Postscript," In *Private Life in New Kingdom Egypt*. Princeton and Oxford: Princeton University Press, 2002.

Metzner, Ralph. *The Well of Remembrance: Rediscovering the Earth Wisdom Myths of Northern Europe*. Boston: Shambhala Press, 1994.

Alfonso Montuori. "Five Dimensions of Applied Transdisciplinarity." *Integral Leadership Review* 12, no. 4 (August 2012).

———. "Gregory Bateson and the Promise of Transdisciplinarity." *Cybernetics and Human Knowing* 12, nos. 1–2 (2005): 147–158.

Moss, Marina L. *The Minoan Pantheon: Towards an Understanding of its Nature and Extent*. BAR International Series 1343. Oxford: British Archaeological Reports, 2005.

Patton, Laurie L., and Wendy Donniger, eds. *Myth and Method*. Charlottesville, VA and London: University Press of Virginia, 1996.

Price, Neil. *The Archaeology of Shamanism*. London: Routledge, 2001.

Read, Donna, and Starhawk. *Signs out of Time: The Story of Archaeologist Marija Gimbutas* Video, 2004. Narrated by Olympia Dukakis.

Renfrew, Colin, and Paul Bahn. *Archaeology: Theories, Methods and Practice*. 3rd ed. New York: Thames and Hudson, 2000.

Roller, Lynn E. *In Search of God the Mother: The Cult of Anatolian Cybele*. Berkeley: University of California Press, 1999.

Ruether, Rosemary Radford. *Goddesses and the Divine Feminine*. Berkeley and Los Angeles: University of California Press, 2005.

Spretnak, Charlene. "Anatomy of a Backlash: Concerning the Work of Marija Gimbutas." *The Journal of Archaeomythology* 7 (2011): 25–51. Accessed January 4, 2016. www.archaeomythology.org/publications/ the-journal-of-archaeomythology/2011-volume-7/2011-volume-7-article-4/.

Steadman, Sharon R. *Archaeology of Religion: Cultures and Their Beliefs*. Walnut Creek, CA: Left Coast Press, 2009.

Wesler, Kit W. *An Archaeology of Religion*. Lanham, MD: University Press of America, 2012.

Endnotes

1 I delivered an earlier version of this article for the panel on "Archaeomythology in Theoretical Elaborations and Multi-Cultural Applications" at the Association for the Study of Women and Mythology conference on Creating the Chalice: Imagination and Integrity in Goddess Studies, in San Francisco, California, May 12, 2012. Many thanks to colleagues Paula Bahn, Lisa Christie, Miriam Robbins Dexter, Joan Marler and Charlene Spretnak for helpful feedback.

2 The publisher had insisted that "gods" needed to come first in the title, even though Gimbutas explained there were many more goddesses compared to gods in the archaeological record of Old Europe.

3 Joan Marler, "Archaeomythology," *From the Realm of the Ancestors: An Anthology in Honor of Marija Gimbutas*, ed. by Joan Marler (Manchester, CT: Knowledge, Ideas & Trends, 1997), 140.

4 Marija Gimbutas, *The Language of the Goddess* (San Francisco: Harper and Row, 1989), xviii.

5 Ibid., xv.

6 Ibid., xviii. See also Joan Marler, "Archaeomythology in Theoretical and Multi-Cultural Contexts" for the panel on "Archaeomythology: Theoretical Elaborations and Multi-Cultural Applications" at the Association for the Study of Women and Mythology conference on Creating the Chalice: Imagination and Integrity in Goddess Studies, in San Francisco, May 12, 2012; in this volume.

7 Gimbutas, *The Language of the Goddess*, 321.

8 Charlene Spretnak, "Anatomy of a Backlash: Concerning the Work of Marija Gimbutas," *Journal of Archaeomythology* 7 (2011): 25–51.

9 Gimbutas, *The Language of the Goddess*, xv.

10 Gimbutas, *The Language of the Goddess*, xv.

11 Marija Gimbutas, *The Civilization of the Goddess*, ed. J. Marler (San Francisco: HarperSanFrancisco, 1991), x.

12 Ibid., viii; see also 396–401.

13 Ibid., viii.

14 Ibid

15 Ibid., viii, 401; 396–401.

16 Marija Gimbutas, *The Living Goddesses*, ed. and supp. by M. Robbins Dexter (Berkeley and Los Angeles: University of California Press, 1999), xix.

17 In addition to Gimbutas's final four works, see Joan Marler, "The Beginnings of Patriarchy in Europe: Reflections on the Kurgan Theory of Marija Gimbutas," *The Rule of Mars: Readings on the Origins, History and Impact of Patriarchy*, ed. C. Biaggi (Manchester, CT: Knowledge, Ideas & Trends, 2005), 53–75.

18 See E. G. Guba and Y. S. Lincoln, "Competing Paradigms in Qualitative Research," *The SAGE Handbook of Qualitative Research*, eds. N. K. Denzin and Y. S. Lincoln (Thousand Oaks, CA: Sage Publications, 1994), 105–117.

19 Nanno Marinatos, *Minoan Religion: Ritual, Image, and Symbol* (University of South Carolina Press, 1993), 10.

20 Ibid

21 Colin Renfrew and Paul Bahn, *Archaeology: Theories, Methods and Practice* (New York: Thames and Hudson, 2000), 13.

22 Ibid., 12.

23 Ibid., 16.

24 Ian Hodder and Scott Hutson. *Reading the Past: Current Approaches to Interpretation in Archaeology* (Cambridge: Cambridge University Press, 2003), 240.

25 Ian Hodder, *The Archaeological Process*, (Oxford: Blackwell, 1999), 83.

26 Ibid., 242. See also Ian Hodder, "Introduction: A Review of Contemporary Theoretical Debates in Archaeology," *Archaeological Theory Today*, ed. Ian Hodder (Cambridge: Polity Press, 2008), 1–13; S. Hamilton, "Lost in Translation? A Comment on the Excavation Report," *Papers from the Institute of Archaeology* 10 (1999): 1–8; Lynn Meskell, "The Interpretive Framework," *Private Life in New Kingdom Egypt* (Princeton and Oxford: Princeton University Press, 2002); and Lynn Meskell, "Postscript," *Private Life in New Kingdom Egypt* (Princeton and Oxford: Princeton University Press, 2002).

27 Renfrew and Bahn, 16.

28 See, for example, Neil Price, *The Archaeology of Shamanism* (London: Routledge, 2001); Marina L. Moss, *The Minoan Pantheon: Towards an Understanding of its Extent*, BAR International Series 1343 (Oxford: British Archaeological Reports, 2005); Debbie Hershman, "In the Beginning: Prehistory and the Origins of Myth," *Beauty and Sanctity: The Israel Museum at 40* (Jerusalem: The Israel Museum, 2005); Joan Bretton Connelly, *Portrait of a Priestess: Women and Ritual in Ancient Greece* (Princeton and Oxford: Princeton University Press, 2007); Anna Lucia D'Agata, M. B. Richardson and Aleydis van de Moortel, *Archaeologies of Cult: Essays of Ritual and Cult in Crete* (Athens: American School of Classical Studies at Athens, 2007).

29 Charlene Spretnak, "Anatomy of a Backlash: Concerning the Work of Marija Gimbutas," *The Journal of Archaeomythology* 7 (2011): 31–36; Joan Marler, "Interview with Ian Hodder," *Journal of Archaeomythology* 3 (2007): 14–24; Timothy Insoll, *Archaeology, Ritual, Religion: Themes in Archaeology* (London: Routledge, 2004), 57.

30 See, for example, Marianne Ferguson, *Women and Religion* (Upper Saddle River, NJ: Prentice Hall, 1994).

31 See, for example, Sharon R. Steadman, *Archaeology of Religion: Cultures and Their Beliefs for Negativism toward Gimbutas* (Walnut Creek, CA: Left Coast Press, 2009). Oddly, the publicity blurb for Steadman's 2009 book states that "Steadman fills *an empty niche* in the

offerings on how archaeology interprets past religions with this useful textbook" (italics added). Accessed January 4, 2016. www.barnesand-noble.com/w/archaeology-of-religion-sharon-r-steadman/1015748355?ean=9781598741544.

32 See, for example, Timothy Insoll, *Archaeology, Ritual, Religion: Themes in Archaeology* (London: Routledge, 2004); and Evangelos Kyriakidis, ed., *Archaeology of Ritual* (Los Angeles: The Cotsen Institute of Archaeology, University of California, Los Angeles, 2007).

33 See also Lynn Meskell, "Goddesses, Gimbutas and New Age Archaeology," *Feminisms in the Academy*, ed. Domna C. Stanton and Abigail J. Steward (Ann Arbor: University of Michigan Press, 1995), 199–247; Lucy Goodison and Christine Morris, eds., *Ancient Goddesses: The Myths and the Evidence* (London: British Museum Press, 1998); Timothy Insoll, *Archaeology, Ritual, Religion: Themes in Archaeology* (London: Routledge, 2004); Rosemary Radford Ruether, *Goddesses and the Divine Feminine* (Berkeley and Los Angeles: University of California Press, 2005); and Kit W. Wesler, *Archaeology of Religion* (Lanham, MD: University Press of America, 2012).

34 Charlene Spretnak, "Anatomy of a Backlash: Concerning the Work of Marija Gimbutas," *Journal of Archaeomythology* 7 (2011): 25–51. For other responses to Gimbutas's critics, see Carol P. Christ, "A Different World: The Challenge of the Work of Marija Gimbutas to the Dominant World-View of Western Culture," *Journal of Feminist Studies in Religion* 12, no. 2 (Fall 1966): 53–66; Naomi Goldenberg, "Marija Gimbutas and the King's Archaeologist," *From the Realm of the Ancestors: An Anthology in Honor of Marija Gimbutas*, ed. J. Marler (Manchester, CT: Knowledge, Ideas & Trends, 1997), 67–72; and Mara Lynn Keller, "Gimbutas' Theory of Early European Origins and the Cultural Transformation of Western Civilization," *Journal of Feminist Studies in Religion* 12, no. 2 (Fall 1966): 73–90.

35 Miriam Robbins Dexter, *Whence the Goddesses* (New York: Teachers College Press, 1990), 34–41.

36 Gimbutas, *The Civilization of the Goddess*, ed. J. Marler (San Francisco: HarperSanFrancisco, 1991), 396–401.

37 Ibid., viii.

38 Ian Hodder, ed., *Archaeological Theory Today* (Cambridge: Polity Press, 2008).

39 See the cultural transformation theory created by cultural historian and economist Riane Eisler in her works *The Chalice and the Blade: Our History, Our Future* (San Francisco: Harper and Row, 1987); *Sacred Pleasure, Sex, Myth and the Politics of the Body: New Paths to Power and Love* (San Francisco: Harper and Row, 1995); and *The Real Wealth of Nations: Creating a Caring Economics* (San Francisco: Barrett-Koehler Publishers, 2007).

40 Gimbutas, *The Language of the Goddess*, xxv.

41 Joan Marler, "Introduction to Archaeomythology," *ReVision: A Journal of Consciousness and Transformation* 23, no. 1 (Summer 2000): 2. I have reconfigured these working assumptions into a list, so the ideas can more easily be considered individually and as a group.

42 Jane Ellen Harrison, *Ancient Art and Ritual* (New York: Henry Holt, 1913), 50.

43 Clifford Geertz, *The Interpretation of Cultures* (New York: Basic Books, 1973), 89.

44 Spretnak, 25–51.

45 Marija Gimbutas, *The World of the Goddess* (video, with Ralph Metzner, Green Earth Foundation, 1993.) www.youtube.com/watch?v=GMutw5CNiRQ.

46 Ralph Metzner, *The Well of Remembrance: Rediscovering the Earth Wisdom Myths of Northern Europe* (Boston: Shambhala Press, 1994).

47 Joan Marler, "Cultivating Sacred Ground," *Foremothers of Women's Spirituality: Elders and Visionaries*, eds. M. Robbins Dexter and V. Noble (Amherst and New York, NY: Teneo Press, 2015), 99.

48 *The Journal of Archaeomythology* is published by the Institute of Archaeomythology: www.archaeomythology.org/publications/the-journal-of-archaeomythology/.

49 See *Reclaiming Quarterly*. www.reclaimingquarterly.org/web/gimbutas/gimbutas1.html. As director of the Women's Spirituality graduate program of the California Institute of Integral Studies, I produced

the West Coast Premiere gala for *Signs out of Time: The Story of Archaeologist Marija Gimbutas* (video, 2004), by Donna Read and Starhawk, narrated by Olympia Dukakis. It can also be viewed at www. youtube.com/watch?v=whfGbPFAy4w.

50 Heide Goettner-Abendroth, "The Deep Structure of Matriarchal Society," *Societies of Peace*, ed. H. Goettner-Abendroth (Toronto: Inanna Publications and Education, 2009), 17.

51 Joan Marie Chichon, "Matriarchy in Ancient Crete: A Perspective from Archaeomythology and Modern Matriarchal Studies," PhD diss., California Institute of Integral Studies, 2013. This dissertation is open access at ProQuest.com.

52 Harald Haarman, *Interacting with Figurines: Seven Dimensions in the Study of Imagery* (West Hartford, VT: Full Circle Press, 2009), 12.

53 Helen E. Longino, *Science as Social Knowledge: Values and Objectivity in Scientific Inquiry* (Princeton: Princeton University Press, 1990).

54 See John Heron and Peter Reason, "A Participatory Inquiry Paradigm," *Qualitative Inquiry Journal* 3, no. 3 (1997): 274–294; and Jorge N. Ferrer and Jacob H. Sherman, *The Participatory Turn: Spirituality, Mysticism, Religious Studies* (Albany: State University of New York, 2008).

55 See Alfonso Montuori, "Gregory Bateson and the Promise of Transdisciplinarity," *Cybernetics and Human Knowing* 12, nos. 1–2 (2005): 147–158.

56 Alfonso Montuori, "Five Dimensions of Applied Transdisciplinarity," *Integral Leadership Review* 12, no. 4 (August 2012).

57 Joseph Campbell, "The First Storytellers." *The Power of Myth* (video, 1988), by Bill Moyers. http://billmoyers.com/content/

58 I use this term to contrast the global North West (the United States, Canada and Europe) with the global South or global East (Asia).

ARCHAEOMYTHOLOGY FROM NEOLITHIC MALTA TO MODERN POLAND: APPREHENDING THE MATERIAL AND SPIRITUAL REALITIES OF ANCIENT AND PRESENT-DAY CULTURES

Joan M. Cichon

Was a Goddess worshipped in ancient Malta? Were women pre-eminent in Neolithic Çatal Hüyük? What was the purpose of the great stone monuments built by the Neolithic peoples of the British Isles? Why has the Black Madonna of Czestochowa been so deeply venerated in Poland? Archaeomythology, according to Marija Gimbutas, gives us "the possibility for apprehending both the material and spiritual realities of prehistoric cultures."[1] This article looks at the methodology of archaeomythology, the worldview of its founder, Marija Gimbutas, how the methodology of the discipline has been elaborated upon by theorists since Gimbutas, and how the discipline of archaeomythology can provide possible and probable answers to the questions posed above.

Marija Gimbutas, the mother of archaeomythology, defined her methodology as "a combination of fields—archaeology, mythology, linguistics and historical data."[2] In *The Language of the Goddess*, calling her work "interdisciplinary," she wrote, "For this work [*The Language of the Goddess*] I lean heavily on comparative mythology, early historical sources, and linguistics as well as on folk lore and historical ethnography."[3]

Out of her methodology, Gimbutas developed a worldview that she presented in her four works: *The Gods and Goddesses of Old Europe* (1976), *The Language of the Goddess* (1989), *The Civilization of the*

Goddess (1991) and *The Living Goddesses* (1999). That worldview may be outlined in the following four points:

- An understanding of the Goddess as one with Nature and as manifesting in three aspects: Life Giver, Death Wielder and Regeneratrix.

- A reinterpretation of Neolithic Europe or "Old Europe/Anatolia" as a "true civilization in the best meaning of the word, an egalitarian, matrilineal, peaceful and artistic one."[4]

- The deciphering of a complex symbolic system formulated around the worship of the Goddess in her various aspects.

- An explanation as to how and why the civilization of the Goddess was amalgamated into the patriarchal, sky-god-worshipping civilization that overtook it.

These are views to which I am partial. I understand that Gimbutas's unorthodox views remain controversial. After extensive study of the details and patterns of her work, I find her interpretations of Old European/ Anatolian artifacts to be persuasive and compelling.

In further trying to understand the methodology of archaeomythology and Gimbutas's contribution as the mother of the discipline, it is helpful to see the discipline "as a bridge between archaeology and mythology, which is to say between science and religion."[5] "She was endeavoring to discover with scientific empirical methods the spiritual beliefs of the ancient Old Europeans."[6]

Because Gimbutas did not elaborate extensively upon her methodology, I find it helpful to review what Mara Keller has written in "The Interface of Archaeology and Mythology: A Philosophical Examination of the Gimbutas Paradigm"[7]: "Gimbutas's archaeomythology scientifically analyzes the material database for Old Europe and draws possible and probable inferences from these analyses, mediated by the application of her knowledge of mythology, folklore, history of religion and linguistics, to reconstruct the symbolic, religious ideology of Old Europe." Keller goes on to say that, unlike the cognitive archaeologists, "Gimbutas grapples with the possible and probable reality of an immanent and transcendent goddess mythology and its implications for gendered social relations in Neolithic Old Europe."[8]

The following comments by feminist thealogian Carol P. Christ also elaborate upon Gimbutas's methodology:

> Recognizing the relation between Neolithic images, practices reported in classical sources, and folk tradition depends on noticing a similar gestalt and hypothesizing a connection. There is a certain selectivity and circularity involved: Knowledge about ancient religion funds our understanding of folk practice and our reading of classical sources, while information about folk practice gleaned from contemporary and classical sources shapes our understanding of ancient religion. I think it is fair to say that conclusions reached on the basis of this sort of logic are not proved in the same way as scientific hypotheses, detail by detail. Rather, Gimbutas offers to the imagination a gestalt that makes sense of a variety of data. The truth or falsity of her vision will be shown, not by the proving or disproving of individual details but by whether the gestalt as a whole makes more convincing sense of the data than alternative interpretive frameworks.[9]

What I have done in my research for the last twenty years is to use archaeology and the database that archaeologists have created for ancient Malta, Neolithic England and Neolithic Çatal Hüyük to draw possible and probable inferences mediated by the application of mythology, folklore, history of religion and linguistics to come to an understanding of the religious ideologies of those societies. I have also used archaeomythology to understand the spiritual realities of modern-day cultures, such as that of Poland.

So how does one use archaeomythology to answer the questions I posed at the beginning of this article? I begin with the question Was a Goddess worshipped in ancient Malta (3,800–2,500 BCE)?

The Maltese archipelago lies 50 miles off the coast of Sicily and covers an area of about 93 square miles. During the period under review, the people of Malta built more than forty megalithic temples and created numerous artifacts portraying and symbolizing their deity. Indeed, one archaeologist has called Malta an "archaeological paradise."

Archaeologists, who have been working in Malta since the early 20th century, have developed a number of theories to explain the existence of the temples and the artifacts found there. The father of Maltese archaeology, Themistocles Zammit, determined that the ancient Maltese practiced a primitive religion.[10] As for the sex of the deity or deities the Temple Builders worshipped, Zammit referred in his works to a "god."

David H. Trump and John D. Evans, the two men who dominated Maltese archaeology during the 1950s and 1960s, proposed no unified theory about the religion of the Temple Builders or how that religion related to their lives. Essentially, they saw a fertility deity or deities at the center of Maltese religion, but they either refused to say whether the deity was male or female (Evans) or changed their minds (Trump), first placing a female deity at the center and then arguing that "we do not really know the sex of the deity worshiped by the Maltese."[11]

Archaeologist Colin Renfrew, writing in the 1970s, ignored the issue of the religion of the Temple Builders and the gender of the Maltese deity altogether and focused instead on understanding the temples as the territorial markers of chieftains. With his "chiefdom thesis," Renfrew argued that ancient Malta was divided into six territories, each representing a chiefdom in which one individual with enormous prestige had a leading social and economic role. According to Renfrew, the ability of such chiefs to control resources and labor made possible such undertakings as the construction of temples.[12] For Renfrew, the temples are simply rival centers of power, foci of competing groups, led by men. When he does address the question of the religion of the Maltese in an article titled "The Prehistoric Maltese Achievement and Its Interpretation," Renfrew is often confusing and contradictory.[13]

The most recent archaeological studies posit that the religion of ancient Malta originally centered upon the worship of human and agricultural fertility but that over a 1,000-year period the religion changed to one obsessed with human propagation. This change occurred, according to the cognitive processualist archaeologists, for environmental reasons—due to soil erosion, the island was no longer able to support the population—and for economic reasons—Maltese trade had dwindled to almost nil because the Maltese had used up the available timber and no longer were able to build seaworthy vessels.[14] I have suggested some problems with the theories of the post-processualists in a paper titled "The Temple Builders of Malta: Traditional and Archaeomythological Perspectives."[15]

If one looks at the archaeological database of Malta mediated by folklore, anthropology, mythology and historical data, one comes up with entirely different interpretations of the Maltese temples and their artifacts. Marija Gimbutas, using an archaeomythological approach, was able to propose a decipherment of the symbolism of Old Europe/Anatolia. As she analyzed the symbols, she discovered that they had an "intrinsic order." "They constitute a complex system in which every unit is interlocked with every other in what appear to be specific categories."[16] She hypothesized that certain symbols represented death and regeneration. One of those symbols was the egg that appears on a myriad of artifacts from 4,000–1,500 BCE in Old Europe/Anatolia.

Looking at the temples of Malta and their egg shape, Gimbutas argued that the temples were modeled on the form of the Goddess's body that emphasized her regenerative function: her egg-shaped buttocks.[17] Gimbutas also noted that the same image—the egg—is repeated in numerous stone sculptures of the Goddess in Malta. (More than thirty such sculptures have been found. All exhibit the egg motif in some way.)

Gimbutas went on to look at other symbols (for example, snakes, pubic triangles and spirals) on the temples and artifacts of Malta and argued, based on her decipherment of the "intrinsic order" of the symbols of Old Europe/ Anatolia, that they were all related to regeneration as well. She ultimately concluded that the Goddess, in her function as Regeneratrix, was the primary focus of the worship of the Old European Maltese.

Archaeomythologist Cristina Biaggi, continuing from where Gimbutas began and using the history of religion, argued that not only was Malta a Goddess-worshipping society but also that the Maltese temples did not merely reflect the body of the Goddess. Rather, they were her body—as temples were in other ancient religions. "The temple reflected and was the body of the Goddess. A temple is not only the place where the deity is worshipped. It is the habitation of the deity and, as such, it is an extension of the deity. It is meant to embody the deity."[18]

An Italian scholar, the late Giulia Battiti Sorlini, agreed with Biaggi: "These buildings [the Maltese temples] reproduce, in a fixed symbolic form, the body of the Great Mother, as medieval churches reproduce the cross of Christ."[19] Sorlini carried the argument another step further by using mythology and anthropology. First, she recounted the legend that the temple of Ggantjia was built by a woman and that Malta was ruled by a woman, a story that is still alive today. Then she turned to anthropology, looking for ethnographic parallels for the belief that the temple was the embodiment of the deity, and she found one in the Fang people of Africa.

Summarizing some of the religious practices of the Fang, Sorlini described a ritual dance. The Fang perform ritual dances at the entrance to and outside their cult house. The women, as part of a ceremony, carry a stone representing their Goddess—"the stone of birth"—and go right inside the cult house. The men, on the other hand, do a dance in which they move toward the cult house, halt, back up, go forward again, halt at the entrance, back up, go forward again and finally proceed into the cult house. This action repeats until all of the men are finally inside the cult house:

> These ritual actions at the birth entrance are variously explained as 1) the difficult birth of men out of this life and into the spiritual world of the ancestors, and 2) the entrance of the male organ into the female body. . . . The spiritual reality that exists within the cult house of the Fang might have existed in the temples of Malta, and the plan of the temples might represent the shape of the body of the Goddess. . . . Psychoanalyst Erich Neumann too described the temple as . . . "a symbol of the Great Goddess" . . . and the temple gate as . . . "entrance into the Goddess."[20]

Finally, I mention Veronica Veen, who, bringing in the disciplines of art history and cultural anthropology, devoted a whole book to the stories of the Giantess who built the temple of Ggantija. Veen believes that it is certainly possible that the story is very ancient. "It is known that stories can sometimes go back thousands of years and can thus prove useful in discovering archaeological remains that would otherwise have never been found."[21] The Giantess story "runs parallel in a very special way to archaeological reality."[22] In a postscript to her book, Veen detailed recent archaeological findings on Gozo, one of the islands of the Maltese archipelago, and correlated them to one or another of the variations on the Giantess story. "Thus, a complicated relationship exists between the oral tradition . . . and the archaeological reality, so complicated that only continuously integrated research into both of these can contribute to achieving more sensible results."[23]

For Veen, the continued existence of this ancient story was proof that the Goddess "lives on in the form of the Giantess in the lives of Maltese women, just as the goddess lives on through Mary in the official religion:"[24]

> Both Our Lady and the Giantess are exemplary models in women's daily life. All passive, heavenly and unattainable features of Maria are balanced by an active, chthonic and far more realistic Giantess. Although the subterranean-Neolithic goddess has been transformed now into Maria as Lady of Heaven, the women of Gozo have managed to retain the chthonic side of life with their Giantess.[25]

With the interpretations of Gimbutas, Biaggi, Sorlini and Veen, we have come a long way from the theories that point to the worship of a god, the worship of fertility, worship based on scarcity and fear, and the territorial markers of chieftains as a way to understand the temples and the Temple Builders of Neolithic Malta. Was a Goddess worshipped in ancient Malta? I think the archaeomythological evidence demonstrates that it is quite possible and probable that she was.

Were Women Pre-eminent in Neolithic Çatal Hüyük?

Çatal Hüyük is a large Neolithic site located in central Turkey. Continuously inhabited for about 1,400 years, between 7,400 and 6,000 BCE, it first was excavated in the 1960s by British archaeologist James Mellaart. It was reopened in 1993 by British archaeologist Ian Hodder, with work continuing today.

In Mellaart's four seasons of excavation at Çatal Hüyük, he uncovered a settlement that had attained an extraordinarily high level of technical achievement, extensive economic development, specialized crafts, and a rich religious life with no sign of warfare or invasion. A large number of the 300 rooms he excavated contained elaborate wall paintings, cult statuettes, and plaster reliefs on the walls and benches, portraying deities, animal heads and the horns of cattle. The most widely known and illustrated of the cult statuettes is that of a woman seated on a throne between two leopards. She appears to be giving birth. Mellaart interpreted all of these pieces of art as having religious or ritual significance.

Human remains were found at Çatal Hüyük and studied as well. Burials were inside the houses under the platforms. Most of the skeletons Mellaart found were of women and children. The women and some of the children were buried under the main platform against the east wall. Men were buried under the smaller platform in the northeast corner. Children were also found buried under subsidiary platforms. The dead were buried in a fetal position on their left sides with their feet toward the wall.

What was the religion that was practiced at Çatal Hüyük? Mellaart based his reconstruction of the religion upon the statuettes, burials and shrines and hypothesized that the religion of Çatal Hüyük included the veneration of a Goddess in her aspects as Birth Giver and Death Wielder,[26] although he did not use those exact words. He interpreted the preponderance of female figurines to mean that women created the religion and played the primary role in it.[27] He also included in his understanding of the religion of Çatal Hüyük the veneration a male god, albeit of lesser importance than the Goddess.[28] Mellaart did not recognize the regenerative aspect of the Goddess. For Gimbutas, that aspect—the regenerative—was of prime importance at Çatal Hüyük:

> The central theme of all painting is the Goddess. . . . She appears in panels or niches as a central figure, most frequently frog-shaped with uplifted arms and widespread legs, flanked with leopards or other animals, sometimes as a double goddess . . . and usually in association with bullheads, vultures, and bee. Her symbolic associations emphasize the theme of regeneration, not merely birth-giving as Mellaart sees it. The Çatal Hüyük Goddess, as my studies of European symbolism suggest, is a transformative deity who can change into a myriad of shapes. The vulture, the bullhead (the uterus), and the bee or butterfly are her most frequent transformations. The latter are not merely symbols associated with the Goddess; they are manifestations of Her. As a vulture She is a death-wielder, as a frog She is a birth-giver and regenerator, as a bee or butterfly She symbolizes a regenerated life. The triangle

or double-triangle are also Her manifestations . . . . In the religion of Neolithic Anatolia, also of Europe, death and regeneration are seen to be two interrelated, inter-dependent, contiguous aspects of one deity. She is part of the religion of the "Sacred Round" and is beautifully represented by Çatal Hüyük artists. . . . The Çatal Hüyük shrines, with their reliefs and paintings, are through and through associated with the idea of death and regenera-tion and very probably with the rituals of regeneration that must have been performed constantly.[29]

The importance of women in Çatal Hüyük society was originally noted by Mellaart.[30] He based this observation on several factors: the fact that male cult statuettes are absent after Level VI[31] (Mellaart excavated twelve levels at Çatal Hüyük); the fact that women were buried under the main platforms in the houses, this pointing in Mellaart's mind to the existence of a matrilineal, matrilocal society; the fact that statuettes of a female deity far outnumber those of male deities; and the existence of wall paintings and other artifacts containing primarily female symbolism.

Gimbutas, who used the architecture, artifacts, burials and wall paint-ings uncovered by Mellaart to develop some of her ideas about Old Europe/ Neolithic Anatolia, also found it extremely significant that women were buried under the main platforms, often with ocher, and that the walls underneath which they were buried were the most richly decorated—with iconography of the Goddess, especially in her aspects as Regeneratrix and Death Wielder. Such findings were in accord with Gimbutas's hypothesis that Old Europe/Anatolia was a matrilineal/matrilocal society, one which she also described as gynocentric.[32]

Thus, using the discipline of archaeomythology, Gimbutas was able to take Mellaart's interpretations of Çatal Hüyük a step further and to find the Neolithic Goddess manifest there in all three of her aspects, not just in two as Mellaart had. She also was—and this is the important part for answering the question I posed at the beginning of the article—able to affirm his depiction of Çatal Hüyük as a matrilineal/matrilocal society in which women were pre-eminent.

How do archaeologists such as Ian Hodder, the current excavator of Çatal Hüyük and a post-processualist (an archaeologist who is interested in highlighting the variety of possible interpretations of artifacts and the sites at which they are found and is sensitive to the artifacts' and sites' political implications), view the position of women at Çatal Hüyük? Hodder and his team have reinterpreted many of Mellaart's conclusions. As regards the position of women in society, they reported that in their excavations they do not always find women buried under the main platform.[33] Invalidating the idea that men were never buried under main platforms, as the Hodder group has attempted to do, weakens the argument for a matrilocal, matrilineal Çatal Hüyük and may put into question one of Mellaart's and Gimbutas's main pieces of evidence in support of women's pre-eminence at Çatal Hüyük. However, it must be kept in mind that Hodder and his team have uncovered no evidence to overturn Gimbutas's hypothesis that Çatal Hüyük, like other Old European/ Anatolian societies, was an egalitarian society.

Perhaps most interesting in regards to this question of women's pre-eminence is the Hodder team's interpretation of the art of Çatal Hüyük. Rather than viewing it as female-centered, as Mellaart, Gimbutas, and others have, they found it male-centered and focused on the hunting or teasing of wild animals. Indeed, when I visited Çatal Hüyük in 2010 with a group of women led by Lydia Ruyle and we were shown around the site by Hodder, he drew our attention to and spent some time discussing a reproduction of a wall painting that he interpreted as a large bull being hunted by men.

Archaeomythologist Joan Marler has written, in an article published in the *Journal of Archaeomythology,* that Hodder has spoken of a "new approach" that he is taking to explore the symbolism of Çatal Hüyük. This "new approach," which is positioned at the opposite extreme from Mellaart and Gimbutas, focuses on the importance of "dangerous" wild animals which Hodder associates with male "hunting-feasting-prowess-ancestry" rituals that, in his view, "dominated much of the symbolism at Çatalhöyük." In shifting the emphasis from female to male, he wrote, "We can talk about the violence, sex and death of the imagery at Çatalhöyük simply in terms of male prowess."[34]

It remains to be seen whose interpretation of Çatal Hüyük—that of Mellaart and Gimbutas or that of the current team—will hold sway. In the meantime, I believe one can make a probable and plausible argument based on archaeomythological evidence that women were pre-eminent in Neolithic Çatal Hüyük.

What Was the Purpose of the Great Stone Monuments Built by the Neolithic Peoples of the British Isles?

When one approaches this question from a strictly archaeological point of view, one finds very few satisfying answers. Most archaeologists of the Neolithic Britain are guilty of what Colin Renfrew accused the profession of in the early 1970s: They are long on description but short on analysis.

Archaeologist Geoffrey Wainwright's work is illustrative of what Renfrew criticized: the failure to interpret. Analyzing his rescue excavations of three of Britain's four largest henge monuments—Durrington Walls, Marden and Mount Pleasant—Wainwright concluded that the stone monuments had timber ancestors (an important find), that there may have been domestic structures within the henges as well (an intriguing hypothesis) and that the purpose of the henges was probably ritualistic. He based the conclusion that they were probably used for ritual on three factors: "the transformation of timber structures into stone indicates some special [ritual] function for the multi-ring buildings . . . which made it necessary for their ruins to be permanently indicated by stone rings;"[35] the fact that some were approached via "avenues;" and the nature and condition of the artifacts—especially the pottery—found at the sites, which was found shattered, indicative of ritual use.[36] Although Wainwright asked, "Were these structures "temples"? he left his question unanswered.

Slightly more interpretation is found in an English Heritage pamphlet about the stone circle at Stanton Drew:

> Stone circles such as those here are known to date broadly to the late Neolithic and early Bronze Age . . . and many examples are known. . . . The circles are believed to have played an important part in contemporary social and religious life and there is evidence that some were aligned with major events of the solar and lunar calendar. They are difficult subjects to tackle archaeologically, though, and their interpretation is the subject of much discussion.[37]

Colin Renfrew has proposed a function for stone circles other than as ritual centers or meeting places. For him they have one overarching meaning: "The building of communal monuments . . . was a deliberate strategy by those holding power to maintain that social order and to increase their control over it."[38] As he did for the temples of Malta, Renfrew argued that henges of the British Isles were territorial markers of chiefdom societies: "For so great an investment of labor, it is necessary to think of some central organizing authority."[39]

In contrast, Marija Gimbutas wrote the following about the henge monuments of Old Europe: "They were not built for the protection of people and their property, as it was believed earlier, but as festival centers and meeting places for funerary rituals, including music and dances, perhaps also as grounds and courses for sports and games."[40]

Gimbutas pointed out that, based on archaeological findings—artifacts, wild and domestic animal bones, which indicate feasting, and cremation deposits found in some circles—the stone monuments were ritual centers. The cremation deposits argue for death and regeneration rituals being celebrated at the henge monuments. The argument for ritual use, and especially the celebration of death and regeneration, is further strengthened by the fact that at some of the sites "clean grain, hazelnuts and crab apples" were found, signifying "the use of the monuments in autumn or after the harvest."[41]

British folklore substantiates Gimbutas's hypothesis that the monuments served as centers for death and regeneration rituals: "The abundance of folklore regarding the prehistoric henges . . . must reflect their importance in prehistoric rituals. They are believed to be inhabited by fairies or witches; music and laughter are heard there, and dances are seen in the moonlight."[42] Even in the present day, Gimbutas noted, there are rituals such as the burial of the Old Year's Bones, ring dances, going around the houses, and making noise to protect against winter/death powers.

In Gimbutas's last work, *The Living Goddesses*, incorporating archaeological findings unavailable earlier, she offered us her most thorough interpretation of the British monuments:

> The British roundels [stone circles] appear related in function to each other and to those found in central Europe, as evidenced by their similar designs, their ceremonial artifacts and the sacrificial or ritual nature of their human remains. It is very possible that roundels were sacred places, dedicated to the goddess. Aligned with the cosmos, the territory of the roundel may have replicated a

symbolic universe. Thus a cosmic ideology may have motivated these Old European cultures to build such large-scale monuments. Through ritual in these monuments, they would have honored the Old European goddess of death and regeneration.[43]

Gimbutas made several important points in the above paragraph. One is the idea of a symbolic universe, which I shall return to in a moment. The other is that the monuments were dedicated to the Goddess, especially in her aspect of Death and Regeneration.

The archaeological literature makes no mention of the worship of a Goddess of Death and Regeneration. Some archaeologists believe it unlikely that a Goddess was worshipped in Neolithic Britain at all. Their main argument against the worship of a Goddess rests on the fact that few Neolithic female figurines have been found in the British Isles. It is not as though no figurines have been found. They have. One now famous chalk figurine was recovered near Silbury Hill, others come from Neolithic sites at Maiden Castle, Dorset, The Trundle, and Sussex and from under the Bell Track, Somerset.[44] Yet archaeologist Aubrey Burl wrote the following:

There are only a few carvings from the chambered tombs of Brittany that can confidently be interpreted as depicting any sort of woman, and there are even fewer from Ireland and virtually none elsewhere in Great Britain. In the British Isles, apart from some strange carvings of hands, feet and axes . . ., the megalithic art is non-representational. The abstract compositions of spirals, cupmarks, chevrons, meanders, rays and circles intermingle in a bewilderment of patterns where the relationship of even one triangle to an adjacent straight line is questionable. To "see" in this confusion some kind of formalized female figure is fanciful.[45]

This quotation from Burl illustrates how thoroughly unfamiliar he was with "the language of the Goddess." Spirals, cupmarks, chevrons and meanders do not make up a female figure; rather, "they are the grammar and syntax of a kind of meta-language by which an entire constellation of meanings is transmitted. They reveal the basic worldview of Old European . . . culture."[46] Chevrons, spirals, cupmarks and meanders are part of the complex symbolic system formulated around the worship of the Goddess in Her various aspects. Unless a female figurine looking like "the elegantly dressed Mediterranean goddess"[47] is found, Burl would not consider the worship of a female deity in Neolithic Britain a possibility.

Addressing the question of the lack of female figurines, archaeomythologist Cheryl Straffon has pointed out that perhaps Neolithic figurines were indeed rare or were ruthlessly destroyed by Christians, thus leaving us only isolated examples. There are many Goddess statues and friezes remaining from the Roman period, Straffon noted, so perhaps prior to the Roman period celebration of the Goddess was done by means of ceremonial monuments in the landscape or perishable offerings.[48] Here Straffon brought up a key point—ceremonial monuments in the landscape—and touched on the other important point made in the above paragraph from *The Living Goddesses*—the symbolic universe.

Gimbutas and archaeomythologists Cheryl Straffon and Michael Dames all found that the Neolithic monuments of Great Britain are inherently symbolic and that, as Vincent Scully learned from his study of ancient Greece, they served to amplify the deity's presence—a presence that had already been recognized in the natural topography.[49] They were symbols of the divine body. Moreover, in some cases, the monuments were created to stage a religious drama that took place over a year's time. The seasonal rites or religious drama re-enacted the cycle of the life and death of nature. Thus, the life of the Goddess and the lives of human beings were portrayed at Avebury, with Silbury Hill, West Kennet Long Barrow, the Sanctuary, the Henge and Stone Circle, and the Avenue all playing their part:

> The overall purpose of the entire ensemble was to celebrate the annual life cycle of the Great Goddess at temples which were her seasonal portraits. The worshippers moved around this extended gallery of symbolic architecture in time with the changing seasons and the farming year, synchronized with the comparable events in the lives of the human community, namely birth, puberty, marriage and death.[50]

How then does archaeomythology answer the question What was the purpose of the great stone monuments built by the Neolithic peoples of the British Isles? They were built to celebrate death and regeneration, honor the ancestors, symbolize the Goddess and provide a container for great religious dramas in which humans could re-enact, within the divine body, the life, death and rebirth of nature and of themselves.

Why Is the Black Madonna of Czestochowa So Highly Venerated in Poland?

Although much more recent in origin than the Neolithic cultures of Malta, Çatal Hüyük and the British Isles, the Black Madonna of Czestochowa, which dates to between the 6th and 9th centuries CE, is included in this discussion because an investigation of her importance illustrates yet another instance in which archaeomythology can be extremely valuable in helping to understand the spiritual realities of a particular culture—whether that culture be ancient or contemporary.

The Black Madonna of Czestochowa in Jasna Gora, Poland is a two-dimensional icon measuring 122 × 82 cm. Her face and hands and those of her child are of a brown or dark brown color. Two large, parallel scars slash down the center of her right cheek and fade underneath her dress. A third, wider scar cuts through and across the other two. She faces the viewer and wears a cape and dress of navy blue decorated with fleurs-de-lis. Her cape, which is trimmed in gold, covers her head, folds around her face and then falls over her shoulders. Her cape is also decorated with a six-pointed star, which appears above Mary's forehead. She holds the Christ child in her left arm. He is represented not as an infant but as a small boy, and he holds a book in his left hand while he raises his right hand in a gesture of blessing. Both mother and child have nimbuses around their heads.

Despite the fact that the Catholic Church "tend[s] to invoke candle smoke or general exposure to the elements"[51] as reasons for the Black Madonnas being black, the explanation offered here is that Black Madonnas are the ancient Earth Goddess converted to Christianity. As Marija Gimbutas put it, "she is our own Earth Mother from European soil since in pre-Indo-European Europe, black meant life and fertility."[52] The blackness of the Black Madonnas also symbolizes wisdom and wholeness. The Black Madonnas are black because they are Christian borrowings from earlier pagan art forms that depicted the Goddesses Demeter, Isis, Artemis and Cybele as black. The Black Madonnas are black because they represent the collective memory of our original mother—a black woman.[53]

We do not know when and by whom the particular Black Madonna in question, the first Black Madonna of Czestochowa, Poland, was painted. Legend has it that she was originally painted by St. Luke on a table that Christ himself built. It is known that the icon was repainted in 1430 after it had been slashed by robbers attempting to steal it from Bright Hill Monastery, where it has rested since being brought to Poland in the 14th century. Hence, the slash marks painted on the Madonna's face.

While there has been much speculation about the icon's origins, scholar Danita Redd has argued that the Black Madonna of Czestochowa is one of those Byzantine Madonnas influenced by images of African Isis. This Black Madonna may even be a literal image of Isis, the Great Goddess of predynastic Egypt whose worship continued until at least the 5th century CE.

Redd tied Mary's origins to the Goddess Isis. She argued that early Christianity survived and thrived because it elevated Mary to the status of the Goddess Isis who, by the 4th century CE, had grown to a position of ascendancy in the ancient world, addressed by such titles as Great Mother, Tender Mother, personification of femininity, Immaculate Virgin, Our Lady, Queen of Heaven, Star of the Sea, and Mother of God[54] and identified by such symbols as the lily, ankh, ears of corn, globe, ship, crescent and full moon. "Images of Isis could also be identified by aspects of clothing. . . . In some depictions, she wears a long, hooded tunic and . . . the hood is drawn over the head, covering the upper forehead."[55]

Redd argued that Christianity needed to raise Mary to the status of the Goddess Isis, because it was competing against other major religions for followers and three important elements were lacking from its early doctrine: resurrection, promise of a better afterlife and salvation of the soul. All three of these were found in the religion of Isis.[56] In addition, elevating Mary to the status of Isis and declaring her Mother of God at the Council of Ephesus, according to Redd, diminished the "patriarchal flavor of Christianity," thus adding to its mass appeal.[57]

Recounting the introduction of the Byzantine art style into Europe, Redd said that it was brought by Greek artists hailing from Egypt and that those artists "frequently borrowed images of the African Isis and Horus to serve as the Virgin Mary and Child."[58] The eyes of Our Lady of Czestochowa are the first clue that the painter of that icon was trained in Egypt in the tradition of the Fayum mummy portrait painters and that the icon dates from the period when Isis was used as a model for the Virgin

Mary. Another clue consists of the elongated faces, figures and fingers of the images. Moreover, there are numerous parallels in the emblems associated with both images.

Thus, the Black Madonna of Czestochowa is very likely a copy of a portrait of Isis and could have been painted sometime between the 6th and 9th centuries. She is literally the image, surviving down to us for thousands of years, of Isis, the Great Goddess.

Finally, Redd reminded us that not only was the image of Isis diffused through the Byzantine-type Black Madonna images but also pagan images of black goddesses were often used to represent the Virgin Mary without any alteration. An image of Isis was simply relabeled as Mary and venerated as the Virgin. Given the legends of the Black Madonna of Czestochowa being hidden in forests and castles and moved about to keep her out of the hands of invading armies, one wonders if she was one of those images of Isis that was brought out of hiding and blessed as an image of the Virgin and Child.

In attempting to understand the veneration of the Black Madonna of Czestochowa, it is important not only to perceive Mary's origins in Isis, which Redd so brilliantly illustrated, but also to look at the history of religion in Poland and at Polish folklore.

Poland was a part of what Gimbutas defined as Old Europe/Anatolia. Although Poland is not part of the territory that Gimbutas included in the term "Balts," I believe that in most ways it was very similar to that region. In *The Living Goddesses*, Gimbutas described:

> . . . the Baltic region as representing perhaps the greatest repository of Old European beliefs and tradition. There pagan religion persisted via oral traditions and customs that endured to the 20th century. The Balts were the last pagans of Europe. As a result, the Christian layer of beliefs among the Balts is very thin.[59]

Much of what Gimbutas said about the Balts applies to the Poles, I believe. The Poles were converted to Christianity in 966, but even until 1918 the Polish peasants practiced many of the old pagan beliefs. William I. Thomas and Florian Znaniecki, two anthropologists studying Polish peasantry in the early 20th century, observed that the religious life of the Polish peasant "contains elements of various origin. There is still the old pagan background."[60] The two scholars broke down their discussion of the religion of the Polish peasant into four parts: general animation of natural objects, solidarity of life in nature, belief in a world of spirits, and mysticism. They noted that among the Polish peasantry there was no separation of the sacred and profane, there was an understanding of the interconnectedness of all life, and there was a belief in the cyclical nature of all life. These beliefs are identical to our understanding of the spiritual beliefs of the peoples of Old Europe/Anatolia.

To substantiate her thesis that Old European beliefs endured among the Balts into the 20th century, Gimbutas cited folklore, tales and rituals. Many of those that she cited have parallels in Poland. Like the Lithuanians, i.e. the Balts, the Poles imaged the hearth-fire deity as a stork who protected the house, hearth, family and village community. The Poles also venerated the snake. Both Lithuanian and Polish folktales contain stories of snakes with crowns, signifying the ability to know or see all, and both kept snakes in the homes, believing that killing a snake would destroy the happiness of the whole family. "Clearly these dim memories of the sacredness of snakes harkens back to the Neolithic snake goddess."[61] Among Polish peasantry, the owl was thought to foretell death or birth.[62] The owl is a common feature in Old European religion. It is an epiphany of the Goddess in her death aspect. Contemporary authors have noted that it is among the peasantry that the Black Madonna of Czestochowa is most highly venerated and that the titles given to Mary (blessed mother of the seeding and planting, blessed mother of hay making and harvests, and blessed mother of flowers and fruits) by the Polish peasantry reflect the ancient practice of honoring the Goddess at the solstices, equinoxes and cross-quarter days.[63]

I have tried to show, based on archaeomythological evidence—archaeology, history, history of art, folklore, and other disciplines—that the Black Madonna of Czestochowa is Isis and, beyond her, the Great Mother Goddess. That the Poles are easily able to connect to her is due to the fact that Christianity came late to Poland and many aspects of the religion of Old Europe/Anatolia were still alive in Poland until the 20th century. Our Lady of Czestochowa is perhaps the last remaining link for the Poles to Old Europe, to Isis, and to the ancient Great Mother Goddess. It is for these reasons that the Black Madonna of Czestochowa is so highly venerated in Poland.

Carol P. Christ wrote that Marija Gimbutas, her methodology and her worldview offer "a gestalt that makes sense of a variety of data. The truth or falsity of her vision will be shown not by proving or disproving individual details, but by determining whether the gestalt as a whole makes more convincing sense of the data than alternative interpretive frameworks."[64] I have attempted to show that the methodology of archaeomythology, as laid out by Gimbutas and scholars following her, makes more convincing sense of the data available and more effectively answers the questions that I posed at the beginning of this article than do the "alternative interpretive frameworks" offered by less multidimensional disciplines.

References

Begg, Ean. *The Cult of the Black Virgin*. London: Arkana, 1996.

Biaggi, Cristina. *Habitations of the Great Goddess*. Manchester, CT: Knowledge, Ideas & Trends, 1994.

Birnbaum, Lucia Chiavola. *Dark Mother: African Origins and Godmothers*. San Jose, CA: iUniverse, 2001.

Bonanno, A., et al. "Monuments in an Island Society: The Maltese Context." *World Archaeology* 22 (October 1990): 190–205.

Burl, Aubrey. *Rites of the Gods*. London: Dent, 1981.

Cichon, Joan. "The Temple Builders of Malta: Traditional and Archaeomythological Perspectives." Unpublished manuscript, California Institute of Integral Studies, 1998.

Christ, Carol P. "A Different World: The Challenge of the Work of Marija Gimbutas to the Dominant Worldview of Western Cultures." In *From the Realm of the Ancestors: An Anthology in Honor of Marija Gimbutas.* Edited by Joan Marler. Manchester, CT: Knowledge, Ideas & Trends, 1997.

Dames, Michael. *The Avebury Cycle*. 2nd ed. London: Thames and Hudson, 1996.

———. *The Silbury Treasure: The Great Goddess Rediscovered*. London: Thames and Hudson, 1976.

Gimbutas, Marija. *The Civilization of the Goddess.* SanFrancisco: HarperSanFrancisco, 1991.

———. *The Language of the Goddess.* San Francisco: Harper and Row, 1989.

———. *The Living Goddesses.* Edited by Miriam Robbins Dexter. Berkeley and Los Angeles: University of California Press, 1999.

———. "Wall Paintings of Çatal Hüyük, 8th–7th Millennia B.C.," *The Review of Archaeology* 11 (Fall 1990): 3–4.

Hamilton, Naomi. "Figurines, Clay Balls, Small Finds and Burials." In *On the Surface: Çatalhöyük 1993–1995.* Edited by I. Hodder. Cambridge: McDonald Institute for Archaeological Research, 1996.

Keller, Mara Lynn. "The Interface of Archaeology and Mythology: A Philosophical Examination of the Gimbutas Paradigm." In *From the Realm of the Ancestors: An Anthology in Honor of Marija Gimbutas.* Edited by Joan Marler. Manchester, CT: Knowledge, Ideas & Trends, 1997.

———. "Women's Spirituality Research Methods Course." Item 20, response 22:25. November 16, 2008. Accessed February 2, 2009. www.ciis.gihost.com/ciisr/swebsock/00149001/0158275/CC50/main/view-itema.cml?797+16.

La Monte, Willow. "Black Madonna Sampler Part Two: From Old Pilgrimage Sites to Contemporary Creative Expression." *Goddessing* (2000): 22.

Malone, C. S., et al. "A House for the Temple Builders: Recent Investigations on Gozo, Malta." *Antiquity* 62 (June 1988): 297–302.

———. "The Death Cults of Prehistoric Malta." *Scientific American* 269 (December 1993): 110–118.

Marler, Joan, and Harald Harrman. "The Goddess and the Bear: Hybrid Imagery and Symbolism at Çatalhöyük." *Journal of Archaeomythology* 3 (Spring/Summer 2007): 50. www.archaeomythology.org/journal.

Mellaart, James. *Çatal Hüyük: A Neolithic Town in Anatolia.* London: Thames and Hudson, 1967.

Ray, B. C. "Stonehenge: A New Theory." *History of Religions* (1987): 225–278.

Redd, Danita. "Black Madonnas of Europe: Diffusion of the African Isis." In *African Presence in Early Europe*. Edited by Ivan Van Sertima. London: Transaction Publishers, 1985.

Renfrew, Colin. "The Prehistoric Maltese Achievement and its Interpretation." *Archaeology and Fertility Cult in the Ancient Mediterranean*. Edited by A. Bonanno. Papers presented at the First International Conference on Archaeology of the Ancient Mediterranean, University of Malta, September 2–5, 1985. Amsterdam: B. R. Gruner Publishing Co., 1986.

————. "The Social Archaeology of Megalithic Monuments." *Scientific American* 248 (November 1983): 157.

Rose, Mark. "Celebrating an Island Heritage." *Archaeology* (July/ August 1997): 45.

Scully, Vincent. *The Earth, the Temple and the Gods: Greek Sacred Architecture*. Revised ed. New Haven, CT: Yale University Press, 1962.

Sorilini, Giulia Battiti. "The Megalithic Temple of Malta," *Archaeology and Fertility Cult in the Ancient Mediterranean*. Edited by A. Bonanno. Papers presented at the First International Conference on Archaeology of the Ancient Mediterranean, University of Malta, September 2–5, 1985. Amsterdam: B. R. Gruner Publishing Co., 1986.

Stoddart, Simon, et al. "Cult in an Island Society: Prehistoric Malta in the Tarxien Period." *Cambridge Archaeological Journal* 3 (April 1993): 3–19.

Straffon, Cheryl. *Earth Goddess: Pagan and Celtic Legacy of the Landscape*. London: Blanford, 1998.

Thomas, W. I., and Florian Znaniecki. *The Polish Peasant in Europe and America*. Vol. 1. New York: Dover, 1958.

Trump, David. "Megalithic Architecture in Malta." In *Antiquity and Man: Essays in Honour of Glyn Daniel*. Edited by John D. Evans, Barry Cunliffe and Colin Renfrew. London: Thames and Hudson, 1981.

Veen, Veronica. *Female Images of Malta: Goddess, Giantress, Farmeress*. Haarlem, Netherlands: Inanna-Fia, 1990.

Wainwright, G. J. *Henge Monuments: Ceremony and Society in Prehistoric Britain.* London: Thames and Hudson, 1989.

———. "Woodhenges." *Scientific American* 233 (1970): 39.

Zalecki, Marian. *Theology of a Marian Shrine: Our Lady of Czestochowa.* Dayton, OH: University of Dayton, 1976.

Zammit, Themistocles. *The Hal-Saflieni Hypogeum Casal Paula-Malta.* Valletta: Malta-Herald Office, 1929.

Endnotes

1. Marija Gimbutas, *The Civilization of the Goddess* (SanFrancisco: HarperSanFrancisco, 1991), x.

2 Ibid.

3 Marija Gimbutas, *The Language of the Goddess* (San Francisco: Harper and Row, 1989), xv.

4 Gimbutas, *The Civilization of the Goddess,* x.

5 Mara Lynn Keller, "Women's Spirituality Research Methods Course," item 20, response 22:25, November 16, 2008, www.ciis.gihost.com/ciisr/swebsock/00149001/0158275/CC50/main/viewitema.cml?797+16.

6 Ibid.

7 Mara Lynn Keller, "The Interface of Archaeology and Mythology: A Philosophical Examination of the Gimbutas Paradigm," *From the Realm of the Ancestors: An Anthology in Honor of Marija Gimbutas,* ed. J. Marler (Manchester, CT: Knowledge, Ideas & Trends, 1997), 391.

8 Ibid.

9 Carol P. Christ, "A Different World: The Challenge of the Work of Marija Gimbutas to the Dominant World-View of Western Cultures," *From the Realm of the Ancestors: An Anthology in Honor of Marija Gimbutas,* ed. J. Marler (Manchester, CT: Knowledge, Ideas & Trends, 1997), 411.

10 Themistocles Zammit, *The Hal-Saflieni Hypogeum Casal Paula-Malta* (Valletta: Malta-Herald Office, 1929), x.

11 David Trump, "Megalithic Architecture in Malta," in *Antiquity and Man: Essays in Honour of Glyn Daniel,* ed. J. D. Evans, B. Cunliffe and C. Renfrew (London: Thames and Hudson, 1981), 135.

12 Mark Rose, "Celebrating an Island Heritage," *Archaeology* 50, no. 4 (July/August 1997): 45.

13 Colin Renfrew, "The Prehistoric Maltese Achievement and Its Interpretation," *Archaeology and Fertility Cult in the Ancient Mediterranean*, ed. A. Bonanno, papers presented at the First International Conference on Archaeology of the Ancient Mediterranean, University of Malta, September 2–5, 1985 (Amsterdam, Netherlands: B. R. Gruner Publishing Co., 1986), 118–130.

14 For a fuller explanation of these theories, see: A. Bonanno et al., "Monuments in an Island Society: The Maltese Context," *World Archaeology* 22 (October 1990): 190–205; Caroline Malone et al., "The Death Cults of Prehistoric Malta," *Scientific American* 269 (December 1993): 110–118; C. S. Malone et al., "A House for the Temple Builders: Recent Investigations on Gozo, Malta," *Antiquity* 62 (June 1988): 297–302; and Simon Stoddart et al., "Cult in an Island Society: Prehistoric Malta in the Tarxien Period," *Cambridge Archaeological Journal* 3 (April 1993): 3–19.

15 Joan Cichon, "The Temple Builders of Malta: Traditional and Archaeomythological Perspectives" (unpublished manuscript, California Institute of Integral Studies, 1998), 14–17.

16 Gimbutas, *The Language of the Goddess*, xv.

17 Ibid., 154, 172.

18 Cristina Biaggi, *Habitations of the Great Goddess* (Manchester, CT: Knowledge, Ideas & Trends, 1994), 144.

19 Giulia Battiti Sorilini, "The Megalithic Temple of Malta," *Archaeology and Fertility Cult in the Ancient Mediterranean*, ed. A. Bonanno, papers presented at the First International Conference on Archaeology of the Ancient Mediterranean, University of Malta, September 2–5, 1985 (Amsterdam: B. R. Gruner Publishing Co., 1986), 144.

20 Ibid., 144–145.

21 Veronica Veen, *Female Images of Malta: Goddess, Giantress, Farmeress* (Haarlem, Netherlands: Inanna-Fia, 1990), 46.

22 Ibid., 45.

23 Ibid., 46.

24 Ibid., 45.

25 Ibid.

26 James Mellaart, *Çatal Hüyük: A Neolithic Town in Anatolia* (London: Thames and Hudson, 1967), 184.

27 Ibid., 203.

28 Ibid., 183.

29 Marija Gimbutas, "Wall Paintings of Çatal Hüyük, 8th–7th Millennia B.C.," *The Review of Archaeology* 11 (Fall 1990): 3–4.

30 Mellaart, 60.

31 Ibid., 181.

32 Gimbutas, *The Civilization of the Goddess,* vii.

33 Naomi Hamilton, "Figurines, Clay Balls, Small Finds and Burials," *On the Surface: Çatalhöyük 1993–1995,* ed. I. Hodder (Cambridge, UK: McDonald Institute for Archaeological Research, 1996), 262.

34 Joan Marler and Harald Harrman, "The Goddess and the Bear: Hybrid Imagery and Symbolism at Çatalhöyük," *Journal of Archaeomythology* 3 (Spring/Summer 2007): 50. www.archaeomythology.org/journal.

35 B. C. Ray, "Stonehenge: A New Theory," *History of Religions* (1987): 235.

36 G. J. Wainwright, "Woodhenges," *Scientific American* 233 (1970): 39.

37 "Stanton Drew Stone Circles." (UK, English Heritage), n.p.

38 G. F. Wainwright, *Henge Monuments: Ceremony and Society in Prehistoric Britain* (London: Thames and Hudson, 1989), 164.

39 Colin Renfrew, "The Social Archaeology of Megalithic Monuments," *Scientific American* 248 (November 1983): 157.

40 Gimbutas, *The Civilization of the Goddess*, 341.

41 Marija Gimbutas, *The Living Goddesses*, ed. M. Robbins Dexter (Berkeley and Los Angeles: University of California Press, 1999), 99–100.

42 Gimbutas, *The Language of the Goddess*, 312.

43 Gimbutas, *The Living Goddesses*, 107.

44 Michael Dames, *The Silbury Treasure: The Great Goddess Rediscovered* (London: Thames and Hudson, 1976), 51–52.

45 Aubrey Burl, *Rites of the Gods* (London: Dent, 1981), 83–84.

46 Gimbutas, *The Language of the Goddess*, xv.

47 Burl, 83.

48 Cheryl Straffon, *Earth Goddess: Pagan and Celtic Legacy of the Landscape* (London: Blanford, 1998), 19–20.

49 Vincent Scully, *The Earth, the Temple and the Gods: Greek Sacred Architecture*, rev. ed. (New Haven: Yale University Press, 1962).

50 Michael Dames, *The Avebury Cycle*, 2nd ed. (London: Thames and Hudson, 1996), 122.

51 Ean Begg, *The Cult of the Black Virgin* (London: Arkana, 1996), 6.

52 Willow La Monte, "Black Madonna Sampler Part Two: From Old Pilgrimage Sites to Contemporary Creative Expression," *Goddessing* (2000): 22.

53 Lucia Chiavola Birnbaum, *Dark Mother: African Origins and Godmothers* (San Jose, CA: Author's Choice Press, 2001).

54 Danita Redd, "Black Madonnas of Europe: Diffusion of the African Isis," *African Presence in Early Europe*, ed. I. Van Sertima (London: Transaction Publishers, 1985), 116.

55 Ibid., 115–116.

56 Ibid., 116.

57 Ibid., 117.

58 Ibid., 120.

59 Gimbutas, *The Living Goddesses,* 197.

60 W. I. Thomas and Florian Znaniecki, *The Polish Peasant in Europe and America,* vol. 1 (New York: Dover, 1958), 205.

61 Gimbutas, *The Living Goddesses,* 204.

62 Thomas and Znaniecki, 219.

63 Marian Zalecki, *Theology of a Marian Shrine: Our Lady of Czestochowa* (Dayton, OH: University of Dayton, 1976), 148.

64. Christ, 411.

HONORING THE WEB: INDIGENOUS WISDOM AND THE POWER OF PLACE

Arieahn Matamonasa-Bennett

This article is an adaptation of the 2013 ASWM Conference keynote address, which examined the ways in which indigenous worldviews and philosophies can inform contemporary studies in mythology and earth-based spirituality. It explores the ways in which ancient concepts converge with modern science, as well as how history and politics influence scholarship and activism.

Introduction: Defining Indigenous

The term *indigenous* is used by definition, experience and worldview. Originally, the term was an adjective from the Latin word *indigen*, meaning "native" or "originating in that place." With a small i, it can refer to things, plants and people that originated in the place being referenced. Here, indigenous refers to any culturally distinct group whose members are descended from the original inhabitants of a region or country prior to its colonization. This definition recognizes the shared experiences of people in groups that have inhabited a country or region for thousands of years, which often contrasts with the experiences of people in groups that have been in the same country for hundreds of years. Typically, indigenous people maintain a historical continuity with precolonial societies and have distinct social, cultural, political and economic structures and ancient, unique knowledge systems. For the individual members of these groups, other terms from their own languages may be preferred to the term indigenous.

The term *indigenous*, as used here, is a relatively recent term that emerged in the 1970s out of the struggles of North America's Native people during the American Indian Movement (AIM) and the Canadian National Indian Brotherhood.[1] This term has political implications in that it allowed colonized, ancient earth-based people, also called First Peoples, Native Peoples, First Nations, and People of the Land, to share a collective voice and to plan, organize and struggle collectively and globally for rights and self-determination.[2] The term is commonly used in North America in a way that includes many diverse communities, language groups and nations, each with its own identification and grouping.

Although indigenous groups have distinct cultures, they share a common worldview that places special significance on the unification of humans with the natural world.[3] Traditionally, they have a profound and deeply rooted sense of place and relationship with the entirety of the natural world. The term indigenous also may be related to the Latin root *indu* or *endo*, meaning "within," or the Greek word *endina*, meaning "entrails," indicating one so completely identified with a place that the place reflects its entrails or soul. Indigenous people do not live on the land, like parasites, but rather in the land, and it lives in them.[4] Many people may relate to being so identified with a place that it feels a part of one's soul. Using that definition and experience, do you identify yourself as indigenous?

There is an interaction between a person's inner reality and outer reality that comes into play when one lives in a place for an extended period of time. The physical makeup and the human psyche are formed in direct ways by the distinct climate, soil, geography and living things of a place. The development of mountain people is distinct from that of desert people and that of people from the plains or north woods. Though the distinctions are not as apparent as in the past, indigenous people from different regions reflect unique physical and psychological characteristics that are the result of generations of interaction with the geographies and ecologies of their respective regions.[5]

People make a place as much as the place makes them. Indigenous people interacted with the places in which they lived for such a long time that the relationship became cocreative and the landscape became a reflection of their very souls. This mindset is particularly challenging for modern people who are highly migratory and, in part, explains the ignorance and insensitivity of many Western governments to indigenous peoples with respect to issues of equality, justice, possession of land and the deep sacredness of place.

There are more than 370 million self-identified indigenous people in approximately seventy countries around the world. In Latin America, there are more than 400 indigenous groups, each with a distinct language and culture. The largest concentration of indigenous people is in Asia and the Pacific, where 70% of the population is indigenous. Although indigenous people make up only 5% of the global population, they represent 15% of the poorest people in the world.[6] On September 13, 2007, the United Nations adopted the United Nations Declaration on the Rights of Indigenous Peoples. This triumph for justice and human dignity followed more than two decades of negotiations between governments and indigenous peoples' representatives. This declaration addressed individual and collective rights, cultural rights and identity, rights to education, rights to health and rights to employment. It outlawed discrimination against indigenous peoples and promoted their full and effective participation in all issues that concern them. Australia, Canada, New Zealand and the United States voted against this measure.[7] The world's indigenous people have rich, ancient cultures and traditional knowledge that deserves to be protected, and they can make invaluable contributions to our world. Indigenous people are among the world's most vulnerable, marginalized and disadvantaged groups, and it is imperative that their rights are respected and their status improved.

The Legacy of Colonization

For many scholars studying mythology and earth-based, indigenous cultures, the history of genocide and the remaining legacy of brutal colonization are social and political realities. I was asked to address this issue, and I can speak about this from my own career and experiences. Early in my teaching career, I was an instructor and coordinator in a Native American studies program at a community college. I struggled with my mixed ancestry and possessing the blood of both the colonized and the colonizers. I found myself attempting to understand and come to terms with history in such a way that would allow for my facilitation of open cultural sharing without activating or triggering pain, guilt or shame in ways that would prevent learning and growth for the students and communities that we visited. I had some pivotal experiences that have led me to my current views on this topic.

In our college program, we frequently invited Native American speakers and activists to visit our campus and hold talks with our students. I observed that those speakers who had achieved healing and balance with their own pain and grief were successful in creating opportunities for cross-cultural sharing and exchange that elevated our students' understanding and appreciation of the strength and wisdom inherent in Native cultures without ignoring the legacy of colonization. Those activists who presented with passion and anger, however, tended to create an atmosphere that shut down the openness of our students. Some speakers managed to create such negativity and animosity among those in attendance that I recall thinking that the event took us backward a few hundred years. These experiences taught me the value and importance of healing one's own wounds before attempting cross-cultural sharing. The displacement of many Native peoples was devastating culturally and spiritually, and there remains a deep *soul wound*, or collective grief, within many communities and individuals. When writing about or practicing earth-based traditions in places that are not our own original places, we indigenous people must acknowledge and have a sensitivity and high degree of awareness of this wound.

In 1999, I traveled with a group of students to the Pine Ridge and Rosebud reservations in South Dakota. Knowing in advance that we would be visiting the cemetery at Wounded Knee, I asked my father, elder Greg Askenette, how I might approach this sorrowful, sacred place in a healing way. He instructed me to "put tobacco down"—to pray for the people who died there *and* to pray for the perpetrators of the massacre. When I did this, I was overcome by an intense, deep grief, well beyond any personal grief I had ever experienced. I believe that what I experienced was the soul wound or collective grief of humanity. At that moment, and in many moments afterward, I had the realization that this was not just about White soldiers perpetrating unthinkable acts of violence against Lakota men, women and children but that humans from every race have done this to each other throughout history. We continue to do this, even at this very moment. I felt it important to share this, because it has become critical in my development as a clinician and a scholar. It set my intention to be a force for understanding, healing and change, and the journey has led me here.

Lessons From Earth-based Cultures

As a part of my journey, I began to expand my knowledge beyond Native studies, and I became interested in the ways in which ancient peoples lived in other places on the planet. I have had the opportunity to travel and meet people from a wide range of cultural backgrounds and earth-based people from many countries. Although it is only possible to theorize about more ancient worldviews, their ideas may have been remarkably similar to those of the remaining indigenous earth-based people. The ideologies and cosmologies of the world's remaining indigenous people contain valuable clues to the ways ancient people may have viewed the world. It is impossible to know exactly the mind of prehistoric, ancient cultures; therefore, our theories about the relationships that our ancestors had with the natural world are largely speculative. The ideology of *traditional ecological knowledge* (TEK)[8] from indigenous earth-based cultures may provide an alternative lens through which to view the findings from mythology, ethnography, archaeology, anthropology and history.

There is great diversity among indigenous peoples in North America and around the globe. Certainly, the influence of geography, culture, history and language assures great variation in ceremonial and symbolic expression of Native worldviews and cosmology. My research suggests that there exists a shared way of thinking and perceiving the world that is defined here, as well as by other scholars, as TEK.[9] In "American Indian Epistemologies," Gregory Cajete stated, "The characteristics of American Indian epistemologies reflect traits that indigenous cultures of the world share. They are really expressions of the ancestral tribal roots of all the families of humankind."[10] Regardless of one's phenotype and the part of the world in which one's ancestors originated, all of our ancestors were from earth-based cultures.

Major revolutions or transformational moments in human development radically altered worldviews and societies from our original, indigenous, earth-based web of interdependent relationships to ladder or dominance worldviews that ultimately subjugated earth-based peoples and destroyed the environment. The combination of the victory of Western forms of Christianity over earth-based cultures and the industrial revolution has led to our current state, which ecophilosophers such as Joanna Macy call the *industrial growth society.* [11]

Over the last several decades, significant thinkers in many disciplines, including philosophy, psychology, ecology, conservation and science, have come to recognize that indigenous philosophy has much to offer contemporary cultures regarding the importance of living in connection and harmony with the natural world. In *Radical Nature: The Soul of Matter*, Philosopher Christian De Quincey described a new paradigm of radical naturalism from the long lineage of supporting arguments from panpsychism, panexperientialism and the sacredness of all life and nature.[12] Astrophysicist Neil deGrasse Tyson has remarked that traditional indigenous perspectives, such as human-like consciousness in animals, extended awareness and communication in plants, and the emotional toll of death on non-human species, are now being given serious scientific consideration. J. Baird Callicott, in *In Defense of the Land Ethic*, suggested that Native American nature wisdom may form the basis for living cultural models for the world to witness and emulate. The late Thomas Berry (1914–2009), theologian and ecologist, was deeply influenced by Native American and indigenous philosophies and proposed an earth-based spirituality and worldview as foundational to our evolution and to create a more sustainable future for the planet.[13]

Other scholars, such as Joanna Macy, Brian Swimme, Daniel McGuire and many other significant ecologists and scientists, assert that the next revolution in human consciousness will involve new ways of living sustainably, a return to ancient shamanic traditions and a return to our understanding of life as a web of interconnected, interdependent relationships.

Indigenous Approaches to Education and Scholarship

Indigenous approaches to education, research and scholarship may be particularly rewarding to those interested in mythology, story and the power of nature and physical place. Understanding the *metaphoric mind* (or "nature mind," as Native scholar Gregory Cajete referred to it)[14] is particularly relevant. The persistence with which indigenous worldviews appear and reappear in human mythologies around the globe can be understood best as the result of the metaphoric mind. The metaphoric mind, our oldest mind, has been developing for about three million years. Its time of greatest development occurred during the Paleolithic era about 70,000 years ago. The development of the mind, from an evolutionary perspective, parallels human development, and the metaphoric mind in individuals develops from birth until the development of language.

As language and the rational mind develop, the holistic experience of the metaphoric mind eventually recedes into the subconscious, but it can still be called on or accessed during creative or spiritual experiences, particularly those in nature. Metaphoric mind processes are tied to creativity, perception, images, physical senses and intuition, and the metaphoric mind reveals itself through abstract symbols, visual spatial reasoning, sound, art, music, dance and myth. As the rational mind develops further and language becomes literacy, the metaphoric mind becomes significantly differentiated from the rational mind, particularly as a part of Western education and social conditioning.[15] Western society and science have been overtly focused on the rational mind—scientific rationalism.[16] The work of Robert Ornstein and Bob Samples suggests that there is clear physiological and psychological evidence that left-brain activity is distinct from right-brain activity and that Western society and its educational systems focus on mainly left-brain functions, such as linear thinking and language. Metaphoric, symbolic perception and intuitive, right-brain activity have been neglected.

Bob Samples stated that around 10,000 years ago stories and myths held the seeds of linearity and that eventually there developed a preference for this in cultural settings. Interestingly, this preference coincided with the end of the subsistence economy and the domestication of animals and plants. He stated that the price of giving up the metaphoric mind was high in that it resulted "in the severing of the umbilicus of humankind from nature."[17] In Native societies, the two minds of human experience are given more equal regard, and the metaphoric mind is the first foundation of Native science and the key to understanding the natural world.[18] This ability to retain and access our more ancient mind may provide us with meaning and connection to our ancient ancestors, as well as reconnection to the world of nature and a deeper human intellectual legacy.

The role of affective, or feeling, elements in education is another stark contrast between indigenous and Western approaches to learning and scholarship. In the indigenous approach, *feeling* and experiencing communal relationships through artistic and mythical dimensions, ritual and ceremony, sacred ecology and psychological and spiritual orientation is the only viable means to acquire wisdom and knowledge. Unlike the *non-feeling*, rational or linear dimensions of Western approaches, these affective elements are not readily quantifiable, observable or verbalized. Perhaps for this reason, they are mostly ignored by mainstream academia. If the mainstream discounts or ignores your work, it may be a positive sign that your scholarship is connected to our indigenous past through deep time.

Mainstream approaches to learning and the creation of knowledge have resulted in many technological advances and material prosperity, which are the primary goals of our industrial growth society. The cost, however, has been very high. We have destroyed the earth and created enormous suffering on the planet. Disconnected from the natural world, those who identify most with the industrial growth society suffer from an image without substance, a technique without soul, and knowledge without context. The psychological result is alienation from the natural world, which is our only true home. We experience a deep loss of community with other humans and the natural world. We suffer from a deep sense of incompleteness. What my peers in the field of psychology view as personal pathologies, I, as an indigenous thinker, view as cultural, social pathologies caused by the values of the industrial growth society and disconnection from who we really are as human beings.

In addition to the affective elements of indigenous education, indigenous approaches emphasize learning through participation and relationships with place and the environmental community of people, plants, animals and the elements. Participation involves being connected to the environment and the earth through the power of breath. For indigenous peoples, breath represents the most tangible expression of spirit in all living things. Breath is an act of prayer. Through each breath, we take in the sacredness of the place where we are and give our breath back to the world. My elders used to say that when we breathe we are breathing "the dust of the bones of our ancestors." From the moment of birth, when we take our first breath, to the moment of death and beyond, it is breath that connects us to the power and sacredness of a place. It connects us, in a direct relationship, to all living things in our community. Acoma Pueblo poet Simon Ortiz talks about the way traditional Native people connect with the special place in their land and their lives through breath in all of its manifestations, which include language, storytelling, singing and chanting.[19]

Mythology:
The Sacredness of Stories and the Sacredness of Place

A value that indigenous people around the world share is that they must preserve their stories, languages, customs, songs and philosophies, because these sustain life—the life of individuals, the life of families, the life of communities and the life of our planet. Stories are particularly important, because they integrate ancestral wisdom and hold the essence of people's spiritual being through time and place. Mythic stories form the script for cultural processes and experience. Gregory Cajete stated, "Culture is the face; myth is the heart; and traditional education is the foundation for indigenous life. . . . *All cultures have indigenous roots* that are bedded in the rich soil of myth from which the most elemental stories of human life spring" [italics mine].[20]

The mythic foundation of indigenous teachings rests upon archetypal stories that describe the cosmology or worldview of the tribe's language and cultural metaphors. The foundation explores the tribe's guiding thoughts, dreams, explanations and orientations to the world. More than just representing the worldview of the tribe, the mythic informs the process of storytelling and presents the script for teaching and learning. Participating in stories guides the people. In tribal cultures, ultimately all education is the expression of storytelling. Myth and stories inform individual psychological and collective spiritual experiences. They can lead to, or form, the practice of rituals and ceremonies of a tribe. They provide a framework for individuals and groups to teach and learn by exploring their inner psychology and collective unconscious.

For traditional Native American people, both historically and today, stories are timeless and sacred. Stories are *medicine* in that they have the power to inform us and transform us in a number of ways. Stories instruct the people about a values system—especially in regard to the nature of our relationships and responsibilities to one another and the rest of creation. Storytelling is used as a teaching tool that allows listeners to draw their own conclusions and internalize life lessons from a personal perspective. In *Research Is Ceremony: Indigenous Research Methods*, Shawn Wilson talks about the difficulties in translating the Native words for myth or story, because in English the words carry the connotation of being make-believe. My elders have explained that there are several levels of storytelling, stories for various purposes and multiple layers and "codes" in stories that reveal themselves over time. In Wilson's work, Cree Elder Jerry Saddleback said that there are three levels of storytelling. At the highest level are sacred stories, which are specific in form and content and are told at various levels according to the stage of initiation of the listener. These stories must be told very specifically, and only those who have been trained, tested and given permission are allowed to tell these stories.[22] These stories would not be shared in books. The second level of story includes indigenous myths or legends that have moral lessons or in which events take place, but story-tellers can shape them according to their own experience and that of the listener. The third level of story consists of the relating of personal experiences of oneself or others. Elders typically use this third level for teaching or counseling. For Native people, all education is the expression of some sort of storytelling. Archetypal stories describe the tribe's cosmology by using the language and cultural metaphors of the tribal culture. The story provides a foundation to guide the thoughts, dreams, explanations and orientations to the world and creates a script for teaching and learning.[23]

An example of the ways in which story provides a script for teaching and learning is the story of White Buffalo Calf Woman from Lakota culture. This story informs Lakota society about the primary ceremonies for maintaining right and reciprocal relations between humans and the rest of the natural world. Embedded in the story are instructions for living in "right relationship" with the earth, other relatives (human and non-human) and the spiritual world. These ceremonies provide opportunities for social cohesion of the group and aid in transitional psychological and spiritual processes, including birth, death, adoption rites of passage from childhood to adulthood and grief/loss. This story is alive within contemporary Lakota culture despite systematic attempts to eradicate and suppress it. In my chapter in volume three of *Goddesses in World Culture*, edited by Patricia Monaghan, I explored the ways in which the essential core teachings of the story are resurfacing in Lakota culture, in response to ecological crisis and the epidemic of violence against Lakota women, to promote healing and change. Contemporary Lakota activists have formed the *White Buffalo Calf Woman Society*, which uses this ancient and spiritual iconic story to guide their contemporary lives and advocate for nonviolence against women.[24]

Although each of the several hundred remaining indigenous cultures has distinct stories, mythologies and ceremonies, there is a strong commonality among all of these cultures. The feminine principle and female creators or cultural icons are found throughout all cultures. Despite 500 years of acculturation, assimilation and contact with Christian and patriarchal worldviews, the feminine principle remains. The power of these myths and stories to shape societies should not be underestimated. Most Native American scholars believe that violence against women is a new problem in these societies and that when and if it did occur in precontact cultures it was severely sanctioned. The loss of traditional feminine, earth-based cosmology, through colonization processes, has resulted in numerous social ills, including violence against women and substance abuse, in contemporary reservation communities.[25]

In my research about Native American men and their perceptions of violence against women, none of these men believe that domestic violence was a part of traditional Native societies. Rather, they believe that a return to traditional Native American values and spiritual traditions is the key to lives of nonviolence and sobriety.

Honoring Myths and Stories

Returning full circle, back to where we began with addressing the legacy of colonization, raises important questions about the role of advocacy or activism within scholarship. For those who dedicate their scholarship and energy to storytelling and myth from an indigenous perspective, this work is sacred work. *It is soul work.* Often there may be conflicting or competing constructs with regard to your role in this soul work. Several scholars have asked, "Where is the place for activism?" Just as we have expanded our definition of indigenous, I want to expand the concept of activism. Activism can take many different forms in scholarship. Helping humanity remember the sacred and imparting ancient ideas or wisdom through scholarly work is activism. Speaking out and educating others about injustice or the destruction of any aspect of the web of life is activism. Using your *breath*, including language, words or your voice, on behalf of those who do not have one is activism. From an indigenous perspective, your "medicine" (gifts, talents and personal power) may find appropriate expression in many different places, and these can change over the course of your career and lifetime

Conclusions

Joanna Macy stated that "the most remarkable feature of this historical moment on Earth is not that we are on the way to destroying the world—we've actually been on the way for quite a while. It is that we are beginning to wake up, as from a millennia-long sleep, to a whole new relationship to our world, to ourselves and each other."[26]

If you are called to a place and you experience its deep connection and power, you are experiencing this shift or transformation of human consciousness. If, in your work, you find yourself powerfully drawn to sacred stories and myths, you are part of this soul work as well. You are helping humanity to remember its connection to the earth and the web of life. The antonym of *indigenous* is alien. Our Elders teach us that we do not live on the earth like parasites but rather that we live *in it* and the earth lives *in us*. We are all connected and all related. As long as we leave anybody out, we are the aliens.

Dedication

The keynote address "Honoring the Web: Indigenous Wisdom and the Power of Place" was dedicated to my dear friend and colleague Pat Monaghan. She was a woman who, like Spider Woman from the Navajo culture, wove webs of interconnection—between like-minded people, between disciplines and between ideas. She truly understood the power of place, and she left a powerful legacy behind. She is greatly missed in the physical world, but I have no doubt that she is still with us in spirit.

References

Anderson, Eugene N. *Ecologies of the Heart: Emotion, Belief and the Environment.* New York: Oxford University Press (1996).

Cajete, Gregory. "A Education for Harmony and Place: American Indian Expressions of Environmentally-Literate Citizenship." *International Research in Geographical and Environmental Education* 5, no. 2, (1996): 136–139.

— "American Indian Epistemologies." *New Directions for Student Services,* 109 (2005).

—*Look to the Mountain: An Ecology of Indigenous Education.* Durango, CO: Kivaki Press, 1994.

—*Native Science: Natural Laws of Interdependence.* Santa Fe, NM: Clear Light Publishers, 2000.

Couture, Joseph. *A Metaphoric Mind: Selected Writings of Joseph Couture.* Edited by Ruth Couture and Virginia McGowan, Edmonton, AB: Athabasca University Press, 2013.

de Quincy, Christian. *Radical Nature: The Soul of Matter.* Rochester, VM: Park Street Press, 2002.

Matamonasa-Bennett, Arieahn. " 'A Disease of the Outside People' :Native American Men's Perceptions of Intimate Partner Violence," *Psychology of Women Quarterly* (July 30, 2014). DOI:10.1177/0361684314543783.

— "The First and Second Coming of White Buffalo Calf Woman." In *Goddesses in World Culture,* Vol. III. Edited by Patricia Monaghan. Santa Barbara, CA: Praeger. 2011: 161–175.

— "Until People Are Given the Right to be Human Again: Voices of American Indian Men on Domestic Violence and Traditional Cultural Values." *American Indian Culture and Research Journal* 37, no. 4. (2013): 25–51.

Ortiz, Simon J.Ortiz, Simon J. "That's the Place Indians Talk About," *Wicazo Sa Review* 1, no. 1 (1985): 45-49. www.jstor.org/stable1409426

Pierotti, Raymond, and Daniel Wildcat, "Traditional Ecological Knowledge: The Third Alternative." *Ecological Applications* 10, no. 5 (2000): 1333–1340.

Salmon, Enrique, "Kincentric Ecology: Indigenous Perceptions of the Human-Nature Relationship." *Ecological Applications* 10, no. 5, (2000) 1327–1332.

Samples, Robert. *The Metaphoric Mind: A Celebration of Creative Consciousness.* Torrence, CA: Jalmar Press, 1992.

Smith, Linda Tuhiwai. *Decolonizing Methodologies: Research and Indigenous Peoples.*2nd Ed. London and New York: Zed Books, 2012: 1–20.

Suzuki, Daniel, and Peter Knudtson. *Wisdom of the Elders: Sacred Native Stories of Nature.* New York: Bantam Books, 1992.

Wilson, Shawn. *Research is Ceremony: Indigenous Research Methods.* Black Point, NS: Fernwood Publishing, 2008.

Endnotes

1 Linda Tuhiwai Smith, *Decolonizing Methodologies: Research and Indigenous Peoples.* 2nd Ed. London and New York: Zed Books, 2012, 1–20

2 Ibid.

3 Daniel Suzuki and Peter Knudtson, *Wisdom of the Elders: Sacred Native Stories of Nature* (New York: Bantam Books,1992).

4 Gregory Cajete, *Look to the Mountain: An Ecology of Indigenous Education.* (Durango, CO: Kivaki Press, 1994); Gregory Cajete, "A Education for Harmony and Place: American Indian Expressions of Environmentally-Literate Citizenship," *International Research in Geographical and Environmental Education* 5, no. 2, (1996), 136–139.

5 Ibid.

6 International Fund for Agricultural Development (IFAD), www.ifad.org/

7 United Nations Office of the High Commissioner, www.ohchr.org/en/Issues/IPeoples/Pages/Declaration.aspx

8 Eugene N. Anderson, *Ecologies of the Heart: Emotion, Belief and the Environment.* (New York: Oxford University Press, 1996); Enrique Salmon, "Kincentric Ecology: Indigenous Perceptions of the Human-Nature Relationship." *Ecological Applications,* 10, 5, (2000), 1327–1332; and Raymond Pierotti and Daniel Wildcat, "Traditional Ecological Knowledge: The Third Alternative." *Ecological Applications* 10, no. 5 (2000), 1333–1340.

9 Ibid.

10 Gregory Cajete, "American Indian Epistemologies," *New Directions for Student Services* 109 (2005), 71.

11 Joanna Macy, 'The Great Turning," Center for Ecological Literacy, www.ecoliteracy.org/essays/great-turning.

12 Christian de Quincy, *Radical Nature: The Soul of Matter.* (Rochester, VM: Park Street Press, 2002).

13 Thomas Berry, "The Meadow Across the Creek," from *The Great Work,* www.thomasberry.org/Essays/MeadowAcrossCreek.html.

14 Gregory Cajete, "American Indian Epistemologies," 71.

15 Gregory Cajete, *Native Science: Natural Laws of Interdependence.* (Santa Fe, NM: Clear Light Publishers, 2000), 71–75; and Joseph Couture, *A Metaphoric Mind: Selected Writings of Joseph Couture,* eds. Ruth Couture and Virginia McGowan (Edmonton, AB: Athabasca University Press, 2013).

16 Cajete, *Native Science,* 29.

17 Robert Samples, *The Metaphoric Mind: A Celebration of Creative Consciousness,* (Torrence, CA: Jalmar Press, 1992), 33.

18 Cajete, *Native Science,* 28.

19 Simon J. Ortiz, "That's the Place Indians Talk About," *Wicazo Sa Review* 1, no. 1 (1985) 45–49. Article Stable URL: www.jstor.org/stable/1409426.

20 Cajete, "American Indian Epistemologies," 76.

21 Shawn Wilson, *Research is Ceremony: Indigenous Research Methods* (Black Point, NS: Fernwood Publishing, 2008), 97–98.

22 Ibid.

23 Cajete, "American Indian Epistemologies," 71–74.

24 Arieahn Matamonasa-Bennett, "The First and Second Coming of White Buffalo Calf Woman," *Goddesses in World Culture*, Vol. III, edited by Patricia Monaghan. (Santa Barbara, CA: Praeger 2011): 161–175.

25 Arieahn Matamonasa-Bennett, "Until People Are Given the Right to be Human Again: Voices of American Indian Men on Domestic Violence and Traditional Cultural Values" *American Indian Culture and Research Journal*, 37, no. 4. (2013): 25–51; Arieahn Matamonasa-Bennett, " ' A Disease of the Outside People,' Native American Men's Perceptions of Intimate Partner Violence," *Psychology of Women Quarterly* (July 30, 2014). DOI:10.1177/0361684314543783.

26 Joanna Macy, www.joannamacy.net

ARIADNE, MISTRESS OF THE LABYRINTH: RECLAIMING ARIADNIAN CRETE

Alexandra K. Cichon

Ancient Crete was once believed to be simply a legendary place in Classical Greece's imagination of its sacred origin, the infamous isle where many goddesses and gods of the Greek pantheon were born.[1] The great bard Homer, in the *Odyssey*, described the island of Crete as "lavishly fruitful, sea-girt, radiant."[2] As portrayed by Jungian scholars Anne Baring and Jules Cashford, its soaring, forest-laden cliffs, cut by deep gorges, concealed from view innumerable caves—cult sites for over 4,000 years—vast caverns penetrating deep into the interior of the mountain, opening to reveal underground waterways, stalactites, and stalagmites, like phantasms of an underground chthonian world.[3] Beyond these cliffs, "out-jutting beaches thundered aloud to the backwash of the saltwater."[4]

In the 8th century BCE, Homer described ancient Crete, and his words once served as the sole surviving depiction of this place of legendary beginnings. This land of hallowed origin remained alive in the Greek imagination, yet no one knew whether the civilization of Bronze Age Crete existed only as the poet's visionary genius or in historical truth.[5] It was a revelation in the early 20th century when archaeological excavations on the island of Crete "lifted the layers of over four millennia of history and laid bare a civilization apparently as magical as Homer had intimated."[6]

Beginning with a Cretan edifice two to three stories in elevation that covered two hectares (five acres) and was the apparent focal point of this culture, Evans's excavations unearthed a great structural complex that he called the "Palace" of Knossos.[7] The topmost structure was found to be built directly upon the layered ruins of two earlier complexes that had been destroyed by earthquakes in 1,700 BCE and again in 1,450 BCE.[8] Decades before the "true nature of Minoan and Old European culture"[9] was determined in subsequent archaeological findings, Evans named the civilization *Minoan* and conjured up the image of Ariadne's father, the legendary king of Greek myth who ruled from his throne at Knossos. Aegean scholar Rodney Castleden[10] used the term *temple-palace* for these centers of wealth and ritual that were presided over by priestesses, comparing their hierarchal function to that of the medieval monastery. Archaeomythologist Marija Gimbutas described these structures as "religious-administrative-economic complexes,"[11] interpreting their function as temples of rebirth and regeneration of the goddess. Gimbutas wrote that the goddess, "in all of her manifestations, was the symbol of the unity of all of life in Nature. Her power was in water and stone, in tomb and cave, in animals and birds, snakes and fish, hills, trees, and flowers."[12]

Gimbutas referred to the governance of Crete as a *theacracy* ruled by a priestess-queen, stressing that "the very name *Minoan* is a misnomer"[13] and that Evans's initial association of kingship with the temple complex at Knossos represented a major obstacle to the accurate perception of the culture. Evans had delineated three broad periods within the arc of this civilization, calling the first *Early Minoan*, or *Pre-Palatial*, representing the Cretan civilization from its beginnings, which some scholars place as early as 3,500 BCE[14] to 2,000 BCE; the second *Middle Minoan*, or *Early Palatial*, the years 2,000 to 1,600 BCE; and the final phase *Late Minoan*, or *High Palatial*, from 1,600 to 1,150 BCE.[15]

In contrast to Evans's delineation, the pictorial, archaeological evidence that provides primary data about the cultural psyche of Bronze Age Crete overwhelmingly reveals the worship of a Great Goddess who may be "experienced as a flowing, dynamic energy that could manifest in a swarm of bees, a dolphin's joyous leap, a flight of birds, the coiling of serpents and sea creatures, as well as in the human gesture."[16] In his monumental work *The Palace of Minos*, which details his thirty-year excavation, Evans himself concluded that the goddess images he found in the excavation of Knossos were representative of "the same Great Mother with her Child or Consort whose worship under various names and titles extended over a large part of Asia Minor and the Syrian regions beyond."[17] Evans's claim was initially contested, but over the intervening century it has been "irrefutably confirmed" by the continuing accumulation of evidence of "similar complexes of images" in locations as disparate as "Mesopotamia, Egypt, northwestern India, Old Europe and Greece."[18]

Extant pieces of small-scale sculpture and sealstones that were found in Crete and are now housed at the Heraklion Archaeological Museum depict the goddess as follows:

> Sculpted with serpents entwined around her body or ris-
> ing from her arms, or . . . holding the double axe in her
> hands. Sometimes she has doves or poppies on her head.
> On seals she is engraved resting in the shape of a bee,
> or standing upon her mountain with lions, or raising her
> arms as the wings of the bird goddess, or sitting beneath
> the Tree of Life offering the fruits to her priestesses. She
> was worshipped as the Great Mother of Life, Death,
> and Regeneration, the Goddess of the Animals, and the
> Mistress of the Sea and of the Fruits of the Earth.[19]

The Cretan goddess was also venerated as Mistress of the Labyrinth, an epithet which links her most directly to Ariadne, because the double axe, the *labrys*, often held by the goddess, is etymologically tied to the *labyrinth*, a symbol of the royal house of Knossos.[20] One of the primary religious symbols of Crete, the labrys served as votive object within cave altars and high mountain sanctuaries; its image was carved on sealstones and painted in frescoes and pottery. Philosopher Mara L. Keller wrote that it was "sometimes stylized as a butterfly, a symbol of rebirth."[21] Other scholars recognized in the sacred labrys a ritual implement of sacrifice, particularly of the bull, "the cult animal who embodied the regenerative power of the goddess."[22]

Critically important to a consideration of Bronze Age Crete and Ariadne's role within it is the fact that the symbol script, Linear A, which was developed by the peoples of Crete during the Middle Minoan period (2,000–1,600 BCE) prior to the Mycenaean Greek invasions, has never been deciphered. There are no extant languages to which its template can be compared. Even the later Mycenaean Linear B script was decoded only in 1953. Interpretation of this culture rests upon image: the persistence of image in the architecture and myriad works of art that have survived earthquakes and time.[23]

The Bronze Age Cretan civilization thus speaks to us in imagery, which Jung believed to be the language of the unconscious, the primary mode of the psyche's perception. As philologist and mythographer Martin P. Nilsson remarked about Minoan religious culture, "the evidence is purely archaeological, it has come down to us as a picture book without text, and our first concern is to furnish a text to the pictures—namely, to interpret them."[24] Art historian Henriette Groenewegen-Frankfort beautifully evoked the spirit of the imagery revealed in the art of Crete in the 2nd millennium BCE:

> Here and here alone [in contrast to Egypt and the Near East] the human bid for timelessness was disregarded in the most complete acceptance of the grace of life the world has ever known. For life means movement and the beauty of movement was woven into the intricate web of living forms which we call "scenes of nature"; was revealed in human-bodies acting their serious games, inspired by a transcendent presence, acting in freedom and restraint, unpurposeful as cyclic time itself.[25]

The Labyrinth of Crete: Ariadne's Dancing Ground

Homer wrote of such a scene of beauty, movement and the web of living forms in the first known literary reference to the Labyrinth of Crete. In the *Iliad*, Homer described the *choros*,[26] the marvelous "dancing floor" at Knossos in Crete, which was built for Ariadne. She "with beautiful braids of hair,"[27] according to mythologist Károly Kerényi, is "an ornamental epithet that Homer confers more often on goddesses than on common girls." Kerényi also noted that Ariadne is the "Cretan-Greek form for *Arihagne*, the "utterly pure," from the adjective *adnon* for *hagnon*.[28] Feminist theologian Carol P. Christ reflected that Ariadne "may have been the name of the Goddess of pre-patriarchal Crete. The ending 'ne' signifies that Ariadne is not of Indo-European origin and thus predates the Greek myths."[29] Ronald F. Willetts, a scholar of ancient Crete who culled through extant archaeological evidence of Ariadne's rites and cult practices, acknowledged that "very little, apart from the mythology, is known about Ariadne from Crete." He considered the rites associated with Ariadne's death to be a singular emanation of "Minoan religious genius" and viewed her as a "vegetation goddess who seems to have emanated from the Minoan goddess."[30] This goddess lineage of Crete is most clearly revealed through an analysis of the labyrinth as Ariadne's prime symbol and central to her mythic saga.

Eminent labyrinth scholar Hermann Kern placed the origin of the labyrinth at Knossos in the 2nd or "possibly" 3rd millennium BCE, remarking that its lineage "cannot be traced back any further."[31] Kern defined its earliest meaning and ritual function as a dancing ground. The scene inscribed on Achilles' shield, evoked by Homer a millennium later, "depicted a dancing floor like the one that Daedalos designed in the spacious town of Knossos for Ariadne."[32] Homer captured the image of the labyrinth at a moment in time when he wrote the following:

> Youths and marriageable maidens were dancing on it with their hands on each other's wrists, the girls in fine linen with lovely garlands on their heads, and the men in closely woven tunics showing the faint gleam of oil, and with daggers of gold hanging from their silver belts. Here they ran lightly around, circling as smoothly on their accomplished feet as the wheel of a potter when he sits and works it with his hands to see if it will spin; and there they ran in lines to meet each other. A large crowd stood round enjoying the delightful dance, with a minstrel among them singing divinely to the lyre, while a couple of acrobats, keeping time with his music, threw cart-wheels in and out among the people.[33]

Goddess scholars Anne Baring and Jules Cashford pointed to the "suggestive link" Homer made between the labyrinth and dancing and the veneration of the goddess in "his image of Ariadne's dancing floor at the Palace of Knossos, for, as the daughter of King Minos and Queen Pasiphae in the later Greek story, she would have been the high priestess who conducted the ceremonies."[34] In Egypt, ritual dance and sacred drama as living myth was enacted in the temples. The art of dance was pervasive in early cultures as "a way of communicating with the goddess, drawing her through ritual and ecstatic gesture into the midst of the spiraling forms that became, as they were danced, her epiphany."[35]

Yet the closed labyrinth has retained its association with death, as in its mythic role as prison of the Minotaur and death sentence for the Greek hostages sent within it to be devoured or lost forever within its precincts. Although the form of the Cretan labyrinth is unicursal, having but one way in and out and thus no possibility of one becoming lost in it, the labyrinth has, since the late Hellenistic period,[36] been confounded with the image of a maze. In the *Aeneid*, Virgil provided an evocative literary description of the labyrinth as *inextricabilis error*, the "errant way," the misleading path through which a way cannot be found, the labyrinth experienced as maze:

> The labyrinth in high Crete had a path
>
> built out of blind walls, an ambiguous
>
> maze of a thousand ways, a winding course
>
> that mocked all signs of finding a way out,
>
> a puzzle that was irresolvable
>
> and irretraceable.[37]

Virgil's epithet *inextricabilis error* implies that the labyrinth, as entrance to the realm of soul, may be experienced by ego consciousness in the way contemporary chaos theory describes the "twisted changeability" of nonlinear systems as "like walking through a maze whose walls rearrange themselves with each step you take."[38] Kern believed the graphic and literary forms of the survival and transmission of the labyrinth "to be reflections of this original expression: attempts at recording the ephemeral movements of the dance."[39]

What, then, was built for Ariadne of the beautifully braided hair? Labyrinth scholar Helmut Jaskolski described it as a "man-made marvel,"[40] an "edifice that was only later attributed to the Athenian architect?"[41]:

> The flat dancing ground, the labyrinthine pattern of which was perhaps not built up into walls but just marked by flagstones, becomes in the Greek tales of the Labyrinth, a masterpiece of building, which we conceive of as a cavernous edifice recalling the underworld. But no such thing was to be found on Crete, which had already been announced with regret by the writers of antiquity, and therefore in more recent times the palace of Knossos has been identified with the Labyrinth as the supposed "house

of the double-axe" (*labrys*), a speculation introduced to the world by archaeologist Sir Arthur Evans.[42]

Upon unearthing the remains of this culture at Knossos, Evans christened this civilization *Minoan*, after Minos, the "king" of Crete and father to Ariadne in the Greek myth, despite overwhelming archaeological evidence that pointed to a culture centered on the worship of a Great Goddess and her priestesses. Although andro-ethnocentric interpreters of the iconography attributed power to the young males as priest-kings, such as Evan's "imaginatively" reconstructed Prince of Lilies, there is a notable absence in the archaeological evidence of a dominant male figure of a king within the "palace" of Knossos. Gimbutas made the following observations about Evans's excavations:

> From the first discovery of this culture at Knossos in the beginning of the 20th century, the self-possessed independence and confidence of women was noticed. Frescoes, to the great astonishment of the scholarly world, revealed beautiful, elegant women dressed in exquisite costumes, frequently bare breasted. They are shown mixing freely with men in festivals, riding in chariots driven by female charioteers, and participating as athletes during the ritual bull games. . . . There are great numbers of outstanding women portrayed as priestesses and goddesses, and it cannot be doubted that women maintained a centrality in religion until Mycenaean times.[43]

The time has come to reclaim Ariadnian Crete and, as Carol P. Christ suggested, engage in a new naming, for "the words we use affect our thinking"[44] and shape our understanding of history. In re-imagining Bronze Age Crete, we must choose to avoid the repetition of the misnomers *Minoan, King Minos, priest-king,* and *Palace* of Knossos, said Christ, when we know these terms to be inaccurate.

The Greek Version of Ariadne's Myth

In the West, the tale of Ariadne comes down to us as interpreted by the Greeks, in whose hands she is a radically humanized and diminished footnote to the hero's quest. The Greek myths, transmitted 1,000 years after the civilization of Bronze Age Crete by bards such as Homer, Aeschylus, and Hesiod, represent tales spun from the patriarchal point of view, a perspective, said mythologist Christine Downing, "that issues in the reduction of ancient Goddesses into figures with whom men can safely deal."[45] Gimbutas remarked that although the goddesses deemed most important by the Greeks "found their way into the Olympic male pantheon," these androgynous, parthenogenetic goddesses, who created life without male participation, became over time the "brides, wives, and daughters of the Indo-European gods."[46]

So it is with Ariadne. In the Greek telling of her myth, a millennium after Bronze Age Crete, Ariadne is the "royal princess" of Crete, daughter of Queen Pasiphae and King Minos to whom sovereignty is attributed.[47] Yet Ariadne's ancestry within the myth reveals her mother Pasiphae as "the all-illuminating" daughter of the sun god Helios and moon goddess Perseis.[48] Pasiphae, the lunar "divine cow," was infamous among the Greeks; her erotic union with the bull, the ritual of *hieros gamos* (sacred marriage) turned into a "tragicomic sex-and-crime story connected with the hero saga of Theseus."[49] Kern remarked on the Cretan association of the bull with the sun, noting that "the sun was even portrayed as a bull and the moon was apparently likened to a cow."[50] Jungian Linda Fierz-David observed that Ariadne's mother Pasiphae "is the heavenly cow of the night, and she appears therefore in myths as the spouse of the son of the bull."[51]

According to the Greeks, Ariadne figures into the heroic saga of Theseus when the Athenian hostages—seven maidens and seven youths—arrive in Crete as payment of the "dreadful tribute" demanded by the Cretan king.[52] There, the hostages are to be sacrificed to the Minotaur, the half-man, half-bull creature born to Ariadne's mother Pasiphae and imprisoned by Minos within the Labyrinth of Crete, who roams the inner precincts of this prison where many enter but few return. Theseus arrives in Crete as one of the Greek hostages on a quest to kill the Minotaur. Ariadne, seeing the hero, falls instantly in love with him. Betraying her own half brother, the Minotaur, Ariadne relinquishes to Theseus her clew of thread, her weapon and her lighted crown—gifts of power that allow the hero to penetrate to the center of the labyrinth and to return safely from its precincts. For the love of Theseus, she forsakes Crete, her royal family, her status as princess and all the underpinnings of her ego-position to return with him to Athens where he has pledged to marry her. She thus also betrays, in most variants of the myth, a prior vow to Dionysos.

Because of Ariadne's gifts, Theseus succeeds in his quest and kills the Minotaur. Ariadne and Theseus flee Crete and, during their voyage to Athens, they stop on the island of Naxos for the night. In the pivotal moment of the myth, Ariadne is abandoned by the hero for whom she has given up everything. He sets sail without her—she is forgotten. In despair, Ariadne attempts suicide, plunging into the sea to drown herself; in another suicidal variant, she hangs herself from a tree. In yet another variant, Ariadne is killed by Artemis for her faithlessness to Dionysos. Variations of her death, by suicide or by another's hand, form the key motif of the myth. Nilsson observed that no other heroine of myth suffers death in so many ways,[53] which is a fitting legacy for the goddess whose true lineage is the triple crown of life, death and regeneration. Ariadne enters a death and love marriage with Dionysos, the unheroic, the god whom Aeschylus called "the womanly one."[54] She enters the realm of the dead with an unborn child in her womb and gives birth in the underworld, in the sole account in Greek myth of birth taking place in the realm of the dead.[55]

Ariadne's Gifts of Power

In mythologist Ginette Paris's wry retelling of the events of the myth, "Ariadne looked like the archetypal Dupe, the Deserted Woman, the Woman Wronged, . . . [the] first in a long line of women who participate in the success of the hero-husband only to find . . . he asks for a divorce" and, in postmodern terms, "leaves her with the kids, without a job, or a car, or money, on the shore of some desolate suburban island."[56]

Ariadne's bestowal of iconic gifts to the Greek hero can be seen to represent, in microcosm, the cultural-historical shift from a matrilineal civilization[57] to the heroic ideal of conquest and a patriarchal sky god. This is echoed in her own betrayal by the heroic masculine and underscored by the nature of the gifts Ariadne bestows upon the hero. "Giving away her power" also mythically illustrates the material and psychological pitfalls of women living under patriarchy.

Ariadne's clew of thread is not a mere ball of yarn to unravel in the passages of the labyrinth but carries the meaning to "point out or trace [as] by a clue or clew . . . a thing which guides through perplexity, a difficult investigation, an intricate structure. The mythological thread of life spun by the Fates."[58] Ariadne gives up to Theseus her lighted crown, a token of her sovereignty and of that which illumines the blackness of the bowels of the earth as *viscera terrae* within her underground laby-rinth[59] and lights the night sky in the form of the constellation *Corona Borealis*. This alchemical *lumen naturae* is described by phenome-nologist Robert D. Romanyshyn as "the light of nature, a dark-light, a luminosity in the darkness of matter" linked with "the soul of the world."[60] Ariadne relinquishes to Theseus her weapon, we may presume the double axe, its twin blades reflecting Logos's symbol of the penetrat-ing, severing function of the intellect, the "cutting edge that can dissect and differentiate on the one hand and can kill on the other."[61] She thus seems an archetypal fool for love, but as poet William Blake observed in 1790, "if the fool would persist in . . . [her] folly, [s]he would become wise."[62] Ariadne persists and, thus, even radically humanized in the myth as told by the Greeks, she embodies the vicissitudes of love that lead to the transformation of consciousness.

Birth in Death: Matrilineal Cretan Origins of the Myth

Kerényi made the following remarks about Ariadne as witnessed by the Greeks:

> Even in this story, which has become so human, Ariadne discloses a close relationship, such as only the Minoan "mistress of the labyrinth" could have had to both aspects of the labyrinth: the home of the Minotaur and the scene of the winding and unwinding dance. In the legend, the Great Goddess has become a king's daughter, but there can be no doubt as to her identity. In the Greek period of the island she bore a name—although, as we shall soon see, she also had others—that is not a name at all but an epithet and an indication of her nature. "Ariadne" is a Cretan-Greek form for "Arihagne," the "utterly pure," from the adjective *adnon* for *hagnon*.[63]

Classical scholar Walter Otto found "the words 'untouched' or 'untouch-able'" closer to the true meaning of the epithet, in the sense of "a nature which is removed from man and is foreign to his concepts of good as well as of evil" and "simultaneously . . . that which inspires worship."[64] He noted that this title, awarded in the *cultus* and ancient Greek sources solely to female deities, is further limited "only to those who belong to the mysterious domain of the earth, of the element of moisture, of Becoming, and of death: Artemis, Kore, Demeter, and Aphrodite."[65] Ariadne, said Otto, is "close to them all, because she is similar in nature."[66]

Returning to the matrilineal foundation of the myth, Kerényi asserted that Ariadne "was no doubt the Great Moon Goddess of the Aegean world, but . . . the dimensions of the celestial phenomena cannot encompass such a goddess."[67] Holding a single strand of Ariadne's thread that traces one motif of the myth, the moment of her supposed death, finds her in the underworld, in labor with her unborn child in the two-dimensional realm of the shades.[68] Ariadne dies pregnant or, in variant tales, while giving birth in the underworld.[69] Kerényi interpreted this event as follows:

A birth in death is something that must be termed "mystic" in the ancient sense, since the Mysteries of Eleusis revolved around such a birth. How much more "mystical" it was if Ariadne was impregnated by Dionysos . . . and if, like Semele, she gave birth to Dionysos! Such a widening of the "ancient mystic" realm must be taken into consideration.[70]

According to Downing, the child born in the underworld, "like the thread Ariadne holds for Theseus, unites this world and the other, the outer and the inner, life and death. Birth is not opposed to death; they are not even to be understood as following one another sequentially."[71] Kerényi's assertion that the child born in the underworld must himself be Dionysos places the event within the mythological frame of the son-lover motif of the matriarchal goddess tradition, restoring Ariadne from hapless, hard-done-by mortal girl to her lineage as a Great Goddess of Crete, triple goddess of birth, death and regeneration. Ariadne, said Kerényi, "not only mirrored Great Goddesses like Artemis, Aphrodite, and Persephone, she was Persephone and Ariadne in one person."[72] In giving birth to Dionysos, Ariadne mirrors Persephone's role as the mother of Dionysos in the Orphic tradition. Dionysos remains, even in the classical period of Greek mythology, the "dying and rising god," reflecting the matrilineal origins of the myth and serving "to remind us of the time when gods were sons and then lovers, who died and then reappeared as newborn sons, became lovers again and died, again and again."[73]

Ariadne mythically enacts fateful moments of psychological transformation as goddess of life, death and regeneration. As Jungian theorist Greg Mogenson reflected regarding our lived experience as humans, "the ways we have been spurned, betrayed, abandoned, and killed . . . both phylogenetically and ontogenetically, determine the ways in which our perceptual system construes all subsequent events."[74] Within the underworld—the locus of psyche—"everything we see is filtered through the apertures of dead love. Everything we see, we see through the eyes of the dead."[75] Ariadne, who dies in so many ways, thus embodies her matrilineal heritage as a triple goddess of life, death and regeneration; her singular connection to death is "preeminently represented" by the labyrinth, "from which most never return but some return transformed."[76]

Ariadne's birth in death, which does not take place in the "real" world of consensual reality, can be witnessed as birth into the imaginal world. As Downing said, "a birth in death, a birth in soul, a birth of the soul."[77] In Kerényi's words, "Ariadne is the archetypal reality of the bestowal of soul, of what makes a living creature an individual."[78] Following this single motif reveals the child born in the underworld, like Ariadne's thread, uniting this world with the imperishable other worlds.

Goddess Ariadne and the Emerging Cosmic Worldview

Within the Greek transmission of her myth, Ariadne's abandonment and suicide/murder embody the deepest lived experiences, the sufferings of these "primal levels" of love; simultaneously, Ariadne and the labyrinth embody the highest aspects of love in the re-emerging worldview, the goddess's "vision of life as a living unity"[79] in our own epoch-shifting times.

Jungian psychotherapist Veronica Goodchild [80] articulated a vision of this unifying force of love that is anchored in Jung's concept of *synchronicity*[81] and in quantum physics. She pointed to the coordinates of this emerging reality, which build upon our current foundation in rational consciousness: the reuniting of psyche and matter (in Jungian terminology, *unus mundus* or one world) and the eroding of the conventional

Cartesian boundaries of time and space. Humans are no longer the "detached observer[s]" behind the glass, a position which the new physics has shown to be an illusion, but are instead participators in the creation of reality, seizing the *kairos*, the "right or propitious moment," and embracing the continuous act of creation born of their ongoing reciprocity with the *One world*[82] or implicate order.[83] Underlying all of these shifts is the eruption of Eros awareness, awakening a sense of oneness without diminishing individual differentiation. Such acts of imagination, said Goodchild, erode "the barriers between the seen and unseen worlds to arrive at the mysteries of the unitary background world, a third domain comprised of a subtle psychophysical reality and its inhabitants."[84] The pathway to such knowledge in the past, she said, "was through the ancient, precarious, and unavoidable initiatory processes of death and rebirth."[85]

This, I propose, is the path of return laid down for us by Ariadne's thread. Ariadne's labyrinth—with its global re-emergence representing her epiphany—provides an entrance into the imaginal world, a portal into the Goddess's "holistic and mythopoetic perception of the sacredness and mystery of all there is on Earth."[86] Ariadne's subtle thread is the erotic tie that binds us to the Goddess, like the physical umbilical cord that once formed our symbiotic tie to a human mother, held fast until the moment of incarnation. Ariadne's imperishable thread is now expressed by the physicist's cosmic web, interweaving all forms of life. Her labyrinth is a *temenos*, where one may enter "the realm of the living imagination, the timeless realm of soul, where nothing is ever lost until it is no longer re-membered."[87] As postmodern ritual ground, the labyrinth holds the possibility of being, for a certain period of time, the meeting place between the visible and invisible worlds.

References

Baring, Anne, and Jules Cashford. *The Myth of the Goddess: Evolution of an Image.* London: Arkana, 1991.

Blake, William. *The Marriage of Heaven and Hell.* Coral Gables, FL: University of Miami Press, 1793/1963.

Bohm, David. *Wholeness and the Implicate Order.* London: Routledge, 1980.

Castleden, Rodney. *The Knossos Labyrinth: A New View of the "Palace of Minos" at Knossos.* London: Routledge, 1990.

Christ, Carol P. "A New Glossary for Crete: The Power of Naming and the Study of History." *In Feminism and Religion* (blog). September 9, 2013. www.feminismandreligion.com/2013/09/09/a-new-glossary-the-power-of-naming-and-the-study-of-history-by-carol-p-christ.

Downing, Christine. "Ariadne Mistress of the Labyrinth." In *Facing the Gods,* edited by James Hillman, 135–149. Dallas: Spring Journal Books, 1980.

———. *The Goddess: Mythological Images of the Feminine.* New York: Crossroad, 1981.

Edinger, Edward F. *Anatomy of the Psyche: Alchemical Symbolism in Psychotherapy.* La Salle, IL: Open Court, 1985.

Evans, Arthur. *The Palace of Minos: A Comparative Account of the Successive Stages of the Early Cretan Civilization as Illustrated by the Discoveries at Knossos.* 4 vols. London: Macmillan, 1921–1935.

———. *The Palace of Minos: A Comparative Account of the Successive Stages of the Early Cretan Civilization as Illustrated by the Discoveries at Knossos.* Vol. 2. London: Macmillan, 1928.

Evasdaughter, Susan. *Crete Reclaimed: A Feminist Exploration of Bronze Age Crete.* Loughborough, UK: Heart of Albion Press, 1996.

Fierz-David, Linda. *Women's Dionysian Initiation: The Villa of Mysteries in Pompeii.* Translated by Gladys Phelan. Dallas: Spring, 1988.

Gimbutas, Marija. *The Civilization of the Goddess: The World of Old Europe.* San Francisco: HarperSanFrancisco, 1991.

———. *The Language of the Goddess.* San Francisco: Harper and Row, 1989.

———. *The Living Goddesses.* Edited by Miriam Robbins Dexter. Berkeley and Los Angeles: University of California Press, 1999.

Gleick, James. *Chaos: Making a New Science.* New York: Penguin Books, 1987.

Goodchild, Veronica. "Psychoid, Psychophysical, P-subtle! Alchemy and a New Worldview." *A Journal of Archetype and Culture* 74 (Spring 2006): 63–89.

Groenewegen-Frankfort, Henriette A. *Arrest and Movement: An Essay on Space and Time in the Representational Art of the Ancient Near East.* New York: Hacker Art Books, 1951.

Hillman, James. *The Dream and the Underworld.* New York: Harper and Row, 1979.

Homer. *The Iliad.* Translated by Emile V. Rieu. Harmondsworth, UK: Penguin Classics, 1956.

———. *The Iliad.* Translated by Richmond Lattimore. Chicago: Phoenix Books, 1961.

Jaskolski, Helmut. *The Labyrinth: Symbol of Fear, Rebirth and Liberation.* Translated by Michael H. Kohn. Boston: Shambhala, 1997.

Keller, Mara L. "Crete of the Mother Goddess: Communal Rituals and Sacred Art." *ReVision: A Journal of Consciousness and Transformation* 20, no. 3 (Winter 1998): 12–16.

Kerényi, Carl. *Dionysos: Archetypal Image of Indestructible Life.* Translated by Ralph Manheim. Princeton: Princeton University Press, 1976.

Kern, Hermann. *Through the Labyrinth: Designs and Meanings Over 5,000 Years.* Translated by Abigail H. Clay, Sandra Burns Thomson and Kathrin A. Velder. New York: Prestel, 2000.

Krontira, Lyda. *In the Days of King Minos.* Translated by Philip Ramp. Athens: Edotike Athenon, 1987.

Mogenson, Greg. *Greeting the Angels: An Imaginal View of the Mourning Process.* Amityville, NY: Baywood, 1992.

Nilsson, Martin P. *The Minoan-Mycenaean Religion and its Survival in Greek Religion.* 2nd rev. ed. New York: Biblo and Tannen, 1971.

Otto, Walter F. *Dionysus: Myth and Cult.* Translated by Robert B. Palmer. Dallas: Spring, 1981.

Paris, Ginette. *Pagan Grace: Dionysos, Hermes and Goddess Memory in Daily Life*. Translated by Joanna Mott. Dallas: Spring, 1990.

Romanyshyn, Robert D. *The Wounded Researcher: Research with Soul in Mind*. New Orleans: Spring Journal Books, 2007.

Virgil. *The Aeneid of Virgil*. Translated by Allen Mandelbaum. New York: Bantam Dell Random House, 2004.

Willetts, Ronald F. *Everyday Life in Ancient Crete*. New York: Putnam, 1969.

Endnotes

1 Anne Baring and Jules Cashford, *The Myth of the Goddess: Evolution of an Image* (London: Viking Arkana, 1991).

2 Quoted in Lyda Krontira, *In the Days of King Minos*, trans. Philip Ramp (Athens: Edotike Athenon, 1987), 3.

3 Baring and Cashford, 106.

4 Quoted in Lyda Krontira, *Op. Cit.*, 3.

5 Arthur Evans, *The Palace of Minos: A Comparative Account of the Successive Stages of the Early Cretan Civilization as Illustrated by the Discoveries at Knossos* (London: Macmillan, 1928).

6 Baring and Cashford, 108.

7 Evans, 2.

8 Ibid.

9 Marija Gimbutas, *The Living Goddesses*, ed. M. Robbins Dexter (Berkeley and Los Angeles: University of California Press, 1999), 135.

10 Rodney Castleden, *The Knossos Labyrinth: A New View of the "Palace of Minos" at Knossos* (London: Routledge, 1990).

11 Gimbutas, 134.

12 Marija Gimbutas, *The Language of the Goddess* (San Francisco: Harper and Row, 1989), 321.

13 Gimbutas, *The Living Goddesses*, 135.

14 Susan Evasdaughter, *Crete Reclaimed: A Feminist Exploration of Bronze Age Crete* (Loughborough, UK: Heart of Albion Press, 1996).

15 Baring and Cashford, Op. Cit.

16 Ibid., 107.

17 Ibid., 110.

18 Ibid., 110–111.

19 Ibid., 107.

20 Ibid.

21 Mara L. Keller, "Crete of the Mother Goddess: Communal Rituals and Sacred Art," *ReVision: A Journal of Consciousness and Transformation* 20, no. 3 (1998, Winter): 13.

22 Baring and Cashford, 113.

23 Ibid.

24 Martin P. Nilsson, *The Minoan-Mycenaean Religion and its Survival in Greek Religion*, 2nd rev. ed. (New York: Biblo and Tannen, 1971), 20.

25 Henriette A. Groenewegen-Frankfort, *Arrest and Movement: An Essay on Space and Time in the Representational Art of the Ancient Near East* (New York: Hacker Art Books, 1951), 186.

26 *Choros* (Greek) is a dance, dance form or dance movement and a place or surface for the performance of a dance. See Hermann Kern, *Through the Labyrinth: Designs and Meanings Over 5,000 Years*, trans. A. H. Clay, S. Burns Thomson and K. A. Velder (New York: Prestel, 2000), 44.

27 Homer, *The Iliad*, trans. E. V. Rieu (Harmondsworth: Penguin Classics, 1956), xviii, 590–593.

28 Carl Kerényi, *Dionysos: Archetypal Image of Indestructible Life*, trans. R. Manheim (Princeton: Princeton University Press, 1976), 98–99.

29 Carol P. Christ, "A New Glossary for Crete: The Power of Naming and the Study of History," *Feminism and Religion* (blog), September 9, 2013, www.feminismandreligion.com/2013/09/09/a-new-glossary-the-power-of-naming-and-the-study-of-history-by-carol-p-christ/.

30 Ronald F. Willetts, *Everyday Life in Ancient Crete* (New York: Putnam, 1969), 176.

31 Kern, 176.

32 Homer, *The Iliad*, trans. R. Lattimore (Chicago: Phoenix Books, 1961), 252.

33 Ibid., 252–253.

34 Baring and Cashford, 135.

35 Ibid., 135–136.

36 Kern, 26.

37 Virgil, *The Aeneid of Virgil*, trans. A. Mandelbaum (New York: Bantam Dell / Random House, 2004), 121–122.

38 James Gleick, *Chaos: Making a New Science* (New York: Penguin Books, 1987), 24.

39 Kern, 27.

40 Ibid., 44.

41 Kerényi, 100.

42 Helmut Jaskolski, *The Labyrinth: Symbol of Fear, Rebirth and Liberation*, trans. M. H. Kohn (Boston: Shambhala, 1997), 37.

43 Marija Gimbutas, *The Civilization of the Goddess: The World of Old Europe* (San Francisco: HarperSanFrancisco, 1991), 346.

44 Christ, Op. Cit.

45 Christine Downing, "Ariadne Mistress of the Labyrinth," *Facing the Gods*, ed. J.Hillman (Dallas: Spring Journal Books, 1980), 141.

46 Gimbutas, 164.

47 Jaskolski, 36.

48 Ibid., 36.

49 Ibid., 40.

50 Kern, 46.

51 Linda Fierz-David, *Women's Dionysian Initiation: The Villa of Mysteries in Pompeii*, trans. G. Phelan (Dallas: Spring, 1988), 22.

52 Jaskolski, 18.

53 Nilsson, Op. Cit.

54 Walter F. Otto, *Dionysus: Myth and Cult*, trans. R. B. Palmer (Dallas: Spring, 1981), 176.

55 Christine Downing, *The Goddess: Mythological Images of the Feminine* (New York: Crossroad, 1981), 64–65.

56 Ginette Paris, *Pagan Grace: Dionysos, Hermes and Goddess Memory in Daily Life*, trans. J. Mott (Dallas: Spring, 1990), 41.

57 This shift reflected the changing political realities of the increasing Mycenaean—Indo-European or Aryan people from the Greek mainland—incursions into the matrilineal civilization of Bronze Age Crete. By 1600 BCE, relations were established with the Mycenaeans, who travelled back and forth from the mainland, absorbing the Cretan culture, bringing with them the early form of the Greek language—a script known as Linear B, deciphered only in 1953. By 1450 BCE, following the destruction of the temple palaces by earthquakes and tidal waves subsequent to the volcanic eruption of Thera to the north, the Mycenaeans settled permanently in Crete. The next wave of invaders, the Dorians, in 1150 BCE, brought the Cretan civilization to an end (Baring & Cashford, *Myth of the Goddess*, 108).

58 *The New Shorter Oxford English Dictionary,* 4th rev. ed., vol. 1, s. v., "clew."

59 Kern, 31.

60 Robert D. Romanyshyn, *The Wounded Researcher: Research with Soul in Mind* (New Orleans: Spring Journal Books, 2007), 8.

61 Edward F. Edinger, *Anatomy of the Psyche: Alchemical Symbolism in Psychotherapy* (La Salle, IL: Open Court, 1985), 191.

62 William Blake, *The Marriage of Heaven and Hell* (Coral Gables, FL: University of Miami Press, 1793/1963), 7.

63 Kerényi, 98–99.

64 Otto, 183.

65 Ibid.

66 Ibid.

67 Kerényi, 124.

68 To enter the underworld is to make a radical shift from material to psychical perspective. Three dimensions morph into two. We are desubstantialized, and flesh, blood, matter and the worldview of nature falls away. The shade is "dead" of natural life, yet in shape, size and sense, it's the precise replica of the figure in life, the immaterial, mirror-like image—*eidola*. It is the realm of soul. James Hillman, *The Dream and the Underworld* (New York: Harper and Row, 1979), 51, 46.

69 Downing, *The Goddess*, 64–65.

70 Kerényi, 108.

71 Downing, *The Goddess,* 65.

72 Kerényi,107.

73 Downing, *The Goddess,* 63.

74 Greg Mogenson, *Greeting the Angels: An Imaginal View of the Mourning Process* (Amityville, NY: Baywood, 1992), 8.

75. Ibid.

76 Downing, "Ariadne Mistress of the Labyrinth," 146.

77 Downing, *The Goddess,* 65.

78 Kerényi, 124.

79 Baring and Cashford, xi.

80 Veronica Goodchild, "Psychoid, Psychophysical, P-subtle! Alchemy and a New Worldview," S*pring: A Journal of Archetype and Culture* 74 (2006): 51–75.

81 Ibid., 81. "The phenomenon of synchronicity, . . . bypassing the time/

space continuum, opens us to the subtle body of the world, points us toward evidence of continuing creation based on an acausal foundation, and relies on the co-creative contribution of consciousness through 'meaning' to this on-going creation."

82 Ibid., 65–66.

83 David Bohm, *Wholeness and the Implicate Order* (London: Routledge, 1980).

84 Goodchild, 66.

85 Ibid.

86 Gimbutas, *The Language of the Goddess*, 321.

87. Romanyshyn, 79.

WILD WOMEN OF THE WATERS: REMEMBERING THE ANGUANE OF THE ITALIAN ALPS

Mary Beth Moser

Folk stories told across the ages in the Italian Alps feature female characters who demonstrate everyday spiritual agency. With characteristics that seem to bridge the human and other-than-human worlds, these females dwell in the wild and embody the very mystery and awe of nature. They are important, because village women told and listened to stories about them in the nightly winter gathering of the filò, a dialect word that comes from the verb filare, which means "to spin." It was a place of entertainment where customs and rules were collectively elaborated. My great grandmothers could have heard and told some of these stories; my grandmothers could have heard them before they left their motherland as young women to immigrate to the United States. The magical actions of the characters in the folk stories lend insight into folk women's everyday activities that gave their lives meaning. I propose that the female protagonists of these stories and their actions convey the long memory of female power. They communicate values that call for the respect of women and of nature and the consequences of violating that respect. The females in the stories specifically ask to be remembered.

This article focuses on the *Anguane*, "women of the waters." They can be regarded as embodied nature deities, associated with the cycles of life and the sources of life, and holders of beneficent and terrifying power. By analyzing the folk stories, I present evidence of the Anguane's agency in their characteristics and roles, address how their agency has been negated, and discern what values they communicate. These females, when considered in all of their forms, embody and enforce the rules regarding the full cycle of life: birth, life, death and renewal.

The Anguane

The Anguane, embodied females who dwell primarily in or near water, are primary characters that appear, by various names, in "hundreds and hundreds" of folk stories in the region of Trentino and throughout the Alps.[1] Although their actions can seem mysterious or even dangerous, in the examples I present they can be viewed as indications of female power. Anguane demonstrate their agency through their strong affinity with and knowledge of nature and its wildness, as well as through the cosmos. Their roles of queen, ancestress and mother indicate their status. Anguane are daughters of the sun and are associated with the moon and the stars. Although the Anguane have been labeled as witches in some stories, even their negated powers demonstrate their embodied knowledge of the forces of nature.

For this analysis, the publications of authors in Trentino and Alto Adige (South Tyrol) have provided the primary sources of information. Specifically, these publications include the research of Mauro Neri, Giovanna Borzaga, Gari Monfosco, Giovanna Zangrandi, Andrea Foches, Brunamaria Dal Lago Veneri, Dino Coltro and Adriano Vanin. Also utilized are the collections of Karl (or Carl) Felix Wolff (born in 1879), translated from German into English by two separate authors, as well as stories reported by Rachel Harriet Busk, who traveled through the region, and published in 1874. By drawing primarily on the stories recorded by or interpreted by people within the Alpine culture, the goal is to glean a representative cultural context.

Names of Anguane in the Folk Stories and Related Place Names

Before discussing the folk stories in which Anguane appear, it is revealing to review the multitude of their names and the prevalence of their place names. Like the rivers and streams that flow with their own intelligence from the mountain waters where they originate, Anguane are not contained by geopolitical borders, which have shifted over time, although their stories likely do reflect political influences. Thus, I include folk stories from the eastern Dolomites in provinces and regions near Trentino, whose people share common values. In the introduction to an English-language version of a compilation of stories focusing on females, the translator, Father Marco Bagnarol, acknowledged that Trentino / Alto Adige, Veneto and Friuli-Venezia Giulia are three "sister" regions of northeastern Italy that share common values, ethics and ideals.[2]

Anguane are known by dozens of names in the folk stories of the Alpine mountain areas, depending on the local dialect of the place the story is told. Similar names in their plural form include the following: *Angane, Agane, Longane, Gane, Aquane, Naquane* and *Pantegane*.[3] In his dictionary of mythological characters, Mauro Neri adds the following: *Aguane, Anghiane, Guane, Inguane, Bèle Putèle* (Beautiful Girls), *Fade* (Fairies) and *Fòle*.[4] Anguane are similar to the females known as *Salinghe*[5] and *Vivane*,[6] with variations including *Aivane, Vane, Vivene,* and *Valdane*.[7] *Selvane* (from *selva*, meaning "wild"), *Salvadeghe* and *Bregostane* also appear in the stories.

In areas with German influence in and near Trentino, they may be known as *sàighele bàibele* or *beate donnette* (literally, "blessed little women").[8] As Donna Berta (Italian for Lady Berta) and Froberta (from Frau Berta, German for "Lady Berta") in Trentino, we see a form of Perchta, a German goddess of winter. Andrea Foches has compiled the names of Anguane in Trentino by location and placed them on a map, illustrated in his book *Leggende delle Anguane*.[9] I shall use the name Anguane for simplicity and consistency in general discussion, with variations by story as appropriate.

Although Neri described them as *fate delle acque* (fairies of the waters),[10] and Giovanna Borzaga referred to them as "creatures of the water,"[11] I prefer the term *donne dell'acque* (women of the waters), used by Brunamaria Dal Lago Veneri and Adriano Vanin, which acknowledges their embodied status.[12] Like other women, they enjoy the pleasures of life, bear and raise children, suffer great loss and die. Although at times they may seem to mysteriously disappear from the view of men who violate their rules, I maintain that they are not disembodied spirits, because their children often continue to see them and to receive their care.

Anguane are primarily of the mountain waters (streams, lakes, rivers and springs), but they also can live in rock crevices, in the wild or in the woods. Citing the proximity of actual bodies of water to the location of their stories, Borzaga said that the Latin word for "water," *aqua*, is related to the words *ega* and *aga* in Trentino dialect.[13] Giovanni Kezich included the derivation *angue* (serpent) as a possible source of their name, noting that Anguane have been assimilated at times with serpents in other traditions.[14]

In addition to their prevalence in the oral tradition of the folk stories, Anguane have left their memory in place names in Trentino and beyond: There are numerous *busi de le Anguane* (literally, "holes of the Anguane" in dialect, most likely "rock crevices" or "caves") and *cròzi de le vivane* (rocks of the Vivane),[15] one of which is located in the hamlet of Martinei,[16] not far from my paternal grandmother's village of Bedollo, and told of in the folk story "El Caradór e le Vivane" (The Cart Driver and the Vivane).[17] Another story, "La Bella Aguana" (The Beautiful Aguane), presented by Borzaga, begins as follows: "Everyone in Valsugana knows that the great rocks near Maso Fraineri of Roncegno are not other than the ancient habitation of the 'aguane.'"[18] The crevices and small caves in the rocks of Combra are known as *ghiana*—similar to one of their names, anghiana.[19]

At the locale of Naquane, in Valle Camonica, whose name is very similar to Anguane, there is a petroglyph that shows a row of females in apparent ritual, with water marks indicating the flow of water over a reclined figure.[20] Mermaids with twin tails are carved at the top of the column near the entry of the church of San Siro in Cemmo, Valle Camonica. Other twin-tailed figures include a fresco, with tails crossed, on the walls of the church of St. Jakob near Tramin in South Tyrol, built on the foundation of a Roman temple to the Goddess Isis.[21] The Anguane, in all of their manifestations across time, seem to remember that the entire area—where stories and place names of Anguane still linger—was once an ancient sea.[22] Monte Concarena and the Dolomites still bear the physical evidence of marine fossils.[23]

Primordial water deities were painted on rocks in Africa nearly 28,000 years ago; a contemporary double-tailed water spirit known as Mami Wata is said to swim there still.[24] In their multicultural presence across the ages, female water beings seem to be shimmering reminders of a shared ancestral African origin, and even earlier, of the primordial waters that are the source of life.

A Framework for Analyzing the Agency of Anguane

Based upon the characterizations of the Anguane by the regional experts and my own analysis of the folk stories, I propose that Anguane are embodied nature deities in sacred relationship with the essential cycles of life. This framework, discussed briefly here and developed in more detail through my analysis of their characteristics and roles, provides insight into the agency of the Anguane. The taboos associated with them demonstrate a rule-keeping or regulatory aspect, which can be viewed as their beneficent and terrifying power. Their negation as witches seems to come from fear of their agency—their embodied knowledge of nature, which includes the ability to merge with plants and animals, and their ability to utilize nature as an ally for punishment.

Embodied Nature Deity

Anguane, as characterized, embody divine—in the sense of all-giving—and human characteristics, firmly connected to nature. Their characteristics are not static over time, however, cautioned Adriano Vanin, who has catalogued dozens of their attributes and explored the caves of their dwelling places. And yet they seem to retain some elemental authentic character that places them in contact with what is essential, he said.[25] Giovanna Zangrandi, who collected folk stories in the Dolomites, described Anguane as "part wild, part divine, part human"—what I am calling an embodied nature deity—and "one of the elements most ancient and alive" in the folk stories; even after alteration, she said, they retained an aspect of "original alpine deity."[26] Gari Monfosco also characterized them as goddesses, proposing that at one time Anguane were honored as divinity of the woods and protectors of the fields, animals and family.[27] The Anguane's actions (bringing forth life and fertility, caring for children, protecting nature, giving gifts, bestowing hidden knowledge and maintaining the rules), roles (queen, mother and virgin), and cosmic connections (sun, moon and stars) in the folk stories that I have analyzed evoke the power of a self-generating and protective deity or ancestress.

These characteristics evoke the numerous images that survive from Neolithic Europe of the female, whom archaeologist Marija Gimbutas described as the source of life, "parthenogenetic, creating life out of herself . . . a primeval, self-fertilizing 'Virgin Goddess' who has survived in numerous culture forms to the present day."[28] Gimbutas characterized the main theme of the symbolism of the Goddess as the:

> cyclic mystery of birth, death, and the renewal of life, involving not only human life, but all life on earth. Symbols and images cluster around the parthenogenetic (self-generating) Goddess who is the single source of all life. Her energy is manifest in springs and wells, in the moon, sun and earth, and in all animals and plants. She is the Giver-of-Life, Wielder-of-Death, Regeneratrix, and the Earth Fertility Goddess, rising and dying with the plants. Male gods also exist, not as creators, but as guardians of wild nature, or as metaphors of life energy and the spirits of seasonal vegetation.[29]

Associated with the Cycles of Life and the Sources of Life

Anguane are associated with the cycles of life and the sources of life; their stories spiral around and through the processes of renewal, fertility and life/death/rebirth. Anguane are associated with the moon and lunar deities, in the assessment of Brunamaria Dal Lago Veneri. They have miraculous capabilities in laundry, she noted, which I view as a cycle of renewal. In their acquired attributes or other guises, they exhibit special abilities in spinning, which she associated with menstrual initiation. The Anguana is midwife and mourner, present at the passage of life and death, and represents a transition from the old year to the new year.[30]

Anguane are often found in groups of three, like the Fates of mythology, according to Kezich, who noted their association with spinning, presiding over life and death with the *la rocca, il fuso* and *le forbici* (the rod or staff, the spindle and the scissors).[31] The presence of triple deities, venerated for the past two millennia, was widespread in Germanic Europe, according to the recent research of Dawn E. Work-MaKinne. Described as "goddesses of the entire life continuum," they include the Deae Matronae of the Romans; the *Norns*, goddesses of fate from the Viking Age in Scandinavia; the *Dísir*, goddesses of guidance and protection; and the *Drei Heiligen Jungfrauen*, the Three Holy Maidens of medieval Catholicism who offer healing, protection and help.[32] Roberto Gremmo claimed that the Matronae, the Mothers, were "the most important divinities of the Cisalpine Gaul," citing evidence of a Celtic cult to them in nearby Piedmont.[33]

Anguane are associated with the source of life, specifically the water and the sun. Contemporary visual images of Anguane convey their strong relationship with the watery realm. The painting *Racconto di Anguane* (Story of Anguane), by Trentino artist Rosanna Cavallini, portrays four white female figures in motion, their flowing hair and mermaid-tail gowns rising up in the blue watery depths from a luminous form, with an umbilical-like ribbon that also rises up and spins around and through them. In another contemporary illustration by an unknown artist, three Anguane circle a central white light in a sea of dark blue.[34]

Vanin characterized Anguane by their "cult of the sun."[35] For people in northern latitudes, the longer days resulting from the return of the sun heralded life. One town in Valle di Ledro in Trentino is completely without sun for almost three months during the winter due to the steep valley walls; the villagers celebrate the sun's return with a parade of an enthroned Sun King accompanied by the most beautiful woman of the village, who is designated the queen, and a great feast.[36] Ancient sundials still appear painted on the outside of some buildings. In Neolithic Europe, the sun was "a symbol of regeneration and one of the manifestations of the Goddess of Regeneration," according to Marija Gimbutas, who noted that the gender of the sun is female in Celtic, Germanic, Baltic, and Slavic languages.[37] The Sun Goddess is African, according to Lucia Chiavola Birnbaum, who noted that in ancient African belief, the light and warmth of the sun are birthed out of the darkness. The sun is personified as the mother, a solar goddess who is the precursor to the light-bringing figure of Santa Lucia.[38]

Beneficent—and Terrifying—Power

Several authors have noted the ambiguous nature of the Anguane. According to Vanin, their desire to interact with humans, even if there are "mysterious taboos" that are usually violated, is an important characteristic.[39] In Neri's characterization, they are ever-ready to help humans, but their nature is at times good and generous but at other times that of the most evil witches.[40] Veneri wrote that they can charm, bewitch and seduce; she characterized the power of the Anguane as "beneficent" and "terrifying," especially when seen through the eyes of men.[41] Monfosco described their actions as "avenging atrocity," a phrase that implies their severe acts are done "in response to" rather than for no reason.[42] The Anguane of the Novella, a stream in Val di Non, are described *as mezze fate e mezze streghe* (part fairy, part witch).[43] Fairies are good, a Trentino woman told me when I asked her about folk stories, and witches are bad—and the witches are always women. As I will further discuss later in this article, I propose that the "mysterious taboos" can be understood as the rules regarding menstruation and the consequences if the rules are not respected. Disrespect of nature, of women's ritual domain or of the rules regarding the greater cycles of life (yearly and agricultural) can result in even more severe consequences.

The Agency of Anguane in Their Actions and Characteristics

In this section, I analyze and present examples of folk stories in which Anguane show agency as embodied nature deities in sacred relationship with the essential cycles of life and close to the sources of life. I also address and bring insight to their associated taboos as indicators of their female power.

In the folk stories presented here, Anguane embody sensual pleasure and wildness; they are of this world (eat cheese, give birth and raise children), they enact cycles of renewal (washing clothes) and acts of transformation (making cheese). They bring forth fertility and abundance. They have affinity with plants and animals. They protect nature's gifts (waters, fields and springs), guard its treasures and offer to teach its secrets to people who have kind hearts. They care for all children. They offer gifts to those who protect them. They maintain rules that I propose protect the creative principle of life and the cycles of life.

Although at times only a summary of the story is presented here, in the interest of brevity, it is important to emphasize that the folk stories are quite specific to place. The village and sometimes even the specific location within the village (such as a farmhouse or a natural feature) is named, which gives the story a sense of authenticity and relevance, especially for those familiar with the location. This cultural specificity has the ability to reach deep within, as well as across time with its genetic resonance. As in traditional cultures, stories tied to the land can give the people a sense of belonging.

For consistency of format, in each of the following paragraphs, the Anguane characteristics are summarized in the title and first sentence. These are followed by examples, from the folk stories, that validate those characteristics.[44] I have utilized the local names for Anguane indicated in each story and have provided the story titles and any other appropriate details in footnotes for ease in readability.

Embody Sensual Pleasure

Anguane like to eat, drink, sing and dance—that is, they enjoy the sensual pleasures of the body. A young Vivana goes home with a man and eats cheese.[45] Salinghe like singing, dancing, and kindhearted herders.[46] A group of Anguane, who live in the mountains among gold and silver, sing a song about drinking the water of love.[47] The *Fade* of Veneto dance inside the caves to the sounds of fifes and drums.[48] Guane live in a cave and have "orgies" on Friday nights.[49]

Have Children and Care for Children

Anguane are nurturing mothers and foster mothers; they watch over and raise children—even if not their own—sometimes secretly, at their own risk. An Ongana from Lago Scin comes to watch over and secretly raise the five children of a widowed man.[50] An Aguana near Primiero marries a young man and has five children; he breaks a taboo and she must leave, but she comes back to watch over them.[51] An Aguana in the town of Malosco dies from mistreatment in her marriage, but she returns during the days as a beautiful ghost, caring for home and her children, until they are raised.[52]

Enact Cycles of Renewal

Anguane are associated with laundry, which I view as a cycle of renewal. A Salinga emerges at midnight to do laundry with the help of a magic circle, magic words and a fountain.[53] There are numerous stories about Anguane laying laundry out in a field to dry.[54]

Eat Transformed Food; Teach the Process of Transformation

Anguane eat cheese, a traditional food in the Alps, and are associated with the transformational processes involved in making it. A young Anguana goes home with a woodsman and eats cheese.[55] The Fade of Veneto teach the mountain dwellers how to make butter, cheese and ricotta.[56] Out of kindness, an old woman "witch" teaches a poor old woman how to make butter and cheese.[57] A wild man who is the husband of Donna Berta, a wild woman, teaches people how to make cheese.[58]

Bring Forth Fertility and Abundance

The Anguane know how to bring forth abundance in nature. A Vivana of the woods knows how to make barley grain multiply and offers to help others to do so.[59] Fields are fertile and goat's milk is abundant under an Anguana's care.[60] Donna Berta helps women and provides an endless source of thread.[61]

Bring and Become Flowers

Anguane gather, bring, sell or become flowers. Several stories involve forget-me-nots or other beautiful blue flowers. Three young Anguane gather and bring flowers to sell and leave behind fields of forget-me-nots.[62] After she dies, an Anguana near Primiero becomes the wild healing plant of Arnica and comes to her daughter in the fields of flowers.[63] One plant, *Chelidonium majus*, bears a nickname relating it to Anguane.[64]

Become Animals

Anguane become animals (otters, marmots and birds) and turn other people into animals (foxes, badgers and birds). The Anguane of Cismon, who bring beautiful blue flowers to sell, turn into otters.[65] A woman named Jendsana is raised by otters after being thrown into the river as a baby, although she clarifies that she is not one of the Anguane, who are "mysterious forest-women." However, like the Anguane, she brings forget-me-nots and befriends a man named Zompo (meaning "cripple") who has an injured foot.[66] In Andraz, an otter woman marries a man and has many children who live on with the sopranome (a kind of nickname, identifying which family or clan one belongs to) of *Salvatica*, meaning "wild."[67]

In the story "Piè di Capra" (Goat's Feet), many Anguane, in the aspects of otters and marmots, secretly attend a wedding between an Anguana and a young man.[68] An Anguana, surrounded by marmots, greets the sun each morning.[69] In nature, otters are of the water and marmots dwell in the rock. Perhaps they represent sister groups of people, each with their own totem animal.

A young woman artist known as the Filadressa is turned into a vulture; she eventually returns to being a woman, marries, and becomes the ancestress of many over the centuries.[70] The Anguane of Fravort turn all of their prisoners into foxes and badgers after one of the Anguane is stolen as a bride and remains with her captor.[71]

Protect Nature and Guard Its Treasures

Anguane protect what is sacred to them (waters, fields, springs and mountains). They guard the treasures of nature, especially from those who appear to seek personal gain. The fatal ending of the violators seems to indicate the importance of what is being protected. An Angana threatens the shepherds who try to use her verdant fields for grazing.[72] Three Vivane sitting at the top of a rock know of treasures within the mountain, which vanish along with people who try to reach them out of greed.[73] A young woman who is a *fata* (fairy) and has golden hair and blue eyes guards the golden treasure in the cave called Pagan Rock, killing the man who betrays her secret.[74] The Anguane of Lago di Lagole, who used to bathe in a miraculous spring with prodigious virtues, destroy the women of Sabasa who had taken over the pool and the temple to Hecate that *il Capo*, the male leader, had erected there.[75]

Know the Future

Some Anguane have oracular abilities. The *Sibilla*, or *Sibyl*, is listed by Foches as one of the names of the Anguane.[76] In a story titled "The Cavern of the Sibyl," a *maga* (magician or sorceress) named Sibyl has oracular and healing abilities.[77] The Sibyl lives in a deep cave with healing thermal waters known as Comano Terme. People go to her for matters of love and to know the future. She helps a wounded knight, who had protected her from being killed by another knight who had intended to violate her domain, by having him drink and bathe in the waters. In the story, the

Sibyl promises to restore life to the person who will remember her. Many years later, long after she has disappeared, the knight whom she healed as a young man returns to find the healing waters for his sick grandson. He forsakes his wealth, chooses to live in the cave and becomes the dispenser of the water.[78] In Borzaga's version of the story, she refers to the Sibyl as a mysterious prophetess whose origins and age were unknown but who may have been "as old as the Earth."[79]

Sibyls, holy women considered to have oracular power, are portrayed in the iconography of Catholic churches and sanctuaries in the towns of Tirano, Trent and Edolo. In the Sanctuary of the Madonna of Tirano in Valtellina, paintings of Sibyls surround the chapel where the miraculous Madonna is venerated. The marble organ loft in the basilica of Santa Maria Maggiore in Trent (site of the non-plenary meetings of the Council of Trent), sculpted in 1534, depicts a scene of the Virgin Mary being adored by the Magi and a large standing female described as *"la Sibilla"* (the sibyl) on the right.[80] In Edolo, a painting of the Sibyl from the 1530s appears in the church of St. John the Baptist, which is said to be "the most significant monument."[81]

Have Knowledge of Medicines

We can glean from the folk stories that Anguane are close to herbs (making meadows grow, laying out laundry on the fields, and bringing or even turning into flowers). The nickname of a powerful herb known as the "plant of the Anguana" indicates that they understand the healing properties of plants. They also know how to make ointment and salves to "fly," an apparent knowledge of the ecstatic properties of some plants. For example, an Anguana from Cloz in Val di Non, who is also labeled a witch, uses magic salve on her body at midnight to fly to a gathering of witches.[82] Another Anguana uses salve on her hair at night.[83]

Offer Gifts if They Are Protected

Anguane reward those who protect them. An Anguana offers to bring riches, marriage and happiness to a cheesemaker if he protects her against the wild hunter who threatens her.[84] Two *fate* (fairies) are protected from the sun by a boy, in an act of unsolicited kindness, and they repay him with the gift of a whistle, which protects him against misfortune.[85] A young man helps an old woman, whom Busk named as an Angana, to carry water; she rewards him with a precious ring, which helps him to achieve his desires, and a dog and a cat to help him.[86] Froberta protects good families who respect her.[87]

Of the Moon, Sun and Stars

Anguane are in close relationship to the cosmos, specifically to the moon, sun and stars. Veneri associated Anguane with the moon and lunar deity.[88] The Anguane come out and dance frenetically on the full moon.[89] Women who are daughters of the sun share characteristics with Anguane.[90] Although not named as Anguane, additional women who are also in close relationship with the moon, sun, and stars are featured in folk stories.[91]

Maintain Rules That Protect the Creative Principle of Life

Anguane are associated with mysterious taboos, which are broken by men they marry or accompany. Once the taboo is violated, through the man's ignorance, curiosity, thoughtlessness or anger, the woman departs. Although the taboos that surface in the folk stories are sometimes presented as minor actions on the part of the males or as spells placed on the females, I propose that they are repositories of ancient menstrual power. The menstrual-related elements of the taboos, which involve touch, seeing light and speaking, become more evident when viewed with the knowledge of metaformic theory. Cultural theorist Judy Grahn's research of menstrual seclusion rites reveals that there were strict taboos for the menstruant against touching, seeing light and speaking.[92] Grahn proposed that, in their primordial roots, these rites helped re-enact human comprehension of separation and, thus, creation. The disciplined ritual separation of the menstruants from others maintained human consciousness.[93]

Taboo of Touch

In several folk stories, it is forbidden for a man to touch the braid of the Anguana while she is sleeping. Often the long hair is touching the ground and he lifts it, upon which she immediately awakens and leaves him. A young woodsman in Val di Non invites a Vivana home; she falls asleep, but when he reaches over to lift her braid from the ground she gets up silently and leaves.[94] A young man with an oxcart marries a Vivana, and they have children; one night, after he touches her braid to lift it from the floor, she disappears.[95] A typical taboo of menstrual seclusion rites is that menstruants were not allowed to touch water or the earth.[96] Further, a menstruant often was not allowed to touch others or herself, particularly her skin or head.[97] The first proto-human females, Grahn proposed, set themselves apart and did not touch themselves or the earth, to keep separate, and thus sacred—both symbolically and ritually—the surface of the earth. This ritual re-enactment of the creation of the earth kept it solidly in human consciousness.[98]

In the folk story "The Clothes of the Salingas," the villagers understand that they should not touch the dazzling clothes laid out to dry by the Salinga or they will burn up.[99] The cloth, in its ritual care with harmful consequences if touched, evokes the potency and restrictions of menstrual rites.

Hair has strong associations with menstrual flow, according to Grahn's research. The maiden's hair, upon her emergence from seclusion, is meticulously tended in culturally significant ways, including braiding, as part of menarche rites. Control of the maiden's hair symbolizes control of menstrual flow and of chaotic forces; its wetness can affect the weather via its ability to attract moisture.[100] Kezich noted that both hair and yarn are braided.[101] The three-part braid (*treccia* in Italian) of an Anguana is a further association with menstruation. Three is considered a sacred number, because it marks the number of days of menstrual seclusion as well as the conventional period for the dark of the moon during its "menstruation."[102]

In the folk stories, the hair touches the ground at night, which seems to align its power to the darkness of night and of seclusion. Barbara Walker associated hair, water and menstruation in her citation of a "durable myth" that a witch's hair placed in water, especially if she were menstruating, would become a serpent.[103] Combing hair was thought to cause thunderstorms in Tyrol, she noted.[104] One contemporary Trentino woman, Pina Trentini, said that she was taught that hair should not be washed during menstruation, because it would not be good for the hair. Menstruation, she said, was at one time known as *le regole* (the rules); a menstruating woman was said to have her *regole*. This term was used when she was a child, she clarified. "Now it's called menstruation."[105]

Taboo of Light

In the story of "The Matrimony with the Angana," it is forbidden for the Angana's husband to view her at night by candlelight.[106] In another story, Merisana cannot have light fall on her at night.[107] In both stories, the husband violates the taboo; in the first story the Angana departs, and in the second story Merisana dies. This "intrusion" of light into the darkness of night seems to violate a separation, a sacred order of day and night.

Seeing light, particularly during menarche (first menstruation) was a menstrual taboo. Almost universally, at menarche the maiden was secluded and strictly prohibited from seeing light until her emergence into the light, which Grahn proposed was a re-enactment, at its primordial source, of the separation of light and darkness in human consciousness.[108] Women's ritual separation from light was therefore honoring its source and maintaining its creation. Through sacred ritual, women participated in and acted as agents of light's cyclic return.

Taboo of Speech

There are several examples of the male partners speaking the names of their female Anguane wives—intentionally, unintentionally or in anger—even though they are specifically requested never to do so. Often the name is a nickname indicating the Anguane's wildness: Goat's Feet, Lontra (otter) and Crivapeta (inverted foot or blood heel).[109] Two similar stories come from Friuli. In one, a man marries a wild woman who lives in a grotto with water and travels the woods predicting the future; when he calls her Crivapeta, she leaves.[110] In another, a man calls his wife Krivòpetà, and she leaves, never to return.[111] In both cases, the women had begun to harvest before their husbands thought the grain was ready. Once the name is spoken and the women leave, the men must never see them again. Monfosco related a similar story in which an Anguana agrees to marry a young man of Deppe, at his request, if he agrees to never call her piè-di-capra, which he later does one day in anger.[112] Coltro referred to "the taboo of the name" when describing the prohibition regarding marriage to an Anguana.[113] The departure of the Anguane, which is sometimes portrayed as her being under a spell, clearly communicates the consequences of the man breaking his word by uttering a name of disrespect or taboo. Can he be trusted to keep other agreements? When the action is intentional, it seems to convey the need for respecting and honoring verbal agreements, which must have been paramount in an oral culture.

In some stories, the Anguana is described as silent, especially when she leaves after a taboo has been broken.[114] Is she returning to her matriarchal clan where the power of the word is honored? Silence was also a common menarche requirement; in some cases, the menstruant's name could not be spoken during her seclusion, which suggested to Grahn that these rites were enacted as though they came from a time before speech, when only ritual existed.[115]

An Anguane not having a name or having a pejorative nickname could have also been a way of identifying her as separate and "other." In a story from Calalzo, Anguane were baptized with the name *Donne selvareghe* (women of the wild), implying they did not take Christian names.[116] In another story, Redòsola, who is a "reformed witch," asks each spring to be baptized but is denied and is given another year of penance by the priest.[117]

In "La Salvatica di Andraz," a man accidentally learns and speaks the otter woman's name, upon which she disappears. In this case, not naming her seems to safeguard her wildness.[118] A custom in some parts of Germany lends support to this idea: According to Lotte Motz, in December the name of the wolf is not to be spoken.[119]

I propose that these examples of the actions of the Anguane regarding their taboos of touch, light and speech hold the memory of rules of menstrual power and demonstrate the consequences for violation of those rules. Menstrual rules were still remembered by some women of Trentino in the 20th century. This persistence of memory speaks to the rules' importance, not as shameful, as they are sometimes viewed today, but as sacred rites that reflect women's spiritual agency. At their source, the rules maintain the creative principle of life.

Affect Flow, Moisture and Fertility

Anguane, especially in their negated role of witches, can affect the flow of life—that is, the fertile flow of menstrual blood, milk or precipitation. By using metaformic theory, the acts of punishment attributed to Anguane—taking away fertility, causing storms and drying up cows' milk—can be viewed as indications of their menstrual powers. Grahn's research showed that in traditional cultures menstrual blood was considered the primary life force, the generative principle whose flow could affect the fertility of others and the flow of waters. It was considered so powerful that a single drop on a path could take away the fertility of someone who encountered it. A menstruant's gaze, filled with the numinous power of her menstrual blood, could affect bodies of water, cause a stream to go dry or make a cow's milk dry up. Because menstrual rites had created these elements, they could also take them away: "Hers was the power of raveling and of unraveling, since what consciousness (spirit, mystery, and mind) gives us, it can also take back. And the power of creation and destruction, as at one time evidently all humanity believed, was in the woman's blood."[120]

In the folk stories that follow, the Anguane are attributed with the power of taking away fertility, affecting the weather or drying up milk. The Anguane punish men near Valle del Bòite, who hunt and kill an Anguana child, by cursing them such that the babies born to their women during the next several years will die.[121] The Anguane call up a storm in retribution for a young woman whose mother-in-law tricked her into doing laundry using the well of the Anguane (where, we are told, a group of pagans lived, near the Christian community in Serdès).[122] In another story, the old Longhana summons the storms of the Lago Cadin.[123]

It is often the women who bear the label of "witch" who demonstrate what I am calling *negated* menstrual powers, that is, menstrual powers that are presented only as destructive, intentional and harming. There are numerous stories of witches acting in this capacity. The witches of Pilcante, for example, bring hail as revenge during midsummer festival.[124] An old witch who comes begging punishes the selfish girl who refuses her request, drying up the milk of her cow.[125]

The Agency of the Anguane in Their Roles

Now that we have seen some of the characteristics of Anguane, it is useful to step back and name their roles in the stories. They are holders of positions of honor, leadership and the creative life principle. Their roles indicate their status, their autonomy from men, their ties with family and their bond with nature. The Anguane hold what could be termed the sacred offices of ancestress, queen, grandmother, mother, daughter and virgin. They merge with plant and animal; they are of the moon, sun and stars. When viewed through these roles, Anguane are embodied (mother, daughter and granddaughter), of nature (plants and animals) and deity-like (progenitor, leader and being of cosmic origin); they are the source of life (ancestress, sun and moon); and they hold within them the cycles of life (alignment of cosmos and earth).

Ancestress

In the folk story titled "The Beautiful Aguana," the Anguana of Roncegno, Valsugana, is a foremother and ancestress of many. A hand-some, hardworking young man who has two wise oxen meets an Aguane on a Friday while they are spreading their laundry out on the herbs. With the help of his oxen's judgment and the spoken word, he chooses and marries the most beautiful Aguana. They have many beautiful children and grand-children who populate today's world.[126]

Queenship, Female Leadership and Matriarchal Culture

Female leadership of the Anguane takes the office of queen. Foches listed *Regina* (queen) as one of their titles in Trentino.[127] In "The Queen of the Guane," a beautiful queen leads the Guane in procession in the fields and woods; they live in a cave, still known as Bus de le Guane in San Martino.[128] Samblana is the "most beautiful" queen of the Anguane, and she loves the hardworking people of the Dolomites.[129] In Wolff's stories, the queen of winter is Semblana or Samblana,[130] the queen of the Croderes is Tanna,[131] and the ruler of the mountain is Donna Kenina, "the most beautiful lady in all the mountains."[132] Merisàna is the queen of the forest and of the water virgins.[133] In the book *Dietrich of Berne,* the "Virginal" Snow Queen is the female protagonist, "a favorite hero of the early Middle Ages throughout Europe," whose laws forbid her to marry a human.[134]

Princess Aulasa in Mastellina in Val di Sole, although not named as an Anguana, is "beloved by the good spirits of the hills, of the forests, and of the waters." She goes into the heart of the mountain, where she can reign as queen forever rather than having her secrets taken from her and being killed by two princes of nearby castles who are jealous of her happiness.[135]

And finally, the witches too are led by a queen. The young man who is caught intruding, out of curiosity, on the domain of witches in the Vajolett

Valley, where they dance on moonlit nights, is asked by the Striona, the head of the witches, "Who is your queen?"[136]

In Vanin's analysis of the Fanes' saga, he proposed that the Anguane had a matriarchal society, with the marmot as their totemic animal. The queen and her daughters were the religious intermediaries between the Anguane and the animal, and power was handed down matrilineally.[137] Extending Vanin's idea to include otter as a totem animal could account for the report of Anguane as protective mothers, since otters are fierce protectors of their young in the wild.

In the stories of Aguane, there are communities of women with daughters, often unmarried. The wild women occasionally marry wild men of various names throughout Trentino and the Alps.[138] When Anguane marry and live with non-wild men, the marriages often do not work out. Anthropologist Michela Zucca referred to the Alpine culture as a "de facto matriarchy," since the men were often absent or far away.[139] Linguists Alfred Toth and Linus Brunner, who have studied the etymology of the names in the Ladin folk stories, proposed that the Reti, a preconquest tribal group of the possible ancestors of the Ladin, were organized in a matriarchal manner.[140]

In the story of Merisàna's wedding, she is named a Salvadega, presumably a type of Anguana. Merisàna's mother is also a Salvadega; her midwife was La Luce di Meriggio, the Light of Midday.[141] Zangrandi likened the Anguana to bees, noting that the presence of the male is not important.[142]

Virgin

In Wolff's account of Merisàna, she is the queen of the water virgins, lives in the water and wanders over the forest meadows at noon. She eventually marries the "king of rays" at noon, at which time everything is filled with joy and peace.[143] The characterization of Merisàna as a water virgin seems to indicate her ability to bring forth the fertility of nature in her body directly or, in this case, via sacred union with the sun, personified by a male.

Other evidence, in addition to this story, hints at women's perception of being able to receive impregnating energy from their relationship with nature, a practice whose knowledge has persisted in the folk memory. Several "rocks of fertility" are found throughout the Alps, including in Valle Camonica. At Foppe di Nadro, on the autumnal equinox the sun sets directly in a vulva-like opening on the crest of Monte Concarena, in view of a fertility rock with an engraving of a ritual orans figure next to an engraved circle. There is a rock of fertility at the Sanctuary to the Black Madonna of Oropa located in the mountains of Piedmont.[144]

High in the wooded mountains above my grandmother's hamlet of Carciato, where the river known as El Meledrio begins, there was once a sanctuary where women went to pray for fertility. Documentation from 1819 indicates that, at one time, this was a place of a *sacra fonte*, a sacred spring: "It is said that young spouses rushed to this sanctuary with devotion for obtaining fecundity, the virgins prayed for a husband, the poor mothers for procuring some dowry for their daughters, and such discourse according to the needs of the female sex."[145] The manuscript further describes the spring or fountain of fertility as indoor, surrounded by a wall and illuminated from above by a round opening in the roof. It was reached by a portico where no men could set foot, except for the religious men of the chapel there.[146]

Scholars attribute veneration of St. Anne with the continuity of the fertility traditions in the Alps. In Trentino, the church of St. Anne at Montagnaga is an apparition site of the Virgin Mary and a place of pilgrimage. The sanctuary in Pellizzano is dedicated to the birth of Mary, whose mother was St. Anne. The conception of Mary, celebrated on December 8, and the conception of Jesus, celebrated on March 25 as the Annunciation, are major dates of celebration in the Roman Catholic Church.

In Vanin's analysis, he proposed that the Anguane were "priestesses" of an animistic cult of the waters, sun and mountains.[147] Were Anguane the keepers of the mysteries of the creative principle of life, guardians of life-giving practices understood and protected by traditional cultures across the ages? Traditional cultures around the world have stories about a natural element containing an accessible life energy that can become a fertilizing force, for example, sun, tree or pond. In the northwest United States, the gum of the western white pine was thought to give women fertility.[148] Apela Colorado described a sacred pond in Hawaii as "a seed point of life for the Hawaiian culture and the feminine spirituality of the islands"; the powers of conception, cared for by women, include "conception of ideas, conception of babies, conception of every form."[149] The pond is home to the *Kihawahine*, the life energy of fresh water, whose animal form is the lizard. The Kihawahine brings the spiritual and earthly realms together through her heart, according to Colorado.[150]

Dedicated groups of virgin priestesses in ancient Greece were believed to practice parthenogenesis, that is, procreation without males, according to the extensive doctoral research of Marguerite Rigoglioso, published in *The Cult of Divine Birth in Ancient Greece* and *Virgin Mother Goddesses of Antiquity*. Citing numerous examples from mythology of virgin births, Rigoglioso suggested that non-ordinary conception was believed to be possible as a spiritual practice.

Mother, Daughter and Granddaughter

Anguane are mothers, daughters and granddaughters with close ties to nature.[151] In Wolff's multi-part story "Children of the Sun," published in *The Pale Mountains: Folk Tales from the Dolomites*, Elba is a mother of two children: a daughter, Soreghina (who dies when her husband violates taboo) and a son, Tschan-Bolpin.[152] Elba herself is a daughter of the sun. Thus, her daughter, Soreghina, is both a daughter of the sun and a granddaughter of the sun. In the story "Gordo and Vinella," Vinella is the daughter of a Vivana who died in a river and unknowingly left her to be raised by foster parents.[153] This naming of the lineage of mothers seems to denote matrilineal if not matriarchal heritage.

Anguane Become Witches: Negated Powers and Negated Titles

Anguane became equated with or negated as witches in some of the folk stories. *Strega* (witch) is one of the titles included in Foches's summary of names of Anguane in Trentino. Although there are numerous folk stories that refer to witches, here I have focused on stories that refer to Anguane as witches, noting when the stories about *streghe* (witches) do not specifically mention Anguane.

Negated Agency

In my analysis of the folk stories, if Anguane exhibit unexplainable behavior (their children are cared for without the Anguane being visible), have taboos (about touching hair, seeing light or having their name spoken), or exhibit special knowledge (knowing the future or past), they have been referred to as witches. If they show agency through their body (using unguent on their body, knowing magic formulas, dancing or partying), through nature (being wild, using ointment, changing into animals or turning others into something) or through what I am proposing are negated menstrual/fertility powers (stealing babies, taking vengeance on a lover, causing storms, making milk go dry or spoiling wine), they have been referred to as witches.

How Anguane are Negated

There are levels of how Anguane are negated. They may be described with negative titles (temptress or witch) or attributes (mean, cruel or ugly). They may be falsely flattered or deceived by non-Anguane, who are often presented as clever. Ultimately, they are banished, turned to stone or killed.

Negative Labels and Attributes

Anguane have been labeled as wicked, cruel, ugly and witches. In one folk story, an Otter Woman defends herself by saying *non siamo salvarie cattive*, essentially, "we are not wicked wild ones," implying a negative association with being wild or that there are various groups that live in the wild;[154] her descendants bear the *sopranome* (nickname) of *salvatici*, also related to being wild.[155] A Zubiana who is a tavern owner is described as a temptress.[156] A Giobiana is described as an "ogre in a skirt."[157] An Aga (a name that evokes the word hag in English) is described as an old evildoer who reads lines on someone's hand and tells the future.[158] *Streghe*, whose name derives from the Latin word for owl (striga), are women who hold magic power whose source is attributed to the Devil and who bring every type of evildoing, such as storms, abductions and assassinations.[159] Agàne, zubiàne and zabiàne are all witches, along with the Aga and the Niaga in the story "Le Streghe di Roncone" (The Witches of Roncone) in Valle del Chiese.[160] Zobia is the name for Thursday, the day dedicated to the Zobiane, the witches, in the dictionary of the ancient Trentino dialect.[161] Zabiana and Subiana are names for Anguane in Trentino, according to the list compiled by Foches. Coltro said that women with specialized powers met to offer their services to undo spells at the crossroads on Thursdays, which resulted in their labels of *Zobiana* and *Donna del giovedi*, literally woman of the

Thursday.[162] In northern European folk culture, there were spinning prohibitions on Thursdays out of respect to the female deity of spinning.[163]

Deceit and False Flattery

Although Anguane are sometimes characterized as *ingannatrice* (deceitful),[164] there are stories in which *they* have been deceived or falsely flattered, sometimes resulting in their death. Neri relayed a story about a young man who lures an Anguane to his cart, laden with gentian and rhododendrons, and kidnaps her, although they fall in love and end up happily married.[165] In a Cadore folk story with a less happy ending, the people of Calalzo decide to get rid of the Anguane with the help of a hermit, famed as a *stregone*, who arranges a feast and invites them, sending a carriage decorated with wildflowers and tree branches to transport them. When the Anguane, dressed in their finest clothes, arrive at Val d'Oten, where the hermit lives, he holds the plant in hand and speaks the magic words in dialect—"*In nome de Dio e dela Madona ciar e rode e dute de pagogna*" (In the name of God and of the Madonna, wagons and wheels and all of viburnum)—and they disappear.[166]

In "The Three Stone-throws," the Devil's wife is "an ugly witch" (not named as an Anguana) who is visited by a man who seeks to be rich. The Devil, described in the story as "more intelligent than all men," understands the secrets of nature; the man seeks the wife's intercession to learn this information. The man flatters her, feigns sympathy for her troubles and promises that he will do his utmost to help her once his mission is fulfilled—which he does not.[167]

Although the woman has seemingly lost her own agency in this story, by being described as "married" to the Devil, she still has access to this knowledge through him, and she gains the knowledge by querying him in his waking stupor. The witch learns from him how to make springs flow again, the formula for a healing remedy and how to get fruit trees to bear. Notably, in the closing notes we are told that the story has been handed down from grandmother to granddaughter across the ages.[168] Was this story a reminder to females about their access to knowledge, which has been demonized?

Treated with Disrespect

Especially as "old witches," the Anguane have been treated with disrespect. In "La Longagna del Lago Cadin" (The Longagna of Lake Cadin), bold boys climb up and taunt the Longhana, who lives in a rocky grotto under La Croda del Vedòrcia in the Cadore, calling her an old witch; she responds by calling forth a huge storm that brings damaging rains.[169]

It is notable when old women who have been labeled as witches are treated with respect. A clever girl, Caterina, of Val di Sole gains safe passage through the land of the feared witches of Passo Tonale by falsely flattering one of the witches and admiring the rags that she wears. The witch, appreciating the kindness, allows Caterina to pass without harm, and the people of Caterina's town learn, from her act, to treat the witches respectfully.[170]

In Neri's version of the folk story "Gordo e Vinella" Vinella meets an old woman at a *malga*, a mountain hut in the high meadows and used for making cheese, and addresses her as "signora" (lady). The old woman is surprised, noting that it is the first time that she has been called that, and proclaims, "Io sono vecchia e gli anni ti regalano esperienza, saggezza e anche preveggenza!" (I am old, and the years give you experience, wisdom and also foresight!)[171] Her words seem to speak on behalf of all of the old women who have been marginalized.

The fear of the witch, marginalized and condemned, made old women vulnerable. According to Coltro, "Fear often turns into hostility and in the life of the country or region, until recently, the poor old women, not well-dressed and alone, were excluded for the image they were offering or maybe hearsay."[172] A quote in the archives from 1630, by a legal defense advocate reflecting on the Val di Non witch trials of 1612–1615, lends support to the idea that old women were vulnerable: "One can easily blunder in various ways because it is not easy to express judgment and to proceed against any woman for her bad reputation, because such bad reputation easily comes up especially against a woman who is old, wid-owed or ugly."[173]

In Neri's version of the earlier-referenced folk story about the Sibyl of Comano Terme, she is initially described as good-looking but later, by the man who is going to kill her, as old and ugly.[174] In Borzaga's version, with her description of the Sibyl as "old as the earth," antiquity seems to indicate ancestral reverence.[175]

How Anguane React to Negation

Although the infractions against the Anguane are sometimes presented as minor, they are often the one condition that is specified to the future husband: "I will marry you if you never say or do this one thing." Other times, the infraction is presented as an unknown taboo that was violated. In my observation of the stories, if the Anguana willingly enters into partnership with a man and he later violates taboo, the punishment is her withdrawal: She departs, and he can never see her again. In the stories where there has been no willing invitation—that is, the man has transgressed a boundary out of curiosity, bravado, allurement or greed, even though the rules seem to be well known—the punishment of the violator is more severe (becoming non-human or death). As punishment, young women are more likely to withdraw from the person who has broken taboo; "old, mean, and ugly" women are more likely to take revenge.

Vanished, Banished, Turned to Stone, Bottled and Defeated

In the folk stories, the witches vanish, are banished to remote places or are turned to stone by the Council of Trent. Val Genova, a place of striking beauty with a waterfall and scattered massive rocks, is said to be a dwelling place of witches; they, along with devils, are relegated there by the Council.[176] The witches of Valòrz, women who meet periodically near the rocks, are banished to Val di Saènt by the Council of Trent.[177] The Brenta group of the Dolomites is said to be "the remains of witches turned into stone."[178] In the story titled "The Angana's Sack," the witches are utterly defeated. The Angana in Val di Non, through her magic, turns the rocky ravine of Moscabrì valley into a verdant field with grasses and flowers. When shepherds try to graze the field, the Angana—described as evil and a witch and having already killed those who violated her territory—threatens vengeance against them. After a shepherd repeatedly takes his sheep there to graze and she unsuccessfully tries to capture him, she summons all of the witches, wizards and devils in the valley to confront the people of Romeno who, through their "cunning and courage," defeat the wicked creatures. The Angana is bound in a sack and thrown into the Noce River by the shepherds whom she had threatened.[179]

A print from the 16th century illustrates the "ordeal of the sack." It shows a man getting ready to dump a person, bound in a sack closed at the top, in the water, with male authorities (wearing tall hats) and women onlookers standing by.[180] Several people from Romeno, where the battle in the story takes place, were accused of *stregoneria* (witchcraft), according to the archival documents of the Val di Non trials of 1612–1615. Accusations included bringing harm to oxen, the weather, the fertility of the spouses, and the cows' ability to give milk, acts that were perpetrated on Monte Roèn, where the witches met on Thursday nights to feast and dance with the devil.[181]

In Faver, "they still believe in witches," according to immigrant storyteller Clementina Todesco. "Before the Council Trento, there were really evil spirits loose in the world. All the bishops at the council had condemned these evil spirits to the sea and the mountains, where they couldn't hurt people."[182]

In the folk story "La Redòsola," a kind, beautiful young woman is tricked one day by a male giant who teaches her the malignant arts of magic and love. Over time, she becomes a "stria in piena regola," a full-fledged witch: She rides a broom, goes to the great Sabbaths, dances in the clearings of the forest, kidnaps a young man, learns how to turn herself into an animal, goes down a woman's chimney (which the woman had inadvertently left unblessed with holy water) as a dirty and disheveled old woman, threatens to boil children, is given a black basket (which does not hold water) instead of a pot and plots revenge. Eventually, Redòsola and the other evil spirits are called in to negotiate a treaty, whereupon the Bishops of the Council of Trent close them up inside the empty wine bottles they have stored under their chairs. Redòsola dances inside the bottle for centuries until, eventually, the glass is worn down and gives way.[183]

Yet the benevolent figure of the old woman witch persists in popular culture: She decorates the barns of Val di Fassa.[184] A figure of a smiling old woman in black, with long gray hair, a pointed hat, and riding a broom, was for sale in 2009 at the gift shop of a Marian sanctuary. La Befana, sometimes portrayed as an old woman riding a broom, brings the gifts on the eve of the Epiphany.

Coltro devoted a short but informative chapter to La Befana, whose tradition, he said, was suppressed years ago and put back on the calendar by demand of the people. In Coltro's summary, Befana is old and decrepit and dresses in black with a scarf on her head; she is the personification of winter, of the cold that brings death to nature. She becomes *la Vecia* (the Old Woman), who is burned in bonfires, known as the *falò* in many parts of Veneto, symbolizing the death of the old vegetation that allows for the new growth. Like Berchta of Nordic mythology, who protects and blesses the fields, Befana comes on the eve of the Epiphany. She descends the chimney, bringing gifts to the good children.[185]

Possible Causes of Negation

It is important to remember that Anguane are described from the view of those who were likely other than Anguane. Evidence of otherness is indicated by the name of *Donna Straniera* (foreign woman), which Foches included in his list of names of Anguane in Valli del Leno.[186]

If the Anguane were other, to whom were they other? Because elements of the stories may reach across centuries and even millennia, the answer is complex and likely still emerging. Prior to Roman conquest, the Italian Alps were populated by numerous tribes, including the Reti, Euganei and Veneti, and influenced by both Celts and Etruscans. The Reti, or Rhaetians, are likely ancestors to the Ladin people, Vanin said, who retained their language and culture and whose DNA differs from that of their neighbors.[187] Busk noted that the Eugani dwelled in Val Sugana, where there are stories of Anguane.[188] Monfosco proposed that the Anguane were the last of a Celtic race, forced to flee for survival and live hidden in the grottoes; the animal skin boots that they wore, Etruscan in style, could have become the goats' feet they were sometimes said to have in the folk stories.[189]

Although it is difficult to assess the complex political and religious influences across time on the characters in the folk stories, the sources cited here provide some clues. Zangrandi said that at one time there were no laws of "Good and Evil." Although the Romans had altered the characters in the folk stories (for example, by appending goats' feet onto the Anguane), major changes came after the collapse of the Roman Empire, with waves of invaders who used the roads built by the Romans. With them came the sense of evil and sin, waves of invasions, the birth of fear and the transformation of the mythic characters. There were "Witches and Demons, damned souls, the Ogres became incarnations of Satan, the Dragons of the Alpine Lakes . . . vomited fire."[190]

Over time, the wild characters were mixed and confused, Vanin observed, and then Christianity created a dualistic nature: "The advance of Christendom heavily contributed to gradually shift all these figures of a past . . . into the sphere of myth . . . as well as to force them into a devil-ish-angelic ambiguity that was not at all their own at their origins."[191] Luigi Reverdito, the editor of Giovanni Borzaga's *Leggende del Trentino*, differentiated between "Guane or Aguane, related to ancient nymphs, beautiful, bewitching, elusive and at times willing to marry" and "the true witches, *le strie*, cruel old women in combat with Satan."[192] For diverse reasons, he continued, both recall "the dark times of the Counter-reformation when in Tyrol and Trentino tens of innocents—widows, midwives, prostitutes, and herbalists—were tried and burned alive with accusations of witchcraft."[193]

Was Reverdito noting something *characteristically* different between the taboos that the young, fertile Anguane enforce and the fierce power that the old witches hold? If so, this supports my understanding of the old woman who indeed could have been feared, having accumulated the knowledge of her entire life. As a hag, she is a wise woman, *hagia* meaning holy/ wise. She seems to symbolize, and thus hold the power of, the culmination of all the cycles of life: the fertility cycle, the yearly cycle and a woman's life cycle.

Fernando Zampiva, a keeper of folk wisdom about plants, stated that, after the Council of Trent, the magic protagonists of the legends disappeared; the Anguane, mythical woodland goddesses, were no longer able to freely communicate with humans. He described the event as a cultural "watershed," to indicate life before and after the Council, an interesting choice of words that also refers to the flow of water in nature.[194]

Did the Anguane Exist?

Some interesting details imply the real existence of Anguane. Coltro stated that intermarriage between humans and *Fade* (who, as described by him, share characteristics with the Anguane) were prohibited by the Council of Trent: "The Council of Trent banned these mixed unions. It is argued that the Fade belong to a particular and not well-defined species of Witches; there are those who feel that they hold the spirits of women who died in childbirth."[195] Busk, in describing the story of a marriage between a man and an "Enguane" that did not work out, relayed that "a holy hermit" advised him that she "was not a proper wife for a Christian man."[196] One family in Auronzo claimed to have a beautiful embroidered *fazzoletto* (handkerchief or head scarf) of an Anguane.[197] The title of one story evokes their real existence, or at least their memory: "Quande gh'era le vivane," which, translated from dialect, means "When There Were Vivane."[198]

Values Conveyed and Traditional Wisdom

In both their actions and their offices, the Anguane have a close embodied relationship with nature and the cosmos. They are wild and live in the wild.

The folk stories communicate the importance of respect for the sacred, respect for what is wild, helpfulness to others, care for children, self-respect, importance of keeping one's word, the gift given freely (of their knowledge and of nature) and protection of those who are other. The Anguane are not separate from nature but part of it. Their ethics also seem to come from nature, not outside nature, or "supernatural." In Vanin's assessment, when ethical concepts are evident, they seem "not to have any supernatural root" and "to be based on a correctness of human behavior: one must keep his word; collective interest must take priority over the individual's."[199] Vanin continued by writing that the cultic actions directed toward the spirits of nature are "to maintain a relationship of harmony and respect with them"; at times, the spirits incarnate and bestow their gifts to the humans.[200]

This is at the essence of my understanding about the Anguane: women in harmonious relationship with nature and the cosmos, understanding the benefits of being in resonance with them, and facilitating that state in one's self and others through education and protection. They keep the sacred rules. They stress the importance of not violating the rules of nature. They warn against improper use of power.

Do Not Forget Me. . . .

Significantly, the old women and young women in the folk stories ask not to be forgotten. The healer/Sibyl of the thermal spring of Comano promises life to the person who remembers her. The Anguane bring forget-me-nots and ask not be forgotten. The ugly witch, who is "married to the Devil"— even in her twice-negated form of being labeled as a witch and being married to the Devil—reminds the man whom she has helped not to forget her. At the end of the story, the commentary adds that grandmothers told this story to their granddaughters until present times, indicating to me that women were remembering their own access to this knowledge of nature's abundance (water and fruitfulness). In the folk stories, men are also keepers of this knowledge and memory: The knight whom the Sibyl healed repeatedly tells the story to his grandson and, in his later years, chooses to become a hermit and the carrier of the tradition previously held by her, dispensing advice and prayers; the men who were helped by the old woman of Valbona go to find her, name the place after her and place a saint's image there.[201]

I suggest these female characters are asking all of us to remember the generative, regenerative, transformative powers of women and the respect that is due to them. They are asking us to honor the full cycle of life, the diminishing as well as the growing, the elders as well the youth, and ultimately the sources of life whose continuity depends on this cycle.

References

Atlante storico del Trentino. Trento, Italy: Casa Editrice Panorama, 1993.

Autonomous Province of Trento. *Almanacco Trentino.* Trento, Italy: Casa Editrice Publilux, 1985.

Autonomous Province of Trento Department of Emigration. "The Homeland" Monograph Series. In *Songs and Tales: Trentino Folklore.* Trento, Italy: Casa Editrice Panorama, 1992.

Becher, Giovanni Pais. "Auronzo." 2012. www.auronzo.eu/3.html.

Bertoluzza, Aldo. *Abbicci: Dizionario dell'antico dialetto Trentino.* Trento, Italy: l'Adige, 1992.

Birnbaum, Lucia Chiavola. *The Future Has an Ancient Heart.* Bloomington, IN: iUniverse, 2012.

Borzaga, Giovanna. *I teschi d'avorio ad altri racconti Trentini* [The Skulls of Ivory and Other Trentini Stories]. Calliano, Italy: Manfrini Editori, 1981.

———. *Leggende del Trentino: Magici personaggi di valli e boschi* [Legends of Trentino: Magic Characters of the Valleys and Woods]. Matarello, Italy: Reverdito, 2008.

Busk, Rachel Harriet. *The Valleys of Tirol.* New York: AMS Press, 1983.

Chiodin, Silvia, dir. *Magnificent Italia: Trentino,* DVD. Milan: Touring Club Italiano, 2007. www.filmideas.com.

Colorado, Apela. 2012. "Awakening our Indigenous Powers and Moving as One with the Earth." Paper presented at the Inspiring Women Summit, web conference, April 15, 2012. www.inspiringwomensummit.com/sessions/2012/20460.

Coltro, Dino. *Gnomi, anguane e basilischi: Esseri mitici e immaginari del Veneto, del Friuli-Venezia Giulia, del Trentino e dell'Alto Adige.* Verona, Italy: Cierre, 2006.

Davidson, Hilda Ellis. *Roles of the Northern Goddess.* London: Routledge, 1998.

Di Gesaro, Pinuccia. *I Giochi delle Streghe* [The Games of the Witches]. Bolzano, Italy: Praxis 3, 1995.

Drewal, Henry John. *Mami Wata: Arts for Water Spirits in Africa and its Diasporas.* Los Angeles: Fowler Museum, 2008.

Fantelli, Udalrico. *Dimaro: La Carta di Regola.* Trento, Italy: Centro Studi per la Val di Sole, 1990.

Foches, Andrea. *Leggende delle Anguane* [Legends of the Anguane]. Torino: Priuli & Verlucca Editori and San Michele all'Adige: Museo degli Usi e Costumi della Gente Trentina, 2007.

Gimbutas, Marija. *The Civilization of the Goddess: The World of Old Europe.* New York: HarperCollins, 1991.

Grahn, Judy. *Blood, Bread and Roses: How Menstruation Created the World.* Boston: Beacon Press, 1993.

Gremmo, Roberto. *Le grandi pietre magiche: Residui di paganesimo nella religiosità popolare alpina*. Biella, Italy: Storia Ribelle, 2009.

Jones, Kathy. "Calling Kiawahine," *In the Heart of the Goddess* www.kathyjones.co.uk/index. php?option=com_content&view=article&id=97&Itemid=103.

Kezich, Giovanni. "*Le leggende delle Anguane* []." Introduction to *Leggende delle Anguane*, by Andrea Foches, 2–3. Torino: Priuli & Verlucca Editori and San Michele all'Adige: Museo degli Usi e Costumi della Gente Trentina, 2007.

Mathias, Elizabeth, and Richard Raspa. *Italian Folktales in America: The Verbal Art of an Immigrant Woman*. Detroit: Wayne State University Press, 1985.

Monfosco, Gari. *Dolomiti: Storie e Leggende* [Dolomites: Stories and Legends]. Bassano del Grappa, Italy: Ghedina & Tassotti Editori, 1987.

Moser, Mary Beth. *Honoring Darkness: Exploring the Power of Black Madonnas in Italy*. Vashon Island, WA: Dea Madre, 2008.

Motz, Lotte. "The Winter Goddess: Percht, Holda and Related Figures." *Folklore* 95, no. 2 (1984): 151–166.

Neri, Mauro. *Donne e bambine nelle leggende del Trentino*. Trento, Italy: Casa Editrice Panorama, 2008.

———. *Mille leggende del Trentino: Trentino Occidentale* [A Thousand Legends of Trentino: Eastern Trentino]. Trento, Italy: Casa Editrice Panorama, 1997.

———. *The Secret Heart of Trentino: A Calendar of Legends*. 4 vols. Lavis, Italy: Litotipografia Alcione, 2010.

———. *Women and Girls in the Legends of the Trent Region*. Translated by Fr. Marco Bagnarol. Trento, Italy: Alcion Edizioni, 2008.

Pojar, Jim, and Andy MacKinnon, eds. 2004. *Plants of the Pacific Northwest Coast: Washington, Oregon, British Columbia and Alaska*. Vancouver: Lone Pine, 2004.

Provincia di Brescia Assessorato al Turism. *The Camonica Valley: Artistic Historical Itineraries of the Brescia Territory*. Brescia, Italy:

Provincia di Brescia Assessorato al Turismo, 2006. Pamphlet from author's private collection.

Sawyer, Ruth, and Emmy Molles. *Dietrich of Berne and the Dwarf King Laurin: Hero Tales of the Austrian Tirol.* New York: Viking Press, 1963.

Südtirol Marketing Gesellschaft KAG. "Church of San Giacomo/ St. Jakob Kastelaz Termeno/Tramin." 2013.

Toth, Alfred, and Linus Brunner. "Raetic: An Extinct Semitic Language in Central Europe." *Mikes International, Hungarian Periodical for Art, Literature and Science* (online). The Hague, Netherlands: Hungarian Federation in the Netherlands, 2007. Accessed on February 13, 2013. www.federatio.org/mi_bibl/Toth_Brunner_Raetic.pdf.

UNESCO. *2013 Calendario: Dolomiti Patrimonio Mondiale UNESCO [Dolomites UNESCO Calendar 2013].* Trento, Italy: La Fondazione Dolomiti UNESCO, 2010.

Vanin, Adriano. "The Fanes Saga: Analysis of the Legend—Related Legends." *The Kingdom of Fanes: Research on the Fanes Saga.* 2012. www.ilregnodeifanes.it/inglese/analysis5.htm.

———. "The Fanes Saga: The Cultural Background—Cults and Myths." *The Kingdom of Fanes: Research on the Fanes Saga.* 2012. www. ilregnodeifanes.it/inglese/background1.htm/.

———. "The Fanes Saga: Researches on the Legend: A Short History of the Studies of the Legend." *The Kingdom of Fanes: Research on the Fanes Saga.* 2012. www.ilregnodeifanes.it/inglese/research1.htm/.

———. "The Fanes Saga: Short Essays—The Anguane." *The Kingdom of Fanes: Research on the Fanes Saga.* 2012. www.ilregnodeifanes.it/ inglese/essay1.htm/.

———. "The Fanes Saga: Short Essays—The Salvans (Wildmen)." *The Kingdom of Fanes: Research on the Fanes Saga.* 2012. www.ilregno-deifanes.it/inglese/essay3.htm/.

———. "The Fanes Saga: A Summary of the Legend." *The Kingdom of Fanes: Research on the Fanes Saga.* 2012. Last modified December 22, 2012. www.ilregnodeifanes.it/inglese/summary.htm/.

Veneri, Brunamaria Dal Lago. "Tessere e filare e cucire" [Weaving and Spinning and Sewing]. In *Un punto più del diavolo: Eccellenza e curiosità della filatura e tessitura femminili*, edited by Rosanna Cavallini, 11–17. Borgo Valsugana, Italy: Comune di Borgo Valsugana, 2010.

Walker, Barbara. *The Woman's Encyclopedia of Myths and Secrets*. San Francisco: Harper and Row, 1983.

Welcome in Italia.indettglio.it [Welcome to Italy in Detail]. "The Village of Martinei," in "Italian Villages." Accessed January 25, 2013. http://italia.indettaglio.it/eng/trentinoaltoadige/trento_bedollo_martinei.html

Wolff, Carl Felix. *The Dolomites and Their Legends*. Translated by Baroness Lea Rukawina. Bolzano, Italy: Vogelweider, 1930.

———. *The Pale Mountains: Folk Tales from the Dolomites*. Translated by Francesca la Monte. New York: Minton, Balch, 1927.

Work-MaKinne, Dawn E. "Deity in Sisterhood: The Collective Sacred Female in Germanic Europe." PhD diss., Union Institute and University, 2010. [Dolomites UNESCO Calendar 2013] ProQuest (3400970).

Zampiva, Fernando. "Piante sacre e piante maledette" [Sacred Plants and Cursed Plants], *Cimbri-Tzimbar, religiosità e superstizioni: Vita e cultura delle comunità cimbre, rivista del curatorium cimbricum Veronense* 6, no. 14 (1995): 179–201.

Zangrandi, Giovanna. *Leggende delle Dolomiti* [*Legends of the Dolomites*]. Translated by Alma Bevilacqua. Chiari, Italy: Nordpress, 2000.

Zucca, Michela, ed. "The Orgy, the Feast, the Witches' Sabbath: Sexuality in the Alps." In Vol. 3 of *Matriarchy and the Mountains, Convention Proceedings,* 63–89. Italy: Centro di Ecologia Alpina, 1999.

Michela Zucca, ed. "The Orgy, the Feast, the Witches' Sabbath: Sexuality in the Alps." Vol. 3 of Matriarchy and the Mountains, Convention Proceedings, 63. Trento, Italy: Centro di Ecologia Alpina, 1999.

Endnotes

1 Iva Berasi "Introduction," in *Women and Girls in the Legends of the Trent Region*, ed. Mauro Neri, transl. M. Bagnarol (Trento, Italy: Alcion Edizioni, 2008), 13.

2 Mauro Neri, *Women and Girls in the Legends of the Trent Region*, unnumbered. Dino Coltro also addresses the regions of Veneto, Friuli-Venezia Giulia, Trentino and Alto Adige. (See endnote 48.)

3 Gari Monfosco, *Dolomiti: Storie e leggende* [Dolomites: Stories and Legends] (Bassano del Grappa, Italy: Ghedina & Tassotti Editori, 1987), 130. She relates them to the words *gana, gènes, vagàna, sagàna, ssana and bagàna.*

4 Mauro Neri, *Mille leggende del Trentino: Trentino Occidentale* [A Thousand Legends of Trentino: Eastern Trentino] (Trento, Italy: Casa Editrice Panorama, 1997), 326–32. These are the definitions, along with many others. Dialect translations are from Aldo Bertoluzza, *Abbicci: Dizionario dell'antico dialetto Trentino* (Trento, Italy: l'Adige, 1992).

5 Neri, "The Brief of the Vivana," *Women and Girls in the Legends of the Trent Region*, 97. Note: "brief" should have been translated as "braid." In the Italian version of this story it is "La treccia della Vivana." See Neri, Donne e bambine, 90.

6 Neri, "Poor Anguana," *Women and Girls in the Legends of the Trent Region*, 83.

7 Vanin, "The Fanes Saga: Short Essays—The Anguane," *The Kingdom of Fanes: Research on the Fanes Saga*, 2012, paragraph 1, www.ilregnodeifanes.it/inglese/essay1.htm/.

8 Giovanni Kezich, "Le leggende delle Anguane," introduction to *Leggende delle Anguane*, by Andrea Foches (Torino: Priuli & Verlucca, 2007), 2.

9. Andrea Foches, *Leggende delle Anguane* (Torino: Priuli & Verlucca, 2007), in the map "Le Anguane nel Trentino," on page 5.

10 Mauro Neri, *Donne e bambine nelle leggende del Trentino* (Trento, Italy: Casa Editrice Panorama, 2008), 77.

11 Giovanna Borzaga, *Leggende del Trentino: Magici personaggi di valli e boschi* [Legends of Trentino: Magic Characters of the Valleys and Woods] (Matarello, Italy: Reverdito, 2008), 67.

12 Brunamaria Dal Lago Veneri, "Tessere e filare e cucire," [Weaving and Spinning and Sewing], *Un punto più del diavolo: Eccellenza e curiosità della filatura e tessitura femminili*, ed. R. Cavallini (Borgo Valsugana, Italy: Comune di Borgo Valsugana, 2010), 14. Similarly, Vanin uses the term "woman of the water." Vanin, "The Fanes Saga: Short Essays—The Anguane," paragraph 1, www.ilregnodeifanes.it/inglese/essay1.htm/.

13 Borzaga, *Leggende del Trentino*, 67.

14 Kezich, 3.

15 Foches, *Leggende delle Anguane*, 3. *Busi* in dialect is *buchi* in Italian, meaning "holes"; *cròzi* in dialect is *roccie* in Italian, meaning "rocks." Translations from dialect into Italian are from Aldo Bertoluzza, *Abbicci: Dizionario dell'antico dialetto Trentino* (Trento, Italy: l'Adige, 1992).

16 Welcome in Italia.indettglio.it [Welcome to Italy in Detail]. "The Village of Martinei," in "Italian Villages." http://italia.indettaglio.it/eng/trentinoaltoadige/trento_bedollo_martinei.html. The story's location is listed as from Martinei (Regnana); both Regnana (population 79) and Martinei (population of 12) are less than two miles from Bedollo.

17 Andrea Foches, "El caradór e le Vivane" [The Cart-Driver and the Vivane], *Leggende delle Anguane* [Legends of the Anguane] (Torino: Priuli & Verlucca, 2007), 14–23.

18 Borzaga, "La bella anguana" [The Beautiful Anguana], *Leggende del Trentino*, 64.

19 Monfosco, 129–30. Monfosco includes an appendix to the Anguane: "Le favolose Anguanes" [The fabulous Anguanes].

20 Franco Gaudiano, e-mail message to author, January 20, 2010.

21 See Südtirol: The official travel site, " St. Jakob Church in Kastelaz."

22 UNESCO, *2013 Calendario: Dolomiti Patrimonio Mondiale UNESCO* (Trento, Italy: La Fondazione Dolomiti UNESCO, 2010).

23 Franco Gaudiano, e-mail message to author, March 31, 2013.

24 Henry John Drewal, *Mami Wata: Arts for Water Spirits in Africa and its Diasporas* (Los Angeles: Fowler Museum, 2008), 28. Drewal comments that from the first evidence of image making on the continent and throughout the millennia, diverse African cultures have stressed the value and power of water not only as a source of sustenance but also as a focus of spiritual and artistic expression.

25 Vanin, "The Fanes Saga: Short Essays—The Anguane," paragraph 6, 9, www.ilregnodeifanes.it/inglese/essay1.htm/.

26 Giovanna Zangrandi, *Leggende delle Dolomiti* [*Legends of the Dolomites*] trans. Alma Bevilacqua (Chiari, Italy: Nordpress, 2000), 130–31.

27 Monfosco, 130.

28 Marija Gimbutas, *The Civilization of the Goddess: The World of Old Europe* (New York: HarperCollins, 1991), 222–23.

29 Ibid., 399.

30 Dal Lago Veneri, 15–16.

31 Kezich, 2–3.

32 Dawn E. Work-MaKinne, "Deity in Sisterhood: The Collective Sacred Female in Germanic Europe" (PhD diss., Union Institute and University, 2010), i, 1–2.

33 Roberto Gremmo, *Le grandi pietre magiche: Residui di paganesimo nella religiosità popolare alpina* (Biella, Italy: Storia Ribelle, 2009), 84.

34 Foches, 11.

35 Vanin, "The Fanes Saga: Short Essays—The Anguane," www.ilregnodeifanes.it/inglese/essay1.htm/.

36 Autonomous Province of Trento, *Almanacco Trentino* (Trento, Italy: Casa Editrice Publilux, 1985), unnumbered. The text appears between the January and February calendars.

37 Gimbutas, 400.

38 Lucia Chiavola Birnbaum, *The Future Has an Ancient Heart* (Bloomington, IN: iUniverse, 2012), 198.

39 Vanin, "The Fanes Saga: Short Essays—The Anguane," www.ilregno-deifanes.it/inglese/essay1.htm/.

40 Neri, *Mille Leggende del Trentino,* 326.

41 Dal Lago Veneri, 14.

42 Monfosco, 130.

43 Foches, "L'Oro delle Angane" [The Gold of the Angane], *Leggende delle Anguane,* 8.

44 Vanin, "The Fanes Saga: Short Essays—The Anguane," paragraph 9, www.ilregnodeifanes.it/inglese/essay1.htm/. For this general format, I am grateful to the list of characteristics presented by Vanin. Ultimately, I had to do my own analysis, utilizing the sources I had available, for the categories of interest to this study.

45 Mauro Neri, "The Vivana's Plaits," *The Secret Heart of Trentino: A Calendar of Legends,* Summer (Lavis, Italy: Litotipografia Alcione, 2010), 93–94.

46 Neri, "The Stones of the Salinghe," *The Secret Heart of Trentino,* Summer, 37, footnote 1.

47 Neri, "The Defeat of the Anguane," *The Secret Heart of Trentino,* Spring, 15–16.

48 Dino Coltro, *Gnomi, anguane e basilischi: Esseri mitici e immaginari del Veneto, del Friuli-Venezia Giulia, del Trentino e dell'Alto Adige* (Verona: Cierre, 2006), 25.

49 Neri, "The Queen of the Guane," *The Secret Heart of Trentino,* Spring, 33–34.

50 Zangrandi, "L'ongana del Larin" ["The Ongana of Larin "], *Leggende delle Dolomiti,* 60.

51 Borzaga, "Leggenda dell'Arnica" [Legend of the Arnica], *Leggende del Trentino,* 80–83. She is the mother who, after the taboo of not touching her hair is broken, has to leave her five children. She comes back during the day to care for them until her husband hides so he can see her again, and she must leave for good. She becomes the wild healing plant of Arnica. Her daughter, advised by an old woman, comes to a field on the nights of S. Lorenzo and wishes upon a falling star to see her mother,

who comes to her in the fields of flowers. The guane are beautiful and kind, even though one of Arnica's feet is half-reversed.

52 Giovanna Borzaga, "L'aguana dei Comorandi" [The Aguana of the Comorandi], *I teschi d'avorio ad altri racconti Trentini* [The Skulls of Ivory and Other Trentini Stories] (Calliano, Italy: Manfrini Editori, 1981), 65–67.

53 Neri, "The Clothes of the Salingas," *Women and Girls in the Legends of the Trent Region,* 21–23.

54 For example, Monfosco, "Piè di capra," [Goat's Feet], 29; Neri, "The Clothes of the Salingas," *Women and Girls in the Legends of the Trent Region,* 21–23.

55 Neri, "La treccia della Vivana" [The Braid of the Vivana], *Women and Girls in the Legends of the Trent Region,* 90–91.

56 Coltro, 25.

57 Neri, "The Dairy Witch," *The Secret Heart of Trentino,* Summer, 70–71.

58 Neri, "Donna Berta and Her Husband," *The Secret Heart of Trentino,* Winter, 110–11.

59 Mauro Neri, "The Vivana of the Barley Grains," *The Secret Heart of Trentino,* Autumn, 71–72.

60 Monfosco, "Piè di Capra," 30.

61 Neri, "The Generous Donna Berta," *The Secret Heart of Trentino,* Winter, 110.

62 Neri, "The Anguana of the Mysterious Flowers," *The Secret Heart of Trentino,* Spring, 115–16.

63 Borzaga, "Leggenda dell'Arnica," *Leggende del Trentino,* 80–83.

64 Fernando Zampiva, "Piante sacre e piante maledette" [Sacred Plants and Cursed Plants], *Cimbri-Tzimbar, Religiosità e superstizioni: Vita e cultura delle Comunità cimbre, Rivista del Curatorium Cimbricum Veronense* 6, no. 14 (1995): 188. *Chelidonium majus* was known as *erba de le angoane* in Valle del Chiampo "perhaps for its strange hypnotic properties."

65 Foches, "Le Anguane del Cismòn" [The Anguane of Cismon], *Leggende delle Anguane*, 36–42.

66 Carl Felix Wolff, "The Hut of the Forget-Me-Nots," *The Dolomites and Their Legends,* trans. L. Rukawina (Bolzano, Italy: Vogelweider, 1930), 90–92.

67 Zangrandi, "La Salvatica di Andraz" [The Wildwoman of Andraz], *Leggende delle Dolomiti*, 89–95.

68 Monfosco, "Piè di Capra," 30.

69 Vanin, "The Fanes Saga: Short Essays—The Anguane," paragraph 9, www.ilregnodeifanes.it/inglese/essay1.htm/; Vanin, "The Fanes Saga: A Summary of the Legend," www.ilregnodeifanes.it/inglese/summary. htm; and Vanin, "The Fanes Saga: The Cultural Background—Cults and Myths," www.ilregnodeifanes.it/inglese/background1.htm/.

70 Carl Felix Wolff, "The Artist of Faloria," *The Pale Mountains: Folk Tales from the Dolomites,* trans. Francesca la Monte (New York: Minton, Balch, 1927), 83–102. Filadressa meets "Anguans" in the story, so she is not technically one herself, but, as a wild mountain person, she seems to share characteristics with them: her wildness, her knowledge of special skills, which she is willing to share, her animal features and her care for children, even though she steals them.

71 Neri, "The Defeat of the Anguane," *The Secret Heart of Trentino,* Spring, 15–16.

72 Neri, "The Angana's Sack," *The Secret Heart of Trentino,* Summer, 9–10.

73 Neri, "The Hill of the Vivane," Spring, 14–15.

74 Borzaga, "La Fata di Rocca Pagana" [The Fairy of Pagan Rock], *Leggende del Trentino*, 161–67.

75 Monfosco, "Le Anguane del Lago di Lagole," 65–72.

76 Foches, *Leggende delle Anguane*, 5.

77 Neri, "The Cavern of the Sibyl," *Women and Girls in the Legends of the Trent Region*, 15–20.

78 Ibid.

79 Borzaga, "L'antro della Sibilla" [The cavern of the Sibyl], *Leggende del Trentino*, 170.

80 *Atlante Storico del Trentino* [Historical Atlas of Trentino] (Trento, Italy: Casa Editrice Panorama, 1993), 47.

81 *Faith Procured Visions of Madonnas and Witches* (Camonica Valley, Italy: Provincia di Brescia Assessorato al Turismo), 25.

82 Neri, "The World of the Anguane," *The Secret Heart of Trentino*, Spring, 19–20.

83 Rachel Harriet Busk, *The Valleys of Tirol* (New York: AMS Press, 1983), 415.

84 Neri, "The Poor Anguana," *Women and Girls in the Legends of the Trent Region*, 82–83.

85 Autonomous Province of Trento Department of Emigration, "The Whistle," *Songs and Tales: Trentino Folklore* (Trento, Italy: Casa Editrice Panorama, 1992), 51.

86 Autonomous Province of Trento Department of Emigration, "The Ring" (or, "A Dog, a Cat and a Magic Spell"), 66–70. Once he has found happiness, he brings his mother to live with him. See also Busk, 425.

87 Neri, "The Generous Donna Berta," *The Secret Heart of Trentino*, Winter, 110.

88 Dal Lago Veneri, 14.

89 Monfosco, "Le Anguane del Lago di Lagole," 65–72.

90 For example, Elba and Soreghina in Wolff, "Children of the Sun," *The Pale Mountains*, 165–179. A female who is a Daughter of the Sun can be read as "in close alignment with," even suggesting, at some level, that she is the result of female/cosmic union. Vanin notes their similarities with the Anguane in "The Fanes Saga: Analysis of the Legend—Related Legends," www.ilregnodeifanes.it/inglese/analysis5.htm and "The Fanes Saga: Analysis of the Legend—Related Legends," "Elba."

91 For example, the Moon Princess or Daughter of the Moon is a well-known figure. See Wolff. Some priestesses or holders of a sacred office may have become princesses, or royal maidens in the stories, even though some stories are likely about actual figures of nobility. Busk notes

the tie of the people to the cosmos in their use of rhyming riddles. See Busk, 440.

92 Judy Grahn, *Blood, Bread and Roses: How Menstruation Created the World* (Boston: Beacon Press, 1993), 11, 18.

93 Ibid., 38.

94 Neri, "The Vivana's Plaits," *The Secret Heart of Trentino* Summer, 93–94.

95 Foches, "El caradór e le Vivane" [The Cart-Driver and the Vivane], 14–23. In this story from Pinetana, the driver of a cart pulled by oxen uses magic words given to him by his mother to choose one of three Anguane, whom he marries; she later disappears when her hair is touched at night, but returns to care for their daughters unseen by him.

96 Grahn, 11.

97 Ibid., 37–38.

98 Ibid., 38.

99 Neri, "The Clothes of the Salingas," *Women and Girls in the Legends of the Trent Region*, 21. This story takes place in Fierozzo, Valle dei Mocheni. The Salinga emerges from the mountain at midnight to wash her clothes within a magic circle.

100 Grahn, 72, 81.

101 Kezich, 3.

102 Grahn, 155, 158.

103 Barbara Walker, *The Woman's Encyclopedia of Myths and Secrets* (San Francisco: Harper and Row, 1983), 370.

104 Ibid., 368.

105 Pina Trentini, e-mail message to the author, November 28, 2010.

106 Foches, "Il matrimonio coll'Angana," *Leggende delle Anguane*, 25–35. See also Autonomous Province of Trento Department of Emigration, "The Marriage with the Witch," in *Songs and Tales*, 47–48, in which the Anguana is referred to as a witch.

107 Wolff, "Children of the Sun," *The Pale Mountains*, 179.

108 Grahn, 11–18.

109 Coltro, 61. Coltro associates the derivation of *Krivopete* to "blood talons—*criva (sangue)* to "blood," and *peta (tallone)* to"heel—although other scholars relate it to a curved foot.

110 Ibid., 62.

111 Ibid., 61.

112 Monfosco, "Piè di Capra," 29–31.

113 Coltro, 58.

114 Neri, "The Brief of the Vivana," *Women and Girls in the Legends of the Trent Region,* 96. Note: "Brief" should have been translated as "braid." In the Italian version of this story it is "La treccia della Vivana." See Neri, *Donne e bambine*, 90.

115 Grahn, 18.

116 Coltro, 57.

117 Zangrandi, "La Redòsola," *Leggende delle Dolomiti,* 44–51.

118 Zangrandi, "La Salvatica di Andraz" [The Wildwoman of Andraz], *Leggende delle Dolomiti,* 89.

119 Lotte Motz, "The Winter Goddess: Percht, Holda and Related Figures," *Folklore* 95, no. 2 (1984): 160.

120 Grahn, 6, 18.

121 Monfosco, "I Mazzamorelli" [The Mazzamorelli], 41–43. *Mazzamorelli* are the spirits of babies who died before birth.

122 Monfosco, "Il Pozzo delle Anguanes di Senes" [The Well of the Anguane of Senes], *Dolomiti,* 91.

123 Monfosco, *Dolomiti,* 81.

124 Neri, "The Witches' Envy," *The Secret Heart of Trentino,* Summer, 104–105. The witches are not referred to as Anguane.

125 Neri, "La Strega che chiedeva l'elemosina" [The Witch That Was Asking for Alms], *Mille Leggende del Trentino,* 107.

126 Borzaga, "La bella anguana," 64–67.

127 Foches, 5.

128 Neri, "The Queen of the Guane," *The Secret Heart of Trentino,* Summer, 33–34.

129 Monfosco, "Le Sette Cime di Diamante," *Dolomiti*, 24. See also Monfosco, "I Mazzamorelli," 42.

130 Wolff, "Children of the Sun, Soreghina (2)," *The Pale Mountains*, 178. Also, Queen is mentioned in Monfosco, *Dolomiti*, 65.

131 Wolff, "The Queen of the Croderes," *The Pale Mountains*, 123.

132 Wolff, "Children of the Sun, Tschan-Bolpin (3)," *The Pale Mountains*, 185.

133 Wolff, "Merisana's Wedding," *The Dolomites and Their Legends,* 103.

134 Ruth Sawyer and Emmy Molles, *Dietrich of Berne and the Dwarf King Laurin: Hero Tales of the Austrian Tirol* (New York: Viking Press, 1963), 7.

135 Neri, "Princess Aulasa," *Women and Girls in the Legends of the Trent Region,* 65.

136 Wolff, "The Spring of Forgetting," *The Pale Mountains*, 143.

137 Vanin, "The Fanes Saga: The Cultural Background—Cults and Myths," paragraphs 22, 24, www.ilregnodeifanes.it/inglese/background1. htm/

138 Vanin, "The Fanes Saga: Short Essay--The Salvans (Wildmen), paragraph 7, www.ilregnodeifanes.it/inglese/essay3.htm/ Vanin notes the *salvani* and *salvans* in the Fanes' saga who sometimes were married to Wildwomen, known as *vivane* or *Bregostane*. See Vanin, "The Fanes Saga: Short Essays—The Salvans (Wildmen)," www.ilregnodeifanes.it/ inglese/essay3.htm/.

139 Michela Zucca, ed., "The Orgy, the Feast, the Witches' Sabbath: Sexuality in the Alps," vol. 3 of *Matriarchy and the Mountains, Convention Proceedings,* 63 (Trento, Italy: Centro di Ecologia Alpina, 1999).

140 Alfred Toth and Linus Brunner, *Raetic: An Extinct Semitic Language in Central Europe, Mikes International, Hungarian Periodical for Art, Literature and Science* (online). The Hague,

Netherlands: Hungarian Federation in the Netherlands, 2007, 34. Accessed on February 13, 2013. www.federatio.org/mi_bibl/Toth_Brunner_Raetic.pdf.

141 Zangrandi, "Il Velo di Merisana," *Leggende delle Dolomiti*, 7.

142 Ibid.

143 Wolff, "Merisana's Wedding," *The Dolomites and Their Legends*, 102–107.

144 Mary Beth Moser, *Honoring Darkness: Exploring the Power of Black Madonnas in Italy* (Vashon Island, WA: Dea Madre, 2008), 75.

145 Udalrico Fantelli, *Dimaro: La Carta di Regola* author's translation (Trento, Italy: Centro Studi per la Val di Sole, 1990), 209. Citing earlier historical record by Guglielmo W. di Berlino.

146 Ibid.

147 Vanin, "The Fanes Saga: Short Essays—The Salvans (Wildmen)," paragraph 8, www.ilregnodeifanes.it/inglese/essay3.htm/.

148 Among the Kwakwaka'wakw, "The gum was chewed to give women fertility, and it was thought by some to cause pregnancy without intercourse." The botanical designation is *Pinus monticola*. Jim Pojar and Andy MacKinnon, eds., *Plants of the Pacific Northwest Coast: Washington, Oregon, British Columbia and Alaska* (Vancouver: Lone Pine, 2004), 39.

149 Apela Colorado, "Awakening our Indigenous Powers and Moving as One with the Earth," paper presented at the Inspiring Women Summit, web conference, April 15, 2012, starting at 14:30, www.inspiringwomen-summit.com/sessions/2012/20460.

150 Kathy Jones, "Calling Kiawahine," in *In the Heart of the Goddess*, 2011, paragraph 2, www.kathyjones.co.uk/index.php?option=com_content&view=article&id=97&Itemid=103.

151 For reference to Daughter of the Sun, see Vanin, "The Fanes Saga: Analysis of the Legend—Related Legends," www.ilregnodeifanes.it/inglese/analysis5.htm/; "Elba."

152 Wolff, "Children of the Sun," *The Pale Mountains,* 163–204.

153 Wolff, "The Fountain of Oblivion," *The Dolomites and Their Legends,* 123.

154 Zangrandi, "La Salvatica di Andraz," 90.

155 Ibid., 95.

156 Neri, "The Temptation of the Zubiana," *The Secret Heart of Trentino,* Autumn, 88.

157 Neri, *Mille Leggende del Trentino,* 328.

158 Ibid., 326.

159 Ibid., 331. Neri adds that this diabolic association resulted in many women being arrested, horrendously tortured and put to death.

160 Borzaga, "Le Streghe di Roncone" [The Witches of Roncone], *Leggende del Trentino,* 148. One of their punishments included making them laugh until they died. When the shoemaker was drawn to go there one night by their power, he tricked them by falsely praising the beauty of the "hags" and wounding one of them.

161 Bertoluzza, *Abbicci: Dizionario dell'Antico Dialetto Trentino* (Trento, Italy: l'Adige, 1992), 299.

162 They had other gatherings they called a game, *gioco,* or a dance, *ballo.* See Coltro, 91.

163 Specific spinning practices that Hilda Davidson cites include no spinning on Thursdays in Blekinge, as the goddess Frigg did her spinning that day; no spinning on Thursday evenings in Latvia, where the goddess of spinning is Laima; and no spinning on the Thursday before Whit Sunday, the special day to the Rusalkas in Russia. Hilda Ellis Davidson, *Roles of the Northern Goddess* (London: Routledge, 1998), 104.

164 Monfosco, *Dolomiti: Storie e Leggende* [Dolomites: Stories and Legends] (Bassano del Grappa, Italy: Ghedina & Tassotti Editori, 1987), 129.

165 Neri, "The defeat of the Anguane," *The Secret Heart of Trentino* Spring, 15–16.

166 Coltro, 57. After they disappear, they are turned into viburnum, which Coltro names as "magic plant"; translation provided by Erminia

Stanchina, e-mail message to author, November 23, 2012.

167 Autonomous Province of Trento Department of Emigration, "The Homeland" Monograph Series, *Songs and Tales*, 58–62.

168 Ibid.

169 Monfosco, "La Longagna del Lago Cadin" [The Longagna of Lake Cadin], *Dolomiti*, 81.

170 Neri, "The Good Catherine and the Witches," *Women and Girls in the Legends of the Trent Region*, 63–64. In the story, the witches, devils and male witches are said to dwell on Passo Tonale, which served as a place to organize their sabbaths and raids into the valleys on both sides of the pass.

171 Neri, "Gordo e Vinella" [Gordo and Vinella], *Donne e Bambine nelle Leggende del Trentino*, 73. Wolff offers a longer version of this story. "The Spring of Forgetting," *The Pale Mountains and* "The Fountain of Oblivion," *The Dolomites and Their Legends.*

172 Coltro, 93.

173 Pinuccia Di Gesaro, *I Giochi delle Streghe* [The Games of the Witches]. (Bolzano, Italy: Praxis 3, 1995), 121. (My translation.)

174 Neri, "The Cavern of the Sibyl," *Women and Girls in the Legends of the Trent Region,* 16.

175 Borzaga, "L'antro della Sibilla" [The cavern of the Sibyl], *Leggende del Trentino*, 170.

176 Borzaga, *Leggende del Trentino*, 46.

177 Neri, "The Witches of Valòrz," *The Secret Heart of Trentino* Spring, 47–48.

178 Silvia Chiodin, dir., *Magnificent Italia: Trentino*, DVD, 32:25 (Milan: Touring Club Italiano, 2007), www.filmideas.com/.

179 Neri, "The Anguana's Sack," *The Secret Heart of Trentino* Summer, 9–10.

180 Di Gesaro, *I Giochi delle Streghe*, 225.

181 Ibid., 104–105.

182 Elizabeth Mathias and Richard Raspa, *Italian Folktales in America: The Verbal Art of an Immigrant Woman* (Detroit: Wayne State University Press, 1985), 257.

183 Zangrandi, 44–51.

184 Chiodin, www.filmideas.com.

185 Coltro, 88–89.

186 Foches, 5.

187 Vanin, "The Fanes Saga: Researches on the Legend: A Short History of the Studies of the Legend," paragraph 2, www.ilregnodeifanes.it/inglese/research1.htm/

188 Busk, 341.

189 Monfosco, 129.

190 Zangrandi, 134–135.

191 Vanin, "The Fanes Saga: Short Essays—The Salvans (Wildmen)," paragraph 9, www.ilregnodeifanes.it/inglese/essay3.htm/

192 Borzaga, *Leggende del Trentino*, 9.

193 Ibid., 9–10. This refers, presumably, to the events resulting from the Council of Trent discussed in the introduction and again in chapter 10.

194 Zampiva, 181.

195 Coltro, 24–25.

196 Busk, 415–416.

197 Giovanni Pais Becher, "Auronzo," 2012, three paragraphs after "Le anguane," www.auronzo.eu/3.html.

198 Carla Zocchio, "Quande gh'era le vivane" [When there were vivane], cited in Foches, *Leggende delle Anguane* 2007, 45.

199 Vanin, "The Fanes Saga: The Cultural Background—Cults and Myths," paragraph 5, www.ilregnodeifanes.it/inglese/background1.htm.

200 Ibid., paragraph 2.

201 Neri, "The Old Woman of Valbona," *Women and Girls in the Legends of the Trent Region..*

ARTEMIS AS PROTECTRESS OF FEMALE MYSTERIES: MODERN WORSHIP IN THE DIANIC TRADITION IN AMERICA

Denise Saint Arnault

O ver the shadowy hills and windy peaks . . . [Artemis] draws her golden bow, rejoicing in the chase, and sends out grievous shafts. The tops of the high mountains tremble and the tangled wood echoes awesomely with the outcry of beasts: earthquakes and the sea also where fishes shoal. But the goddess, with a bold heart, turns every way, destroying the race of wild beasts: and when she is satisfied and has cheered her heart, this huntress who delights in arrows slackens her supple bow and goes to the great house of her dear brother . . . there to order the lovely dance of the . . . [Muses and Graces]. There she hangs up her curved bow and her arrows and . . . leads the dances.[1]

Worship of the goddess Artemis spanned vast geographical regions, cultures and epochs, from the thousand-breasted Artemis of Ephesus in Turkey (3,000–200 BCE), to the early winged Artemis found in Sparta (8th century BCE)[2] to the stylized, urbane Roman Diana of Italy (3rd century CE). Unfortunately, it is beyond the scope of this article to examine the similarities and differences among these forms in terms of cultural influence, religious migration and other dispersion patterns. Here the focus will be to examine the activities that may have occurred in the Artemisian temples established by the Athenian political center in Greece between 700 and 400 BCE. There, scholars agree that women engaged in exclusively female religious activities organized around the specific lifecycle events in the temples in Greece.

Although Artemis cared for male children and for animals, she was a goddess who specifically guarded women as they moved through life transitions. Within the Wiccan religious movement in America, a feminist branch honors the goddess as the primary and unitary source of all. Many practitioners in these groups hold exclusively female religious activities that celebrate the female body as a reflection of the goddess and the seasons as a reflection of her aspects, from conception through menarche, maturity, cronehood and death. Artemis is an extremely important goddess in this feminist religion, because it is she who presides over the mysteries of the female body. The links between this mythos of Artemis and contemporary goddess-centered cosmology have ignited the spirits of women for decades, providing cosmological and legendary evidence and validity to their religious form. These are the mythological underpinnings for women who aim to claim and reclaim their right to practice a religion, in which their fundamental and unique biological being is honored as divine and holy, in segregated space—a right protected by the goddess herself.

Artemis as the Goddess of Women's Mysteries

Artemis was a goddess who moved and transformed across time (from 3,000 BCE to 300 CE) and across vast regions (from Turkey in the east across southern Europe). Using Artemis's images, motifs and temple locales in Greece between 700 and 400 BCE, this examination focuses on the smallest slice of a vast religious field by painting a conceptual picture, not a linear one, and by exploring common threads that relate to one contemporary goddess religion.

Temples were established at boundaries and edges. Artemis was the inviolable goddess of the wild. There are no accurate counts of the numbers of Artemisian temples throughout Greece during this period; however, estimates are in the hundreds. Because she was the goddess of the wilderness, her temples were established at the margins of the centralized provinces. Artemis's temples were also established on remote edges of marshes, lakes, hillsides and sacred streams. These geographic placements serve as evidence about the function of Artemisian temples in Greek society.

> On the right [of the road from Argos to Arkadia, Argolis]
> is Mount Lykone, which has trees on it, chiefly cypresses.
> On the top of the mountain is built a sanctuary of Artemis
> Orthia [of the Steep]. . . . Saron built the sanctuary [at
> Troizenos, Argolis] for Artemis Saronis by a sea which is
> marshy and shallow, so that for this reason it was called
> the Phoibaian lagoon. . . . Artemis called Daphnaia [of the
> laurel]. By the sea is a temple of Artemis Diktynna on a
> promontory, in whose honor they hold an annual festival.[3]

Artemisian temples varied in size and were regional in character. Central or local governments constructed and maintained these temples and sponsored women-specific activities at them. S.G. Cole and others have hypothesized that these locales, along with the sheer number of Artemisian temples throughout Greece, indicate that the Greek government considered Artemis a remote but important protector of the people.[4] Her guardianship occurred at these edges, where she claimed dominion. Cole focused on how the Greek government may have established Artemisian temples at the margins and edges of Greece's established territory to symbolically protect the borders of its lands. As the protectress of the wild spaces and the guardian of the edges, Artemis protected the Athenian people where they were most vulnerable to invasion.

Cole's argument is convincing: Artemisian temples can be analyzed from a political and economic perspective as carrying strategic importance. However, Herodotus and Pausanias recorded primarily women-focused festivals or other types of women-specific community events taking place at most of these temples.[5] Indeed, although little is known about what happened at Artemis's temples, symbols and art from them suggest that the activities were related to women's transitions. By establishing goddess temples, the Greek polis (city-state) was not only safeguarding its sovereignty but also sponsoring a social form that entitled women to spaces focused on female-specific religious activities.

In day-to-day life in the Greek world, local people may have had vague knowledge about the strategic and political rationale for governmental sponsorship of the temples. However, it is likely that the priestesses who served at these temples felt passion and desire in their service to their goddess. Certainly, the women who traveled to these temples with offerings of their faith were moved by a psychological and spiritual motivation beyond the political desires of the Greek polis. Such women may well have practiced their faith passionately, beseeching Artemis for protection for successful childbirth or sending their daughters to her temples for transitional rituals. These women and girls engaged in religious and symbolic relationships with Artemis. They hoped, prayed and gave offerings from true devotion.

Temples Relate to the Biological Aspect of Womanhood

The next important variable is that the symbology contained in Artemisian temples was, in most cases, primarily or exclusively about women, and activities documented in them were about female-specific life issues, including the safety of the young, the transition of girls into women, childbirth and, in some places, the transition into marriage. One Artemisian temple that has engendered enthusiastic scholarship and debate is the Artemisian sanctuary at Vravrona, now Brauron. Located about fifty miles outside Athens, this temple is of interest for several reasons. It is near Athens, enjoyed a thorough excavation in the 1940s–1960s, and has stone tablet remains (in both Vravrona and the Acropolis) that document the offerings that women brought for the goddess. There were also myths and historic writings about it.[6]

In Greek mythology, a priestess of Artemis, Iphigenia, was credited as having established the temple at Vravrona. During the Trojan War, Agamemnon offended Artemis, and she punished him with ill winds. Myth suggests that Iphigenia was to be killed by her father in exchange for favorable winds. In some versions of the myth, Artemis intervened by replacing Iphigenia with a female deer. Artemis also proclaimed that Iphigenia would henceforth act as priestess of Artemis's temple in Tauris, north of the Black Sea. In a later myth, Iphigenia's brother, Orestes, traveled to Tauris to search for the statue of Artemis. He was also captured, but Iphigenia recognized him, and they escaped. With the help of the goddess Athena, Iphigenia was told to establish and preside over the temple at Vravrona. Iphigenia had an important role in mythology and at the temple, and legend says her tomb is there.

Excavations have found textile offerings, mirrors, jewelry and other items such as garment pins in the sacred spring at the temple. There is evidence that this temple enjoyed an established system of religious activities from 700 BCE until 400 BCE, when it was destroyed by invasion. There is also evidence that the Greek government had slated this temple for reconstruction in the late 4th century BCE. The evidence suggests that this temple had an altar, an inner space for priestesses (*cella*), a house for maidens, a gymnasium, a wrestling school and a stable, as well as a sacred spring and a cave tomb.[7] It was well known throughout Greece that the activities that took place at the temple were female-specific:

> The Pelasgians dwelt at that time in Lemnos [ca. 6th BCE] and desired vengeance on the Athenians. Since they well knew the time of the Athenian festivals, they acquired fifty-oared ships and set an ambush for the Athenian women celebrating the festival of Artemis at Brauron. They seized many of the women, then sailed away with them and brought them to Lemnos to be their concubines.[8]

Artemis's Connection to Childbirth

Written documents, pottery, artwork and stone engravings have been interpreted as indicating that women gave offerings of their weavings and textiles to Artemis to ensure healthy childbirth. This affirms Artemis as a goddess who, specifically, provided protection and care to women during childbirth. One wonders if other childbirth-related rituals, spells or activities might have occurred at this and other Artemisian temples.

> Seldom is it that Artemis goes down to the town . . . I [Artemis] will visit [these cities] only when women vexed by the sharp pang of childbirth call me to their aid—even in the hour when I was born the Moirai [Fates] ordained that I should be their helper, forasmuch as my mother suffered no pain either when she gave me birth or when she carried me in her womb, but without travail put me from her body.[9]

Orpheus said the following in a beautiful poem to Artemis:

> [Artemis Prothyraia] labour pains are thy peculiar care. In thee, when stretched upon the bed of grief, the sex,

as in a mirror, view relief. Guard of the race, imbued with gentle mind, to helpless youth benevolent and kind; benignant nourisher; great nature's key belongs to no divinity but thee. . . . Thine is the task to loose the virgin's zone and thou in every work art seen and known. With births you sympathise, though pleased to see the numerous offspring of fertility. When racked with labour pangs, and sore distressed the sex invoke thee, as the soul's sure rest; for thou Eileithyia [Artemis] alone canst give relief to pain, which art attempts to ease, but tries in vain. Artemis Eileithyia, venerable power, who bringest relief in labour's dreadful hour; hear, Prothyraia and make the infant race thy constant care.[10]

Her Connection to Maidenhood and Menarche

Another function of this temple was related to the maturation of girl children. Early writings suggest that female-specific rituals were held annually or possibly every four years. Determining what ceremonies or rituals took place at the Temple of Vravrona requires examining both the depictions on the vases found at the temple and the documented choruses and poetry about the events. In both the vases and the poems, females in a group competed in contests or races, processed to an altar, carried or wore garlands and participated in choral performances. These age differences among the women and among the girls, as well as the use of torches, suggest that at least some of the events took place at night.[11]

Women playing the bear used to celebrate a festival for Artemis [at Brauron]. . . . The reason was that a wild she-bear [sacred to Artemis] used to come to the . . . Phlauidoi and spend time there; she became tamed and was brought up with the humans. Some virgin was playing with her and, when the girl began acting recklessly, the she-bear was provoked and scratched the virgin; her brothers were angered by this and speared the she-bear, and because of this a pestilential sickness fell upon the Athenians. When the Athenians consulted the oracle, [the god] said that

there would be a release from the evils if, as blood price
for the she-bear that died, they compelled their virgins
to play the bear.[12]

Although records are not consistent, there are suggestions that girls
between the ages of five and ten years old participated in these festivals,
which have been interpreted as maturation rites. These were unlikely to
be specific to menstruation, since the girls were probably too young. In
addition, the facilities at this temple and written evidence suggest that the
girls also stayed at the temple complex to engage in religious service. It is
not known how long the girls stayed, whether their mothers stayed with
them, what the full purpose of this pilgrimage was, or how many girls went
there. Some speculate that the girls who went to the temple were from the
families of the elite in Athens, but most report that all girls would have
been obliged to go to the temple at some time. One legend states that "girls
playing the bear used to celebrate a festival for Artemis dressed in saffron
robes; not older than ten years nor less than five . . . the Athenians decreed
that no virgin might be given in marriage to a man if she had not previously
played the bear for the goddess."[13]

This mythology and archaeological evidence suggest that the girls ran
races and wore the pelts of bears, dancing with torches around an altar to
Artemis. The wildness of these rituals leaves the imagination flying. One
wonders what it would mean to a six- or seven-year-old girl to march more
than fifty miles to a remote temple and to become engaged in enactments
for the goddess and her priestesses. These pre-menarche rites could have
served a host of psychological and spiritual purposes.

Women's Religion in a Misogynous Culture

Several authors have focused on the misogyny of the Greek culture
during this archaic period. It has been speculated that there were only a few
roles that a woman could play in society. Indeed, S.B. Pomeroy maintained
that these were the only options for a female in this society.[14] Records from
Greek medical texts, as well as writings by Plato and Socrates, espouse the
view that women are fundamentally inferior to men, wild in their nature and
prone to insanity.[15] Women were outside the enculturation or domestication
of ordered society; they were wild, untamed, unclaimed and unconstrained.
Artemis's temples also were at the margins of society, and women went to

these places to relate with this untamed, wild goddess. Whatever the political and social benefits this had for the patriarchal society, women knew themselves as apart from men, different because of their biology, experiencing their unique, specific religious rites apart from men. Artemis, living on the edge, outside the center, cared for and protected the wild and the vulnerable: her women.

Dianic Tradition in America

> I am Nature, the universal Mother, mistress of all the elements, primordial child of time, sovereign of all things spiritual, queen of the dead, queen also of the immortals, the single manifestation of all gods and goddesses that are. My nod governs the shining heights of Heaven, the wholesome sea breezes the lamentable silences of the world below. Though I am worshipped in many aspects, known by countless names, and propitiated with all manner of different rites, yet the whole round earth venerates me.[16]

A branch of the American Wiccan tradition referred to as the Dianic tradition does not embrace the concept of the sacred duality of male and female as the most important cosmological principle; however, this duality is an important principle in other Wiccan traditions.[17] Rather, they understand that the goddess is the primary source of all, that both the female and the male biological forms arise from the goddess. She is the sacred, unified divine being, sovereign and inviolable, fundamental and complete. Her dominion is all that is: All of the elements, the heavens, sea, earth and universe are her. She has a million aspects or facets. She can be seen in all that is, and she is known by a myriad of different names, roles, faces, perspectives and cultures. However, her essence is singular and holistic. Everything comes from her and returns to her.

The namesake for the Dianic tradition is Artemis-Diana, because of her specific female-centered cosmology. Her wildness—in the sense that she cannot be claimed, tamed or in any way ruled—is the essence of the understanding of the goddess in the Dianic tradition. Artemis-Diana is not defined by another, and she unflinchingly exemplifies all of the desired attributes of people of *both* genders: strength and tenderness; vengeance and pity;

155

power and grace; beauty and terror. These attributes are equally and fully juxtaposed in her mythology and her symbolism. So, too, in Dianic tradition there is a spiritual, psychological, symbolic and collective emphasis on the wholeness and completeness of a woman outside her relationships with others. This emphasis serves to assist her in claiming or regaining access to all of a woman's complete being. Woman, as goddess, is fully formed, complete and supremely capable of all attributes, regardless of how these attributes have been culturally distributed to each gender.

In addition, Artemis-Diana is completely female-identified. She rejects domination by men, seeking instead to serve nature, animals, the young and women. She does not engage in the politics of men, and she lives entirely outside their control. She is not in any way aggressive to men; her focus is on her women. However, she will retaliate against any man or woman who violates her laws: protection of the weak and vulnerable; clarity in one's own sanctity and purity; protection of her sovereign domain. As in Artemis's myths, Dianics believe that they have the sovereign right to their own space. They identify with women, identify in the world as women and focus their energies on women. There is no issue with their relationships with men; most Dianic practitioners maintain relationships with their fathers, sons, husbands, brothers, lovers and other men. However, they are not defined by or identified by these relationships. Most Dianic practitioners likely would claim as their focus the security of, protection of and stewardship of nature, children, girls and women.

Finally, but perhaps most importantly, Artemis-Diana was a goddess focused on the biological specificity of the female. Her sanctuaries were claimed by women as specific to women and to the biological reality of the female body. The mysteries of being born into a female body were her mysteries. As the guardian of the wild and vulnerable, she cared for the girl-child during her transition into womanhood. She also cared for the woman who suffered the dangerous state of pregnancy and childbirth, taking pity on her by easing her pain. Or, if circumstances required, Artemis would take mercy on the woman by releasing her with her golden arrow.

So it is with Dianic practitioners. Being born into the female body is the foundation of commonality among women, and the focus is on the distinct spiritual mysteries of this separate biological sex. In that specific body knowledge, women share commonality and spiritual mystery. Religious rituals specific to the mysteries arising from the biological reality of being

156

female are the birthright of any woman, granted and protected by the goddess herself. Dianic practitioners celebrate, as manifestations or aspects of her totality, the earth, her seasons, the elements and all that is. In religious rituals throughout the year, they honor the mysteries of being female, by symbolically overlaying the life cycle of a woman on the seasons of the year. In this way, celebrations of spring may be celebrations of the mysteries of maidenhood, even as celebrations of the winter are celebrations of the mysteries of the hag.

The Goddess is all that is, and she is known by 10,000 names and faces. She is essential, unitary and total in herself. However, women can understand the Goddess only by relating to her aspects, and one such aspect that has taken hold in the consciousness of modern witches is the face of Artemis-Diana. In her mythology and cosmology, women and Dianic practitioners can find motifs and symbolism that indicate the female birthright to have separate, sacred space to celebrate uniquely female mysteries

.

References

Apuleius. *The Golden Ass*. New York: Farrar, Straus, 1951.

Barrett, R. *Women's Rites, Women's Mysteries: Intuitive Ritual Creation*. Woodbury, MN: Llewellyn, 2007.

Budapest, Z. *The Holy Book of Women's Mysteries*. San Francisco: Weiser Books, 2007.

Callimachus. *Hymns and Epigrams in Lycophron and Aratus*. Loeb Classical Library 129. London: William Heinemann, 1921.

Cole, S. G. Landscapes, *Gender and Ritual Space*. Los Angeles: University of California Press, 2004.

Hamilton, R. "Alkman and the Athenian Arkteia." *Hesperia* 58, no. 4 (1989): 449–472.

Herodotus. *Histories*. Cambridge: Harvard University Press, 1922.

Hesiod. *Homeric Hymns, Epic Cycle, Homerica*. Translated by H. G. Evelyn-White. Loeb Classical Library 57. Cambridge: Harvard University Press, 1914.

King, H. "Bound to Bleed: Artemis and Greek Women." In *Images of Women in Antiquity*, edited by A. K. Cameron, 109–127. London: Routledge, 1993.

Mountainwater, S. *Ariadne's Thread: A Workbook of Goddess Magic*. Berkeley: Crossing Press, 1991.

Orpheus. *The Hymns of Orpheus*. Translated by T. Taylor. Los Angeles: Philosophical Research Society, 1981.

Papadimitriou, L. "The Sanctuary of Artemis at Brauron." *Scientific American* 208, no. 6 (1963): 110–120.

Pausanias. *Guide to Greece*. Cambridge: Harvard University Press, 1918.

Pomeroy, S. B. *Goddesses, Whores, Wives and Slaves: Women in Classical Antiquity*. New York: Schocken Books, 1995.

Thompson, M. S. "The Asiatic or Winged Artemis." *Journal of Hellenic Studies* 29 (1909): 286–307.

Endnotes

1 Hesiod, *Homeric Hymns, Epic Cycle, Homerica*, trans. H. G. Evelyn-White, Loeb Classical Library 57 (Cambridge: Harvard University Press, 1914), Homeric Hymn 27 to Artemis.

2 M. S. Thompson, "The Asiatic or Winged Artemis," *Journal of Hellenic Studies*, 29 (1909): 286.

3 Pausanias, *Guide to Greece* (Cambridge: Harvard University Press, 1918), 2.24.5, 2.30, 3.24.9.

4 S. G. Cole, *Landscapes, Gender and Ritual Space* (Los Angeles: University of California Press, 2004).

5 See note 3 above; see also Herodotus, *Histories* (Cambridge: Harvard University Press, 1922).

6 L. Papadimitriou, "The Sanctuary of Artemis at Brauron," *Scientific American* 208, no. 6 (1963): 110.

7 Ibid.

8 Herodotus, *Histories* (Cambridge: Harvard University Press 1922), 6.138.

9 Callimachus, *Hymns and Epigrams in Lycophron and Aratus,* Loeb Classical Library 129 (London: William Heinemann, 1921), Hymn 3 to Artemis.

10 Orpheus, *The Hymns of Orpheus*, trans. T. Taylor (Los Angeles: Philosophical Research Society, 1981), Orphic Hymn 2 to Prothyraia.

11 R. Hamilton, "Alkman and the Athenian Arkteia," *Hesperia* 58, no. 4 (1989): 449.

12 Herodotus, *Histories* (Cambridge: Harvard University Press, 1922), Arktos e Brauroniois.

13 Ibid.

14 S. B. Pomeroy, *Goddesses, Whores, Wives and Slaves: Women in Classical Antiquity* (New York: Schocken Books, 1995).

15 H. King, "Bound to Bleed: Artemis and Greek Women," in *Images of Women in Antiquity*, ed. A. K. Cameron (London: Routledge, 1993), 109–127.

16 Apuleius, *The Golden Ass* (New York: Farrar, 1951), 264.

17 R. Barrett, *Women's Rites, Women's Mysteries: Intuitive Ritual Creation* (Woodbury, MN: Llewellyn, 2007); Z. Budapest, *The Holy Book of Women's Mysteries* (San Francisco: Weiser Books, 2007); S. Mountainwater, *Ariadne's Thread: A Workbook of Goddess Magic* (Berkeley: Crossing Press, 1991).

SECURELY ATTACHED: BRAZILIANS AND THEIR BLACK MADONNAS

April Heaslip

Brazilians are born into a culture infused with the Great Mother arche-type. Throughout the country, Yemanjá is worshipped as a thriving African diasporic deity beyond traditional Candomblé *terreiros* (yards) and within mainstream Brazilian culture. Her syncretism with various Catholic versions of Mother Mary—most notably the country's patron saint, *Nossa Senhora Aparecida*—has created a unique living goddess tradition that carries the potential for psychological benefits in the Brazil-ian psyche.[1]

Brazil, like all places, has its shadow side. Its history of slavery, military dictatorship, disappearances, and the infamous abuse of Rio de Janeiro's homeless children is well chronicled. My wish is not to sugarcoat or minimize a nation's archetypal persona but to illuminate a compassionate resilience and persistent positivism in relation to Brazil's devotion to the divine feminine.

As a mythologist, I am especially interested in how these images and stories affect our lives, especially as living traditions. I am drawn to *applied* archetypal and post-Jungian psychological theories and practices that explore trends emerging from our collective unconscious and to con-textualizing these reflections within goddess scholarship. The dark, sacred feminine seems to be an embodied, active symbol for our times. Black Madonnas may represent certain aspects of life: earthy, moist, fecund, decaying, composting, grieving or renewing energies relating to matter. Matter is often dualistically contrasted with spirit; even the word *spiri-tuality* lends itself to the masculine split of honoring spirit over matter.

Perhaps Black Madonnas are not simply ancient and medieval—and typically European— tributes to what was lost; perhaps they represent what is rising.

In Sync: Syncretic Interpretations of Yemanjá

Popular folklore about the Orixá Yemanjá varies greatly in Brazil. Yemanjá is a member of the Yoruban diasporic pantheon known collectively as the Orixás. Originating in Africa, the Orixás have a global influence and grew especially out of the slave trade within the Americas through the Spanish, Portuguese, French and English colonies. Differences in class, race and geography greatly influence how these myths migrate, mutate and infiltrate the collective unconscious. A survey of how she is experienced in modern mainstream culture may yield a plurality of responses that can be challenging to categorize.

I suggest that Yemanjá has had an active, vast and beneficial influence, providing positive images as Mother and protectress, especially augmented as her mythology has become fused with that of Mother Mary—who is highly venerated in Brazil, by both a Catholic majority and the growing Protestant communities—as the mother of the son of God. Regarding

Nossa Senhora Aparecida
by Loona Houck

Mary's titles, I find the term *virgin* problematic for several reasons. The word itself no longer holds the definition of the archaic Greek: a girl or woman whole unto herself. Because it is Mary's maternal role that links her to Yemanjá, the virginal aspect becomes irrelevant to this discussion, and Yemanjá is certainly not virginal in the word's modern usage. Additionally, because the Catholic Church has used the mythology of Mary's virginity as a way of controlling women's sexuality for over two thousand years (most dramatically illustrated in the constructed fallacy of the virgin-whore dichotomy between Mother Mary and Mary

Magdalene), continuing to identify the divine feminine embodied in living traditions in relation to such limiting sexual definitions keeps us repeating misogynistic patterns of oppression and consigns us to cultural amnesia.[2] Although mainstream Christianity may have attempted to eliminate shadow and darkness from its mythology—promoting a sexually virginal and flaw-less holy mother instead—through Yemanjá, we see one way in which Brazil, with its cyclical celebration of darkness that is Carnival, may be a place where darkness is more accepted and even celebrated than in other Roman Catholic cultures.

What is the difference among confusion, conflation and synthesis? When differing forms of belief are fused, the result can be disorienting to a world intent on linear categorization and understanding. Yet it is exactly this bricolage of beliefs that has created the unique composite of a thoroughly Brazilian Yemanjá, who can be described at syncretic. In *Secrets, Gossip, and Gods: The Transformation of Brazilian Candomblé*, Paul Christopher Johnson values the gerund *syncretizing*, which he defines as "the active process of constructing common ground between potentially conflicting entities and so is a form of historical practice to construct identity in relation to specific historical exigencies."[3] A living tradition requires ongoing interaction.

Since arriving in Brazil as an exchange student on August 15, 1984 with a return ticket for the same day a year later, I have been seen as a daughter of Yemanjá. Not only is August 15th celebrated as the day of Mary's Assumption and a secular holiday for the town that hosted me—Araras, São Paulo—but also it is one of several holy days for Yemanjá. In her dissertation titled "The Heartbeat of the Great Mother: The Transformational Birth Archetype in Brazilian Candomblé," Kris Oster explained the significance of August 15th within the Candomblé liturgical calendar:

> The Boa Morte celebrate their main festival in Cachoeira, Brazil, on August 15, the day of the Assumption of the Virgin Mary. . . . The Virgin Mary was syncretized with Iemanjá during the slavery period, and the members of Boa Morte still honor their ancestresses by continuing the tradition of honoring both the Catholic Virgin Mary and African-Brazilian Iemanjá.[4]

Yemanjá is also honored on February 2nd, the feast day of Saint Brigid, which overlaps the Catholic holiday of Candlemas, which was originally layered over the ancient Celtic cross-quarter day of Imbolc. Most popular of all of Yemanjá's days is the coastal celebration on New Year's Eve, when laypeople and committed practitioners alike gather in white (right down to the most important, newly purchased, undergarments) to send small prayer-laden boats out to sea on the waves.

Across Brazil, African diasporic traditions have become interwoven with European and other spiritual traditions in highly accessible, diverse and liberating ways. Greatly affected by the southerly economically and environmentally based migrations of northeasterners—principally from the state of Bahia—toward industrialized, cosmopolitan regions, throughout the past several decades, these traditions have spread in novel, dynamic ways while maintaining regional flavor. My own exposure to these traditions in the southern Brazilian states of São Paulo and Minas Gerais, beginning in the 1980s, was very different from the traditional Candomblé and Umbanda practices in northeastern Brazil. While the word *Macumba* is often used primarily by nonpractitioners as an umbrella term to describe African-based Brazilian religious movements, more exact though somewhat fluid names for spiritual traditions include *Candomblé* and *Umbanda*.

Who Yemanjá most directly relates to in the Catholic pantheon of saints depends largely upon whom you ask. (See Appendix A for a compilation of some syncretic parallels between Yemanjá and aspects of Catholicism together with the Candomblé and Umbanda orixá pantheons in relation to the Orixá Oxúm.) Yemanjá has been connected with several emanations of Mother Mary and is often depicted as light-skinned, haloed and swathed in blue gowns.

This longstanding syncretism is featured in Toni Morrison's novel *Paradise*, in which her creation of parallel and intertwining worlds embodies both African and Catholic mythologies. The story takes place in a convent that serves as a Candomblé *terreiro*, where the female characters worship and embody the divine feminine. La Vinia Delois Jennings explores the novel's mythopoetic structure in *Toni Morrison and the Idea of Africa*, in which she identifies the interconnected complexities of archetypal identity. She points to "Consolata as the Candomblé water priestess Yemanjá, the complement of the African-descended . . . loa of Voudoun, La Sirène, (an aspect of the loa Erzulie) who resides under the sea. She is depicted as a mermaid with ample breasts, the symbol of her maternal, nurturing nature, and her oceanic colors are blue, white, and green."[5] Jennings explained, "Yemanjá is the guardian of women, the womb, childbirth, fertility, and witchcraft,"[6] and she connected her with Catholic emanations of the divine feminine:

> The Virgin Mary is Yemanjá's and therefore Consolata's Christian parallel. . . . A Candomblé manifestation of the Madonna and a complement to Yemanjá, Piedade, or rather her memory, pervades Consolata's consciousness. The cerulean Piedade is the guardian Virgin of the sea who gives safe harbor to those at risk of perishing beneath its flood. Off the coast of Salvador on Itaparica, the largest island in the All Saints Bay, stands the Capela de Nossa Senora de Piedade (Our Lady of Piety Chapel) erected in 1622 in honor of the Virgin. However, Morrison's conflation of Piedade, 'a woman black as firewood,' with the most important Virgin of Brazil, Our Lady Aparecida, centers the representation of Consolata squarely within Brazilian religious iconography and the trope of Yemanjá.[7]

These expansive and varied mythologies of Yemanjá are embodied within living, vital traditions that cross geographical, religious and even archetypal borders. Diasporic movements teem with life as they move into uncharted territories, digest new ideas and offer up fluid, reflexive expressions of meaning that often slip through hands hungry to categorize and define. What is constant is Yemanjá's unfailing maternal nurturing, as well as the devotion of her followers.

Appearing, Our Lady

The name of Brazil's patron saint, *Nossa Senhora Aparecida*, translates as "Our Lady Who Appeared." Considering how she was found, the juxtaposition is interesting. China Galland tells a version of her creation myth in "Raise Up Those Held Down: A Pilgrimage to the Black Madonna, Mother of the Excluded, Aparecida, Brazil" in *The Moonlit Path: Reflections on the Dark Feminine*:

According to legend, in October 1717, a poor fisherman, João Alves, and two companions had been unable to catch any fish in the Paraiba River of Brazil. On the last cast of the day, the fishermen pulled up a net empty but for the broken body of a statue of a Black Virgin Mary. They cast again and pulled up her head. They named the statue *Aparecida*, which means "appeared." They rejoiced in finding the Virgin and resolved to keep her, and thereafter their nets were filled with fish. This was the first "miracle" attributed to this Madonna.[8]

The sculpting of the statue—which is less than three feet tall and dated to ca. 1605—has been attributed to a *carioca* (someone from Rio de Janeiro) monk from São Paulo, Frei Agostino de Jesus. How the statue came to be underwater or how long it had been there is not known, but it apparently was there for years. The face and hands of *Our Lady Aparecida*, the only parts of the statue's body visible as flesh, are dark brown, and she balances herself on a crescent moon. The local town was renamed Aparecida and distinctly grew around her axis of miraculous mythology. The basilica of Nossa Senhora Aparecida, today second only to Saint Peter's in size, is saturated with intense religious commercialization. Nonetheless, the statue, tiny, old and a survivor of prolonged moisture, theft and breakage, brings faith to those on pilgrimage, making the Basílica do Santuário Nacional de Nossa Senhora Aparecida a unique, enormous temple dedicated to the feminine divine, a goddess.

Diasporic Dames as Black Madonnas

In *Black Madonnas: Feminism, Religion and Politics in Italy,* Lucia Chiavola Birnbaum explained Carl Jung's well-documented interest in the Black Madonnas. She viewed his interest as rooted in his "insights that archetypes, notably the archetype of the earth mother, 'were, and still are, living psychic forces that demand to be taken seriously.'"[9] Black Madonnas embody dynamic qualities of the divine feminine while refusing to be easily defined. Some statues are called "black" due to having been darkened by time. Some are so ancient that they lost their original names and were later co-opted into patriarchal roles within the Catholic Church and other institutions. Sometimes, Black Madonnas are termed African in origin, usually referring to another divine diasporic powerhouse, Isis.

Jung's insight into Black Madonnas was further explored by Sheri Parks in *Fierce Angels: The Strong Black Woman in American Life and Culture*. She discussed how Jungian theory and therapy have greatly influenced how we view and work with popular psychology in contemporary culture. Parks identified what she believes Jung saw as the underlying, emerging principle requiring our attention: "The Sacred Dark Feminine has directly or indirectly become part of therapy and self-help of people across the country and around the world."[10]

According to anthropologist Anna Fedele in *Looking for Mary Magdalene: Alternative Pilgrimage and Ritual Creativity at Catholic Shrines in France,* Black Madonnas are often seen as composite representatives of three distinct expressions of the divine feminine—Mother Mary, Mary Magdalene and Mother Earth—all of whom relate to darkness.[11] She also discussed the statues as "cultural surviv[ors] of pre-Christian goddess cults and thus a privileged access to the energy of the Goddess and especially Her dark side."[12] This hybridization may support a unified—if complex and multidimensional—definition of our understanding of who or what a Black Madonna represents. I believe these three facets to be interconnected.

Situating archetypal images and ideas within our larger conversations about aspects of the divine feminine helps to contextualize our experiences. For example, post-Gimbutas conversations within feminist archaeology offer us a terrific range of questions to reflect upon. Who are the Black Madonnas? Lost Earth goddesses? Other recognizable deities such as Inanna, Persephone and Isis? What does it mean to venerate a mother goddess? (What are the benefits? What does it mean for other archetypes?) What does the archetype of "Mother" mean to us? We may acknowledge an entire continuum of responses, from devouring to nurturing to indifferent. Who exactly do these statues and figurines represent? Goddesses? Or is there just one Goddess? Priestesses? Women? Archetypes? Ourselves? The Other (in Jungian terms, the receiver of our own disowned shadow qualities, our projections)? How do these statues relate to place? Is she out there somewhere in the world? Is she tied to a specific place? Or is she inside me? How does "evidence" of her affect my life? Do I have to be "earthy" or a mother to relate to her? (This question provides an example of how biological terms may restrict our understanding of womanhood as it relates to motherhood.) Could there be a soaring, transcendent aspect to these Black Madonnas, too, that contradicts or compliments the chthonic, matter (*mater*) aspects? How do we combat essentialism while deeply exploring our own experiences with the divine feminine?

My own interest in Black Madonnas is in relation to the lineage of ancient Mediterranean fertility cults embodying the alchemical sacred marriage, particularly in regard to Mary Magdalene as the lost and returning archetypal bride of Western cultures. Her re-emerging mythology presupposes the need for her heresy to have gone underground—into the dark and hidden places of Gaia herself—in order to survive. Birnbaum wrote of the survival, despite the condemnation of the Catholic Church, of pilgrimages dedicated to the Magdalene. Magdalene pilgrimage "persists (notably in the pilgrimage of the Gypsies of Europe to the black Sarah-Kali and her two white half-sisters at Stes-Maries-de-la-Mer in France). In popular Easter-week rituals, many women, identifying with Mary [Magdalene], accompany her."[13]

Regarding the two Brazilian Black Madonnas, Jennings offered complex, often conflicting information about the archetypal importance of water within their mythologies:

> In the African-Brazilian tradition, the Black Madonna Aparecida is connected with the *orixá* Oxum [Oshun], the Mother of Africa and the patroness of pregnancy, children, rivers, seas, beauty, seduction, shrewdness, and wisdom. Oxum rules the sweet waters—rivers, brooks, and streams—and is closely related to Yemanjá. Consolata's celebration of Piedade underscores her affiliation with the Candomblé orixá Yemanjá who is associated with the Virgin Mary and is a symbol of motherhood.[14]

Again, the powerful fusion between Yemanjá and Nossa Senhora Aparecida, based on their common qualities, is amplified. Both are protectresses, mother figures, patronesses of fishermen and goddesses of the waters (unique among Black Madonnas, who are more consistently associated with the fecundity of the black earth).[15] However, Birnbaum discussed how the blackness of such Madonnas "taps very deep emotions,"[16] and I am reminded of our ladies' active aqueous powers. Yemanjá and Nossa Senhora Aparecida are the *only* Black Madonnas I am aware of who are associated with water, offering an academic field day for archetypal psychologists interested in exploring the depths of emotional intelligence and the submerged unconscious of our collective divine feminine.

Archetypes are inherently multifaceted and beg not to be reduced to rational, logos-oriented "clarity." None is more complex than the Black Madonna, whose very embodiment is dark, fecund and perhaps unknowable. I suggest that she is all that has not been seen. I suggest that, rather than look for simple or unifying definitions of who she or they might be for us, we look in situ at how these two Brazilian Black Madonnas are very much part of living spirituality. I even would go so far as to suggest that they—or she, if they are treated as one and the same—have infused the culture with something unique and palpable.

Great Mother as Psychological Protectress

In *Jung: A Feminist Revision*, Susan Rowland explored post-Jungian feminisms as vehicles for vibrant mythological interpretation. In her chapter titled "The Goddess and the Feminine Principle," she examined the emergence of critical scholarly voices determined to excavate Jungian material in service of liberation:

> A remarkable amplification of Jung's feminine within the numinous (in archetypes) is the rejection of masculine-dominated monotheistic culture in favour of a 'return' to the divine as a great mother. 'She' infuses and makes sacred the natural world. She is the divine within or immanent in the world, not apart and transcendent of it. Here Jungian feminism becomes a most ambitious feminist myth of history, culture, aesthetics and psyche.[17]

With this perspective in mind, what might Yemanjá and Nossa Senhora Aparecida—as powerful Black Madonnas of our deep psychic waters—offer us through their living mythology? Further, what are these embodiments of the Great Mother inviting us to cocreate?

There is something unshakable in the Brazilian psyche. Not only is there a deep devotion to their collective culture, but I also experience Brazilians as generally at peace, rooted in a sense of self, family and community and in connection with life. Over the past thirty years, the countless conversations I have enjoyed have revealed core Brazilian beliefs that we are being cared for, held and guided by the divine. Although dialogues can certainly involve God as father and Jesus as savior, they are just as likely to be centered on how Mother Mary and Yemanjá look out for us. Having often wondered where this engaged sense of surety came from, I suggest that most Brazilians, regardless of religious affiliation, believe that a great Mother Goddess—some aspect of the divine feminine—protects Brazil and her people. In addition to holding this cultural belief, they feel this protection on both a personal and a collective level. Furthermore, perhaps this implied vigilance (i.e., "Mama is watching out for us") allows and, indeed, provides for a secure sense of being.

Secure attachment, as defined by Jasmin Lee Cori in *The Emotionally Absent Mother: A Guide to Self-Healing and Getting the Love You Missed*, holds a similar resonance. "When the world (generally in the person of Mother) meets our needs consistently, we develop trust that we will have what we need and the world is perceived to be a safe place."[18] There are enormous benefits to a strong attachment bond, most importantly high self-esteem. Specifically, "secure individuals learn to perceive themselves as strong and competent, valuable, lovable and special—thanks to being valued, loved, and viewed as special by caring attachment figures."[19] I believe that, culturally, Brazilians exhibit an extraordinarily high rate of these secure attachment benefits, and I suggest that this may relate to their strong belief in a Mother Goddess archetype, generally a composite of Mother Mary and Yemanjá. Furthermore, their daily dialogue is infused with this belief, verbally amplifying its effect as they consistently and calmly reassure one another through daily practice.

I suggest that Brazil's relationship with female deities as mother goddesses—both African and Christian in origin—offers their collective unconscious tangible and useful psychic security, as attachment theory would suggest. Perhaps Brazil's unique history and conditioning—including tolerance, multiculturalism, syncretism and shadow work—has resulted in a culture infused with reverence for the divine feminine and a belief that the female divine watches over all.

References

Birnbaum, Lucia Chiavola. *Black Madonnnas: Feminism, Religion and Politics in Italy*. Boston: Northeastern UP, 1993.

Cori, Jasmin Lee. *The Emotionally Absent Mother: A Guide to Self-Healing and Getting the Love You Missed.* New York: The Experiment, 2010.

Fedele, Anna. *Looking for Mary Magdalene: Alternative Pilgrimage and Ritual Creativity at Catholic Shrines in France*. Oxford: Oxford Un, 2013.

Gustafson, Fred, ed. *The Moonlit Path: Reflections on the Dark Feminine*. Berwick: Nicolas-Hays, 2003.

Jennings, La Vinia Delois. *Toni Morrison and the Idea of Africa*. Cambridge: Cambridge University Press, 2008.

Johnson, Paul Christopher. *Secrets, Gossip and Gods: The Transformation of Brazilian Candomblé*. New York: Oxford University Press, 2002.

Omari-Tunkara, Mikelle Smith. *Manipulating the Sacred: Yorùbá Art, Ritual, and Resistance in Brazilian Candomblé*. Detroit: Wayne State University Press, 2005.

Oster, Kris Katsuko. *The Heartbeat of the Great Mother: The Transformational Birth Archetype in Brazilian Candomblé*. PhD diss., Pacifica Graduate Institute, 2011.

Parks, Sheri. *Fierce Angels: The Strong Black Woman in American Life and Culture*. New York: One World/Ballantine Books, 2010.

Rowland, Susan. *Jung: A Feminist Revision*. Oxford University Press: Polity, 2002.

Shulman, Mary Watkins, and Helene Shulman. *Toward Psychologies of Liberation: Critical Theory and Practice in Psychology and the Human Sciences*. New York: Palgrave Macmillan, 2010.

Appendix A: Yemanjá & Oxúm Syncretisms
Comparisons found in *Manipulating the Sacred: Yorùbá Art, Ritual, and Resistance in Brazilian Candomblé* by Mikelle Smith Omari-Tunkara and *Secrets, Gossip and Gods: The Transformation of Brazilian Candomblé* by Paul Christopher Johnson.

Source	Aspect	Yemanjá	Oxúm
Omari-Tunkara (149)	Catholic saint	Virgin Mary (Nossa Senhora de Conceição)	Nossa Senhora das Candeias
(69)	Water attribute	Goddess of the sea and river	
(72)	Catholic saint	Nossa Senhora de Conceição da Praia / Our Lady of Immaculate Conception of the Beach	
(74-5)	Catholic saint	Virgin Mary	
(75)	Water attribute	Iemanjá lives in the middle of the waters	Lives on the surface of the water
(76)	Water attribute	Her adé (crown) represents her sovereignty of the sea and, according to some initiates, all water.	
(77)	Catholic saint	Dona Janaina	
Johnson (43)	Water Attribute	Stumbled as she fled Oungan, bursting her great breasts and giving birth to freshwater rivers	
(205)	Mother/Fecundity & Fertility Aspects	Female *orixá* of the sea (in Brazil) and fecundity; Mother of other *orixás* in some cosmogonic myths	Female *orixá* of fresh waters and rivers. Associated with divinatory skill, sex appeal, fertility, and the love of wealth & refinement
(205)	Calendric Worship	Revered on New Year's Eve in many coastal cities of Brazil	

Appendix B: Preoccupied Attachment Style

The following is from *The Emotionally Absent Mother: A Guide to Self-Healing and Getting the Love You Missed* by Jasmin Lee Cori. Portions of this list can be found on pages 50–51 of that book; the remainder was gleaned and synthesized from the entire book.)

When a mother's love is intermittently reinforced, children walk on eggshells in response to her changing moods, never knowing whether they will meet the good mother or the absent mother. In response, a child can develop the following feelings, behaviors, and problem-solving techniques:

- A heightened need for closeness
- Anger and rejection qualities when another is not available to the child emotionally (as an adult, he or she can be anxiously tied up with how available others are)
- Hypervigilance about attachment signals
- Questioning and testing the commitment of others
- Emphasis of need and helplessness in order to convince others to stay
- Punishment of others for not providing what he or she wants
- Anger when attachment needs are not met
- Extreme upset at being alone during times of distress
- Feeling of abandonment when attachment figures go away
- Constant search for love
- So caught up in attachment concerns that he or she cannot explore the world
- Such preoccupation with relationships that he or she becomes an underachiever
- Alternating between cutting off feelings and plunging into them headlong (vacillation between detachment and self-sufficiency, and then collapse into a dependent pattern)
- Lack of confidence that others will be emotionally available and can be counted on to provide support

When the mother was not emotionally present, the child had three choices: follow her into her black hole of no feeling, sever some of the connection to avoid the hole, or become her rescuer, her antidepressant, by making the extraordinary effort to charm her.

Endnotes

1 While a literal translation of Nossa Senhora Aparecida effectively identifies her relation to place, her Portuguese name might be more accurately translated to read Our Lady who Appeared. The town Aparecida was named for her appearance and subsequent "miracles."

2 Mary Watkins and Helene Shulman. *Toward Psychologies of Liberation: Critical Theory and Practice in Psychology and the Human Sciences* (New York: Palgrave Macmillan, 2001), 234.

3 Paul Christopher Johnson, *Secrets, Gossip and Gods: The Transformation of Brazilian Candomblé* (New York: Oxford University Press, 2002), 71.

4 Kris Katsuko Oster, *The Heartbeat of the Great Mother: The Transformational Birth Archetype in Brazilian Candomblé,* (PhD diss., Pacifica Graduate Institute, 2011), chapter 3.

5 La Vinia Delois Jennings, *Toni Morrison and the Idea of Africa* (Cambridge: Cambridge University Press, 2008), 168.

6. Ibid., 169.

7 Ibid., 168–169.

8 China Galland, "Raise Up Those Held Down: A Pilgrimage to the Black Madonna, Mother of the Excluded, Aparecida, Brazil," in *The Moonlit Path: Reflections on the Dark Feminine, ed. F. Gustafson* (Berwick: Nicolas-Hays, 2003), 215–216.

9 Lucia Chiavola Birnbaum, *Black Madonnas: Feminism, Religion and Politics in Italy* (Boston: Northeastern University Press, 1993), 12.

10. Anna Fedele, *Looking for Mary Magdalene: Alternative Pilgrimage and Ritual Creativity at Catholic Shrines in France* (Oxford: Oxford University Press, 2013), 26.

11 Ibid., 238.

12 Ibid.

13 Lucia Chiavola Birnbaum, *Black Madonnas: Feminism, Religion and Politics in Italy* (Boston: Northeastern University Press, 1993), 144–145.

14 Ibid., 168–169.

15 Ibid., 11.

16 Ibid., 146.

17 Susan Rowland, *Jung: A Feminist Revision* (Oxford: Polity, 2002), 47–48.

18 Jasmin Lee Cori, *The Emotionally Absent Mother: A Guide to Self-Healing and Getting the Love You Missed* (New York: The Experiment, 2010), 44.

19 Ibid., 44.

WEAVING CROSS-CULTURAL NARRATIVES: CURANDERISMO AND PSYCHOTHERAPY

Natasha Redina

Introduction

When the stories of our ancestors are edited or lost, we lose some vital way of seeing and understanding the world in which we live. I remember as a young child, when I was unwell, my Greek grandmother dimming the lights and lighting candles on her altar, which was filled with images of Greek Orthodox saints, serene faces watching me as their golden halos glimmered in the candlelight. I recall her reciting strange prayers, rubbing me down with herbs and alcohol, splashing me with holy water, salt and oil and my drifting off to sleep enveloped by the smell of rose and frankincense burning in the corner of the room. Whether the ceremonies she performed or the care and attention I received made me better is unknown. But what the experience provided was a narrative within which the power to heal was situated within the homestead, given freely and with love, weaving some invisible thread of interconnectivity between the seen world and the unseen world. The rest of the family saw this as superstitious nonsense. Unfortunately, my grandmother's craft died with her, which is a story repeated over and over again as traditional medicinal practices are lost and forgotten in the wake of modern medical advances, which often place the locus of healing externally, in the hands of depersonalized experts and large pharmaceutical companies.

Modern medicine has saved countless lives, and this discussion is not about turning our back on these advances but rather about inviting into awareness an alternative, grassroots-based narrative into the dialogue. Within the modern medical framework, there lies the danger of rejecting traditional healing practices altogether and, in so doing, losing deep, rich philosophies that can offer affordable, accessible healthcare. In addition to the practical application of old ceremonies come the associated narratives, which have formed part of our collective psyche for millennia and offer portals through which expanded ways of seeing ourselves and our communities can be viewed—a key into an archetypal world beyond the personal and a connection to our own mythic stories. By preserving this wisdom and the voices of marginalized peoples, we can incorporate an integral aspect of our collective psyches, which has the potential to sustain a more balanced way of living.

It is hoped that further research into the effects of traditional healing techniques may contribute to a better and more culturally fulfilling understanding and encourage a greater respect and appreciation of *curanderismo* (traditional Mexican healing) as a valid, affordable system of healthcare throughout the Americas.

Lost Traditional Narratives

I remember, a few years ago while walking through the Acropolis museum in Athens, being overcome by an intense wave of sadness as I gazed upon the broken remains of many of the female statues housed there. Disembodied limbs, missing heads, shattered torsos, these fragmentary images spoke to me of the beauty and craftsmanship of times gone by but equally of the great gaps reflecting the knowledge and narratives that had been lost—the stories of women and healing.

In the writing of European history, the majority of female voices and voices from borderland cultures have been omitted. During the Middle Ages, earth-based healing practices were systematically destroyed, with many practitioners facing persecution for practicing the old ways; ceremonies were abolished and sacred sites replaced with churches; the Renaissance and the Enlightenment further cemented the Cartesian split. These movements displaced healthcare practices from the accessibility and affordability of the homestead and put them in the hands of "experts," where they were then practiced from a position of superiority and based on monetary exchange.

The Mexihka tradition has kept alive many of the wisdoms that had been thought lost, providing a narrative which is helping many to find a more integrated way of living in harmony with their natural environment. Miahuatzin said the following[1]:

> *I believe and was taught by the grandparents, and I trust in my experiences too, that we are all one human race—that we all want the same thing, we are all looking for the same things—our health, our strength and happiness. We may all have different paths maybe and so sometimes it may seem as though we are different, but we are not different, we are one human race. We all want to be happy—we are here on the earth to be happy— no matter where we live, in an indigenous tribe, in the Federal District of Mexico City, in New York, London or Berlin—we all want the same thing—we are searching for happiness.*

> *What I have noticed is that the closer we live to virtual communication methods, the more we feel different and separate. They try to tell us that we are different—they send us these messages, not as to respect ourselves, but as to justify a sense of separation and alienation from different cultures and each other. The messages we get from the mass media are "Oh I'm educated differently," "Because I live in a city and you in the countryside," "Because I live in America and you live in Mexico," we are different.*

> *But this is the attitude of someone that doesn't want to open up and wants to remain fixed in his or her daily routine. It happens a lot in Europe where many of my students are afraid to use the Mexihka medicine because of the laws surrounding registration of health professionals, and so they are afraid the police will come and they will be punished. But you have to understand the medicine is such a beautiful complete system. The grandparents say that our brain is like a big box—we have to activate*

177

this box—and if you activate it things will come to you. If you think of the police—they will come to you! But if you don't think of them and you do your work, full of love, because you like it, and see your patients because you want to, both you and your patients can find a way down this beautiful path, and they can carry on walking on their paths afterwards with happiness.

Liminality and Soul Loss

Ethnographer Arnold van Gennep postulated that there were three phases within any rites of passage: the ritual of separation (pre-liminal), the ritual of margin (liminal) and the ritual of aggregation (post-liminal). Liminality is a space "betwixt and between,"[2] within which the parameters of daily life are altered and become porous and open to change and transformation. There is often a difficulty in translating these experiences into words, and people who undergo this process often speak in terms of metaphors and analogies, because these approximate the lived experience within liminal space.

Within both depth psychotherapy and *curanderismo*, the practitioner invites the patients to step out of daily life and enter a liminal space, within which shifts, transformations, and healing can take place. The patients will experience this liminal space and often, through introspection or ceremony, encounter not only nonlinear, atemporal spaces within their psyches but also approximate archetypal processes.

Susto (soul loss), as described within the *curandera* tradition, happens after a trauma. It is believed that a part of an individual's spirit jumps out of his or her body and gets lost; it is the role of the *curandera* to bring the soul back and restore it to its rightful place. On a symbolic level, this is very much akin to depth psychotherapeutic practices in which a therapist undertakes a similar journey with the patient, to very painful places, helping him or her to assimilate traumatic incidents and reintegrate fragmented aspects of the psyche so that he or she can be whole again. Memories are stored in associated neural networks within the brain and affect the person's perceptions of the surrounding world. After a trauma, one's information processing is affected neurophysiologically, and some traumatic memories are stored as disconnected fragments. These fragments can become frozen and, therefore, not able to be fully integrated into the person's experiences. These fragments can resurface and provoke intense reactions and further trauma; therefore, often a lot of energy is put into keeping them repressed. This expenditure of energy for repression and disassociation impedes a person from fully engaging in and experiencing his or her emotions.

Psychotherapy

Psychotherapy originates from the Greek words *psyche* (soul) and *terapia* (care of). There is a common misconception that psychotherapy began with Freud, but although he and subsequent psychotherapists contributed a massive body of work toward the understanding of the psyche, in particular in creating a richly descriptive vernacular to express inner psychological dynamics, the care of the soul has been going on for millennia. One form through which this has been expressed is mythic narrative. "Not only does behavior of the unconscious resemble the workings of myth, but we ourselves participate in living and lived myths."[3] Within Greek mythology, Asclepius, a potent archetype of the wounded healer and dream worker, was said to be unceasingly gentle and able to heal with words that alleviated the tormented souls of men and offer them the gift of healing dreams.[4] The Greeks were famous for their healing temples where patients would undergo healing baths, eat special diets, visit shrines, make offerings, ingest herbs and take part in rituals and ceremonies to help heal themselves, but the vast majority of these practices have now been lost.

The mind is complex, and there are many schools of thought and modalities within the psychotherapeutic world. A basic premise is that there exists the surface mind, that of which we are conscious and which is our typical normal waking state. The ego is the verbal, organizing part of the mind and enjoys a sense of control and power; however, in order to do this it often suppresses the subconscious, which it sees as a dangerous realm of untamed instincts. The deep mind, or subconscious, is the intuitive aspect of the mind; it is connected to the body and emotions, and its language is images, dreams, symbols and myths. It also stores painful or shameful memories that the ego has repressed, as well as parts that may have been deemed unacceptable, but it is also a font for creativity and spontaneity. Within transpersonal psychology, the deep center, the core of our being that corresponds to what Jung called the Self, is acknowledged, and the language with which it communicates is symbol and archetype.

Individuals often disassociate or cut themselves off from experiences in order to survive. In myth, a great example of this was Procrustes. He stood on the road to Athens, and all pilgrims had to pass him in order to enter the city. Each pilgrim had to lie on Procrustes's bed, and any parts of the pilgrim that did not fit in the bed had to be chopped off before the pilgrim could proceed. This is often a reflection of what we experience growing up: cutting off parts of ourselves that are deemed unacceptable by our primary caregivers or in order to survive traumatic incidents. What psychotherapy, especially psychosynthesis, does is invite these lost parts back into the patient's consciousness so that they can be integrated and he or she can function as a full psychic being. The more accepting and loving we can be toward ourselves, the happier and more integrated we will be.

I asked Miahuatzin if she felt that psychotherapy played a part in *curanderismo*, and she replied as follows:

> *It plays a big, big role and our grandparents placed great emphasis on it because it is seen as a preventative medicine. Our grandparents tell us a story of Maria Sabina, and it's about the first x-ray machine that arrives at a nearby village. Maria Sabina stood and watched the mules carrying the heavy equipment and asked the local doctor what it was for. Maria Sabina always talked to the doctors and the priests, it is important that healers can be open and talk to different professionals. He explained what it was to her and she asked why he needed this. "It's a way of diagnosing disease in patients," he said. And Maria Sabina was thinking, Why so many instruments? The doctor asked her "How do you carry out your diagnosis then?" She replied, "There are four ways of finding out the diagnosis and I will share one of them with you now."*

> *The first reason a person gets sick is he or she does not fulfill their tasks. They could get diarrhea or a cold or a headache and it's because you are not fulfilling your task. It's not about asking what is good and what is bad,*

it's about being true to yourself and to your path. And you can find all this out just by talking to your patient.

We are all the same—we each have our tasks—but the difference is we each have a different task. Maybe the woman who lives in the countryside was too lazy to make tortillas and this is why she got ill. And maybe the woman in the city did not feel like going out to the shops to buy something to eat—and this is why she got ill.

So the first reason you get ill is when you do not fulfill your tasks. How can you find what are your tasks? The only way is to know yourself. To know yourself and who you really are and what you have to do. This is why I insist on my students knowing the Tonalmaxioto (the Mexihka calendar). Because by knowing the Tonalmaxioto, you know yourself—and by knowing yourself—you know others and by knowing others you know yourself. It's a chain in which we know each other and are not separate. Your principal obligation is your path. You can be daughter, son and a mother, father but your real obligation is to you, to be you and fulfill your task. It does not mean you become selfish and egotistical, saying "I'm well because I want to be well." No. It's saying, "I want to be well because I want all those around me to be well." Always thinking also of the people around us. If you are in a room with 6–7 other people and you have a headache—by the end of the day all the people in the room will have a headache. Jesus was a healer and he spoke with his patients—he asked them, "What's going on with you?"—he didn't just say, "Yes, I will heal you." He spoke with them, he listened to their stories. Curanderismo has a lot to do with psychotherapy. You need to talk, always, always talk.

Curanderismo

There were many healing traditions and cultures from all over Mexico that each went underground in their own way after the Spanish *conquistadores* arrived and that have been resurrected and readopted in many different ways in modern life. The story goes that the real gold that the Spanish were after was the secret medicine that had been kept hidden for about 500 years. The tradition of the Mexihkas, which stored some of this secret healing knowledge, was kept secret until 1970, when the elders decided it was time to share this knowledge with the world.

Mexihkas are *curanderas* who weave the natural world into their practice, inviting in archetypal energies, plants, songs, touch, smoke, objects, words and images, all integrated with ceremony and ritual. *Curanderismo* is a healthcare system that allows for the *curandera* and her patients to fully immerse themselves in mythic worlds but in very grounded, practical ways. Words and ceremonies are not just symbolic; rather, they are alive and lived by the *curandera* and her patients.

The teachings are grounded in the *Filosofía Náhuatl*, which is about living in harmony with ourselves and our environment. Use of these concepts enables us to know our true selves and bring more consciousness to our thinking and behavior. This philosophy is applied to all areas of life and provides the basis for the medical concepts of the *Mexihkas*; Mexihka literally translates as "one who comes from his or her center." It is a deep, multilayered philosophy, and it is not within the scope of this article to go into any great depth in it, but I hope that by elucidating some of the central themes I may begin to paint a picture of this rich multifaceted healthcare system.

In *Nahuatl*, the word *Omoteotl* means "everything in balance" or "duality in balance," indicating two complementary forces that unite and produce life. All ailments are seen as arising from an imbalance, which can be physical, emotional or spiritual. This medicinal system is based on bringing the patient back into a state of equilibrium; there must be balance in mind, body, emotion and spirit for the person to be healed. The *Nahuatl* language can be approached and understood on multiple levels, including literal and symbolic; in addition, when the sacred names of the energies are called upon, the words themselves conjure and manifest those energies. Each healing session consists of a combination of several techniques. Patients may be asked to bring a variety of objects, such as eggs, herbs, flowers, or candles, for the treatment. Usually, the session will begin with a *platica* (talk) so that the *curandera* can decide which treatment is needed. The treatment may be followed by a course of herbs specific to the patient and any further treatments that are necessary. Some of the most common techniques that are used in order to restore the patient to harmony are as follows:

- *Platica*—heart-to-heart talking.
- *Limpia*—cleansing to heal the person from physical, mental, emotional, spiritual or soul illnesses, by using natural objects, such as eggs, flowers or fruit.
- *Tlawayo*—diagnostic and therapeutic massage used to invigorate and improve physical health; hot or cold creams may be used depending on the patient's needs.
- *Susto*—spirit-retrieval ceremony, to bring the individual back into harmony after a fright, shock or trauma.
- *Cura de Alma*—soul-healing ceremony for deep wounds.
- Herbal medicine—traditional teas and tinctures from Mexico and Peru.
- *Temazcalito*—Mexihka sweat lodge ceremony.
- House clearing—ceremony to bless and cleanse a dwelling.

The *curandera* does not work alone, so before any of these rituals can be performed the six directions are shown the proper respect and invited in to assist. The *Nahui Ollin Teotl* (four energies in movement), Father Sun, and Mother Earth each hold potent archetypal energies; by calling *Chimawala* (*Nahuatl* for "come here") following the name of each energy, the *curandera* invites them into the healing space.

In the direction of the east and the rising sun abides *Quetzalcoatl*, the most beautiful snake-bird, who brings in his wake the energy of logic, new beginnings, initiation, light and shining. The power animal in this region is the eagle, associated with the wind and the color white.

In the direction of the west and the setting sun, we encounter *Camaxtli Xipe Totec*, the mouth of fire and shedding of skin; this is the region of the feminine and healing, and it brings with it the energy of instinct, continuity, medicine/healing, female heat and physical, natural answers. The power animal in this region is the coyote, the associated element is water, and the associated color is red.

In the direction of the south, *Tlaloc Huitzilopochtli*, the hummingbird of the left hand and region of thorns, abides. The energy obtained here is willpower, constancy, applied strength and generated answers. The power animal is the hummingbird, with the associated element of fire and color blue.

In the direction of the north is *Tezcantlipoca*, lord of the night, smoky mirror, and region of transformation. Here abides the energy of consciousness, along with completion, integration, discernment and centeredness. The power animal is the jaguar, with the associated element of earth and color yellow/black.

Looking up at the sky, *Totatzin Tonatiuh*, Father Sun, is invited in. Kneeling down on the ground, *Tonanzin Tlali Coatlicue*, respected Mother Earth of the seven snakes is invited in.

A *curandera* has a plethora of complex archetypal energies at her disposal. Votives and other objects act as bridges between the visible and the invisible and between the sacred and the profane. Magic occurs in the space between an object and its spiritual significance or intent.

Embodied Ritual Praxis

Sustained learning occurs best when the body is involved in the process. By a person participating in a ritual praxis, such as setting up an altar or taking part in a ceremony, his or her willpower and intent are engaged in an embodied, multifaceted way, and thus new neural networks are created within the brain. This phenomenon allows for the patient to engage in a radically different way with his or her "systems of condensed experience," known as COEX ("a dynamic constellation of memories and associated fantasy material from different periods of the individual's life, with the common denominator of a strong emotional charge of the same quality, intense physical sensation of the same kind, or the fact that they share some other important elements").[5] Additionally, by inviting in a third force, be it named the observer, the archetypal (transpersonal) or the spiritual, problems are viewed and engaged with in a radically different way from simply talking. By generating an intent and creating a ceremony, a space is created, not merely externally but also within the psyche, through which inner and outer worlds can bleed into each other and either natural innate healing abilities can be accessed or divine help can be given, depending on which perspective is viewed. The following distinguish a ritual from mere acting:

- Transformation occurs (via the three phases of each rite of passage, which includes liminal space).

- Embodied will/intent and focus are present (the dialectic nature of body and mind working in unison and thus strengthening their connection).

- Associated artifacts or votives hold symbolic power and are used as tools to produce a desired outcome.

- The process is "engraved" in the psyche through physical movements.

- A two-way interaction of mind to body and body to mind creates an *ouroboros*, or gestalt of experience, which helps to shift engagement and subsequent perception of the problem.

The creation of any ritual, if viewed from a purely phenomenological perspective, corresponds to the creation of an out-of-the-ordinary environment that facilitates shifts in an individual's perspective and creates a bridge across the various levels of manifestation. Through the conscious enactment of a ritual, an exchange between mind and body is created for the accomplishment of a specific goal.

On a physical level, within a ritual or ceremony, for example during a *Tlawayo* massage, *curanderas* will find that their patients will start talking about an issue while certain parts of their bodies are being worked on. This behavior links into the concept that the body and mind are not separate entities and that emotions can be stored in the body and, as such, released from there by touch.

On a psychological level, within a ritual or ceremony, the mind is engaged via *platica* (heart-to-heart talking), and through this emotions may rise and fall and be expressed and released. The mind also sends and receives multiple messages through the engagement of all six senses and, in so doing, engages in any psychological issues in a radically different way.

On a mythic or archetypal level, nonverbal images and cues are elicited through the use of items such as votives, candles, feathers, songs, or copal and sacred ceremonies such as *limpias* or *sustos*. Often within these rituals, all six senses are engaged; here are a few examples for each:

- Smell—copal, Agua Florida, palo santo
- Taste—chiles, tequila, herbs, Coca-Cola
- Touch—*Tlawayo*, flowers, eggs, medicines
- Sound—rattle, singing, flute playing, prayers, words
- Sight—altar, dress, room, flowers
- Sixth Sense—openness to intuition and spirit

Curanderismo works on both implicit memories (timeless, nonverbal, somatic and affective) and explicit memories (fixed in time, memory, cognitive and functional). Connecting to mythological narratives helps an individual to connect to his or her present problems on a symbolic basis, placing them within a greater context and so engaging with them from a different perspective. This empowers the individual by creating a sense of meaning out of chaotic, seemingly meaningless life traumas.

So, in summary, embodied ritual praxis offers a safe environment within which to access and engage with both conscious and unconscious material. By creating a safe sacred space and utilizing potent symbols, images and metaphors, embodied ritual praxis connects the patient to archetypal processes and emotions and thus bypasses the conscious defenses of the ego. All of these elements combine to facilitate an alteration in the individual's consciousness, which, when combined with the power of healthy intent, can lead to positive mental changes.

Conclusion

Carl Jung described contemporary mental illness as a loss of soul, which only the process of psychic integration can repair. Postmodernity reflects the fragmentary nature and liminal space within which we find ourselves at this point in history. The eradication of traditional narratives shifted healthcare practices from the accessibility and affordability of the homestead and into the hands of "experts." But there is a gradual contraflow against established health care provisions and a re-emergence of traditional healthcare techniques, sometimes due to necessity and other times via conscious choice. Many of the old, outworn meta-narratives are being challenged, and more localized narratives, based on more connected, inclusive concepts, are emerging. The voices of people in borderland cultures are slowly starting to be heard. This opens the opportunity to explore new perspectives, offering us a greater understanding of our common and shared humanity while honoring the uniqueness and wisdom of each.

Psychotherapy and *curanderismo* both aim for integration. They both invite patients to step out of their daily lives and enter a liminal space within which a process of reintegration and transformation occurs and through which patients become more whole and balanced.

Working with both ceremonies of the *curandera* tradition and depth psychotherapy, potent tools are at our disposal to help to welcome home and synthesize aspects of ourselves from which we have disassociated. These processes create a bridge between the seen and the unseen and the conscious world and the subconscious world, opening pathways into the symbolic and portals into the mythic. *Curanderismo* is a deep, complex system, replete with ceremonies and rituals that have been created specifically for the purpose of psychic reintegration and healing of our individual and collective soul loss. It is a system that can teach us how to live in balance with ourselves and our environment at this critical point in history.

Challenging the paradigmatic assumptions upon which we base our concepts of reality brings forth a more integrating and encompassing worldview, one in which we are parts of a whole rather than separate isolated entities. Movements such as deep ecology acknowledge the deep interconnection within the ecosystem and the important implications of understanding who we are in relation to our environment. It revolves around an ecocentric rather than an anthropocentric one, within which humankind is seen as an equal and integral part of its environment.[6]

Traditional healthcare systems such as *curanderismo* have known this wisdom for a long time and have tended to focus on balancing the mind, body and spirit within the context of the community; the community extends to incorporate all elements of nature, including archetypal energies. This holistic approach involves cultivating a sense of connectedness and inclusiveness and, contrary to our Western healthcare system, generally does not try to isolate and heal only one part of the person; the Western approach, in a sense, reflects our fragmentary, disconnected nature. This concept was further elucidated by Miahuatzin:

> The grandparents have educated us so as to know that we are part of a whole. The excuse that we get now in the occidental world is that it's only you—the individual—you have to go out and fight for yourself. It's a good dynamic but not the best, because in so doing we lose the community. And we are always living in a community—always. With trees, with plants, with stones, with animals. We are always living in community. These are parts of the community that never go away—they are always there—we shouldn't forget about them. This is like a sin, it's like a trauma which cannot be healed, you cannot forget this sin—you cannot forget about the task—your task—so that everyone and everything is fine.

> When I was three years old my grandparents took me to the fields and said to me look around—look at everything—you are part of all of this—if you harm something—you do it to yourself—if you love everything you also love yourself. At three years of age I learnt that, so it is a part of me.

> The Mexicaotl is not a hobby—it's a way of life. It's a key in our lives—a beautiful way to live and be happy . . . to see and experience the beauty and connection surrounding us, before we commit more sins against our communities and ourselves. It's so beautiful and sometimes when you think there is no hope - there is surrounding you lots of hope . . . if you want it.

References

Ferrucci, P. *What We May Be: Techniques for Psychological and Spiritual Growth Through Psychosynthesis.* City, ST: Tarcher Penguin Books, 1982/2004.

Grof, G. "Realms of the Human Unconscious." In *Paths Beyond the Ego.* Edited by R. Walsh and F. Vaughn, 9. City, ST: Penguin Putnam, 1993.

Jung, C. G. *Psychology and the East.* In the *Collected Works of C. G. Jung,* vol. 11), London: Ark Paperbacks, 1986.

Jung, C .G. "The Spiritual Problem of Modern Man." In *Modern Man in Search of a Soul.* Tranlsated by W. S. Dell and Carry F. Baynes. London and New York: Routledge, 2001. See esp. "The Spiritual Problem of Modern Man."

Naess, A. *Ecology, Community and Lifestyle: Outline of an Ecosophy.* Oslo, Norway: University of Oslo Press, 1973.

Tick, E. *The Practice of Dream Healing.* Wheaton, IL: Quest Books, 2001.

Turner, V. "Betwixt and Between: The Liminal Period in Rites of Passage." In *Betwixt and Between: Patterns of Masculine and Feminine Initiation.* Edited by Loiuse Carus Mahdi, Steven Foster and Meredith Little. Wheaton, IL: Open Court, 1987.

Endnotes

1 Verbal communication with Miahuatzin Ivonne M. Buendia Sanchez, a Mexican *curandera* and teacher who studied in Mexico and Peru. Since she was 18 years old, she has been working as a healer in San Pablo Tecalco, Mexico. Over 15 years ago she founded the Calpulli Cencalli, a study center for people interested in the teachings of the Mexihkas. There she teaches the philosophy and language Nahuatl, traditional medicine, and Mexihkan astronomy and mathematics. All direct quotes from Miahuatzin have been italicized in this article. Additionally, it can be noted that most references are made towards *curanderas* (female

traditional healers), but the author wishes to acknowledge these references are equally applicable to *curanderos* (male traditional healers).

2 V. Turner, "Betwixt and Between: The Liminal Period in Rites of Passage," in *Betwixt and Between: Patterns of Masculine and Feminine Initiation,* eds. Louise Carus Mahdi, Steven Foster and Meredith Little (La Salle, IL: Open Court, 1987), 3–19.

3 C. G. Jung, *Psychology and the East,* in the *Collected Works of C. G. Jung,* vol. 11. (London, England: Ark, 1986), 96.

4 E. Tick, *The Practice of Dream Healing* (Wheaton, IL: Quest Books, 1986), pp. 18.

5 G. Grof, "Realms of the Human Unconscious," in *Paths Beyond the Ego*, eds. R. Walsh and F. Vaughn (City, ST: Penguin Putnam, 1993), 98.

6 A. Naess, *Ecology, Community and Lifestyle: Outline of an Ecosophy (Oslo, Norway: University of Oslo Press, 1973).*

THE GODDESS AND THE MYTH
OF CITIZEN RIGHTS

Gayatri Devi and Savithri Shanker de Tourreil

The polymorphous and polyvalent goddess

> Come and see the dance of light under the feet of a
> Dark girl,
> Seeing Mother's beauty, Shiva, giver of life and
> Death, lays down his breast,
> The world cannot contain her beauty therefore
> Mother is skyclad.[1]

A *Kali bhajan* by the renowned Bangladeshi national poet Kazi Nazrul Islam tells the story of the great Hindu goddess thusly:

> Mahakaler kole eshe (Coming to [sit on] Mahakala's [Lord Siva's] lap)
> Gauri holo Mahakali (Gauri became Mahakali)

Perhaps the translation does not reveal the synonymy and polysemous playfulness of these words—*Gauri*, *Mahakala* and *Mahakali*—but to an ear familiar with the Sanskrit language, the lyricism of the lines goes hand in hand with the mythical lore about the goddess, particularly the ability of the goddess to assume variant forms. *Gauri* and *Mahakali* refer to two of the three qualities, or *gunas*,[2] associated with the various incarnations of Devi.

191

There is a *sattwik* (peaceful aspect) signified by the descriptive epithet Gauri, a word for "white" in all Indic languages derived from Sanskrit, and a dark, terrifying *tamasik* aspect , signified by the epithet *Mahakali*, a word that literally means "cosmic time." The goddess is known by many names, with each name highlighting a specific aspect or attribute under a particular *guna*, and the goddess herself is a mutable sign that contains both the creative and the destructive *gunas*. Each detail in Devi's iconography seen in temple statues, devotional hymns and in popular representations has a particular meaning resonant with the above three *gunas*. Every detail is what it is but also more than what it is; it is not only as natural as the colors white or black but also simultaneously supernatural as a protective or destructive power. The premise of the song is thus a philosophical proposition, a statement. A practicing devotee of the goddess Kali embraces the philosophical implications of the polymorphic goddess, her naturalism and her supernaturalism.

In Kazi Nazrul Islam's song, the goddess Gauri, who has everything a princess could want, desires to become the Mahakala's consort. *Mahakala* is the masculine form of *Mahakali*; both words mean cosmic time, time that is the primal cause and which existed before the dawn of creation itself. In this song, the goddess falls in love with Siva, the ascetic god, one of the Hindu trinity, the other two being Brahma and Vishnu. Siva, whose abode is in funeral grounds and other inauspicious locations, whose body is smeared with ashes, and whose companions are *bhutas*, *pisacas*, and other cursed and violent spirits of the restless dead, is the god of both destruction and creation, just like the great goddess. In the song, the princess leaves behind her opulent life, for the love of the ascetic Siva: "Bhikku Shiber anurage, bhikka magge rajdulari," which means, "Because of her love for the beggar [ascetic] Siva, a princess begs for alms." In other words, this love story is already invested with a crack, or a divide, at the center—a princess leaves everything for the love of a beggar.

One could read a political plot into this scenario. Such a tendentious reading is not that farfetched to an Indian ear familiar with the class, caste and communal politics in India. The song with a god and a goddess as its characters makes the political subtext symbolic, archetypal and, thus, mythical. Indeed, myths become acutely real and relevant when they shed light on historical events, when societies that gave birth to the mythical stories turn to the myth to understand historical experiences, as with this song or the Indian writer and activist Mahasweta Devi's short story "Draupadi," which is discussed later in this article. In the ensuing discussion, we chart the manner in which Mahasweta Devi used the mythical stories of the great goddess to shed light on the historical and ongoing oppression of the indigenous tribal people of the Indian subcontinent, who are afforded neither the fundamental protections nor the basic human rights of other citizens of India. In turning to the story of Draupadi, the central heroine in India's national epic, the *Mahabharata*, to illuminate the abjection of the indigenous tribes of India, Devi deconstructed the patriarchal myth of Draupadi with a definite feminist emphasis derived from Indian myths about the great goddess. The result is a courageous exposition of the social mechanisms with which Indian society is engineered to oppress the lower tiers, starting with women and the lower castes and tribes and the natural/ supernatural scaffolding of these social structures. The myth of the abject woman rescued by a god—the story of the epic heroine Draupadi as told in patriarchy's favorite narrative—receives its countermyth in Devi's recasting of a tribal Draupadi who reveals the power of the goddess through the body that she shares with the goddess.

In the myth enshrined in the song with which we started the discussion, the great goddess known variously as Devi, Parvathy, Uma, Lalitha, Durga, Kamakhya, Sati, or Kali, all manifestations of the *satwik*, *rajasic*, or *tamasik gunas*—the goddess manifests all three—leaves the opulence of her father's palace for the terrifying cremation grounds of Siva, where he lives with his *ganas*,[3] covered in ash and soot and with a snake wrapped around his neck. The ground is littered with skulls, bones and corpses that are being burned or eaten by vultures. The Divine Mother wants to accompany Lord Siva, whose name signifies auspiciousness, in his dance of destruction and death. Within the space of the couplet of the lyric that opened this article, the myth transforms the *satwik* goddess (Gauri) into the *raudra* (terrifying) goddess called Mahakali. In this article, we explore the mythopoeia of this transformation and its significance for the lived experiences of women who share their bodily form with the goddess. In popular iconography that tells the story of this Siva-Shakti couple—the goddess and her consort—the great blue-black goddess is portrayed with dark, dilated eyes, red, lolling tongue, teeth dripping blood, and wearing a garland of skulls or severed hands across her bare breasts. She holds a cleaver in her hand and dances in the cremation ground. This incarnation, or *avatara*, of the goddess is a complement to the goddess in her benign, creative aspect. At the shrine of Kamakhya in Assam in northeastern India, for instance, the goddess is worshipped as the *Mahayoni*, the sacred vagina or womb. She is believed to be the sole creatrix of the universe. The goddess is polymorphic and polyvalent.

A devotee of the goddess must be able to understand her transformative *avatarana* (descent or incarnation) as Gauri, Parvati, Sati, Durga, Mahakali, and so on. It is a great gift of Hindu metaphysics that we are able to freely draw from the vastness of the mythic lore. It provides us with subjective, objective and symbolic images that enable us to interpret how we perceive and experience our everyday lives as well as our own personal evolution. The myth becomes an integral constituent of epistemology and becomes the language through which we know ourselves and the world we inhabit. Through subjective experience of myths, a devotee accesses the goddess in a singular fashion that enables her to evolve and develop not merely aspects of herself but also the mythic structure of the *murthi* (divine image) at one and the same time. In addition, this process destabilizes and restabilizes the structure and content of these myths across time and space in an inexhaustible cultural reproduction.

Discussing the possibility of a polytheistic Hindu "structure of feeling," the subaltern feminist intellectual Gayatri Chakravorty Spivak described "the unanticipatable emergence of the supernatural in the natural," which is common to the Hindu way of thinking and feeling.[4] Spivak attributed a *dvaita* structure—most readily understandable in Puranic stories as in everyday life, in the instances of *avatara* (coming down from a concomitant "up there").[5] Here, *dvaita* denotes what Spivak described as "two-ness, with the secondary meaning of doubt—in this case about the stability or constancy of the apparent."[6] Spivak noted that "It is not too fanciful to say that a possible *dvaita* 'structure of feeling,' if there are such structures, would be the future anteriority of every being as potentially, unanticipatably *avatar* in the general sense. It is within this general, uneven, unanticipatable possibility of *avatarana* or descent—this cathexis by the ulterior, as it were, that the 'lesser' god or goddess, when fixed in devotion, is as 'great' as the greatest."[7] Women's singular interior experience of the goddess is often indicative of this *dvaita* structure of feeling that Spivak identified as a radical interruption of the premises and practices of orthodox Brahminism, Puranic syncreticism or even reform Hinduism. According to Spivak, "There is no great goddess. When activated, each goddess is the great goddess."[8] Such a notion of *dvaita* interruption is one trope that enables us to understand why, within a country such as India, the goddess still thrives as a singular experience of her devotees and why this relationship does not necessarily have to be validated by mainstream gatekeepers of religion, primarily Brahminical, patriarchal orthodoxy. In order for it to be disruptive, the goddess worship must always contain an element of doubt within itself about the form and authenticity of the goddess herself. Hinduism may be polytheistic, but the Hindu encounter of the divine feminine involves a *dvaita* structure of surprise, shock, doubt, recognition and doubt. The doubt engendered by encountering the divine feminine centers on the polymorphic and polyvalent aspects of the goddess. Who or what is the goddess? Is the goddess *satwik* or *tamasik*? Is the goddess a creatrix, protector or destroyer? For instance, in many folk tales and legends of temple deities, the goddess takes on the forms of an old woman, daughter, cow, tree, and so on. The goddess could be anyone; the goddess might be you.

In a strange paradox for patriarchal India, particular Hindu communities have historically committed themselves to the worship of the goddess in a conspicuously gynocentric manner. A recent critical appraisal of this gynocentric tradition is the highly interesting original study of Kali typology in Indian literature and culture, by author and academic Neela Saxena. In *In the Beginning is Desire: Tracing Kali's Footprints in Indian Literature*, Saxena observed that Kali means "everything to her devotees": To women, knowledge of the Goddess is especially essential, because that knowledge can liberate her from the *avidya* (non-knowledge) of their powerlessness. . . . That gender, and all other distinctions, vanish in the iconographically affirming female body of the great mother who invokes all and devours all.[9] All across India all of the numerous temples devoted to the goddess, the hagiography of women saints, and the public worship of female gurus and *yoginis*—both historical and contemporary—testify to a thriving woman-centered spiritual subculture in which women recognize, accept and absorb within themselves the presence of the divine feminine. In particular, the Tantric Shakta tradition elevates the worship of the goddess to an apotheosis of the divine feminine as the ultimate truth and goal of all knowledge. Though the combination of the words *woman* and *goddess* have not always yielded the most salutary effects for women within mainstream patriarchal Hindu ethos, esoteric Hindu traditions, such as the Tantric Shakta tradition, respected female gurus or *yoginis* as not merely practitioners but also the fully manifest presence of the divine itself. The female form or the body is an *avatara* of the goddess. In the Tantric Shakta tradition, the goddess, or Shakti, is the ultimate godhead, the source and origin of all cosmos, all things manifest and transcendent. A 16th century Shakta text described the rapturous power of the divine feminine thusly:

Woman is the foundation of the world,

She is the true form of the body,

Whatever form she takes . . .

Is the superior form . . .

There is not, nor has been nor will be

Any holy Yoga to compare with woman,

No mystical formula nor asceticism to match a woman.

There is not, nor has been, nor will be

Any riches more valuable than her.[10]

In the Shakta tradition of goddess worship, the Siva-Shakti duality privileges Shakti, the feminine, as the dynamic aspect of Brahma. An iconic representation of the Siva-Shakti pair shows Kali standing astride Siva, as evoked in the epigraph to this article. Siva is the ground, or supreme reality and consciousness, Brahma at rest, and Shakti is Brahma in its dynamic form. *Shakti* is a difficult word to translate into English; its closest English equivalent is "power." Shakti is power with action; the goddess Shakti is power in action. Shakti is always dynamic, never inert.

This cultural reification of the goddess as Shakti offers an alternate paradigm for women's psychosocial development insofar as myth provides us with an imaginative structure to validate or interrogate established epistemologies, such as the status of cultural negotiations about gender balance in the Hindu ethos. In this article, we discuss how the myth of the goddess as Shakti is essentially and necessarily a political myth about the lives of women within the Hindu patriarchal ethos. In addition, we analyze how the representation of the goddess in mythopoeic traditions may help us to understand, capture and argue for the necessity of spiritual power in the ongoing struggle for women's rights across cultures. The goddess is every woman's greatest ally along the route to private and public empowerment. Our discussion of the political power of the goddess myth is centered on the short story "Draupadi," written by one of India's foremost activist writers, Mahasweta Devi. Mahasweta Devi's radical, subversive application of a sacred myth of the birth of the goddess poses a structural challenge to not only Brahminical Hinduism but also the nationalist discourse that was historically nurtured by elite Hindus but which excluded a significant demographic of India's poor, in particular, the *Adivasi*, or tribals. The figure of Devi's Draupadi becomes a sign of two related levels of patriarchal and national oppression: that of women and that of the tribals.

The Goddess as Citizen

We begin this article by outlining a character from the Hindu epic the *Mahabharata*. Let us look at the persona of Draupadi, originally a stunningly beautiful, strong princess of divine origin, much like the great goddess, who rose out of the sacrificial fire, through two narrative frames: the canonical version of the story and its interpretation, followed by a modern retelling with a distinct feminist interpretation of the goddess myth. We will first discuss Draupadi's story as told in the national epic the *Mahabharata*, followed by a modern retelling by one of India's renowned writers and social activists, Mahasweta Devi.

In the epic the *Mahabharata*, the original persona of Princess Draupadi acts as the linchpin of the great conflagration of war in the main story. Without her consent and without warning, Draupadi finds herself committed to a polyandrous marriage to five royal brothers, the Pandavas. Nonetheless, she succeeds perfectly in fulfilling her marital role and duties in relation to each of her five husbands.

Draupadi is included in a traditional list of the five most virtuous, perfect women. Hindu Brahmin men (and perhaps women) recite this list reverently even to this day, although polyandry is by no means a societally sanctioned practice for modern Hindu women. Draupadi, however, is unquestionably accepted as the perfect, chaste, exemplary wife, according to traditional Hindu ethos.

In the *Mahabharata*, Draupadi's five husbands, the Pandava brothers, are tricked into becoming the slaves of their rivals, the Kauravas (100 evil cousins) through deceitful, duplicitous means. These cousins argue that a wife is the property of her husband and has neither autonomy nor absolute rights as a person, and they proceed to claim Queen Draupadi as their slave. Accordingly, Dussasana, one of the brutal cousins, drags Draupadi by brute force into the royal assembly hall, a designated male-only space, and attempts to disrobe her in front of all of the other men.

Draupadi's honor is saved by the miraculous supernatural intervention of Krishna, her chosen deity, who also happens to be her relative.

In revenge, Draupadi demands that Bhīma, the strong arm among her five husbands, kill the evil cousin who tried to dishonor her. Henceforth, Draupadi refuses to bind up her long, beautiful tresses in the fashion prescribed for a virtuous, chaste wife. She takes a solemn oath that she will wear her hair unbound, until her husband slays Dussasana, who insulted her in the august assembly of royal men, and with hands covered in his cousin's blood, binds up her tresses.

In the fullness of time, it comes to pass. A long, gory, bitter war ensues between the two sets of cousins until the five husbands are victorious and utterly destroy the evil cousins and their supporters. Draupadi's famed tresses are, at last, bound up by her giant of a husband, Bhīma, his hands steeped in the blood of the bully Dussasana. Thus, Draupadi and her five husbands salvage their honor.

This is the conflagration of the battle described in the epic the *Mahabharata*. In this manner, Draupadi becomes the linchpin of the bloody action of bringing nemesis to the evil cousins. This war was waiting to happen and was ultimately triggered by the violation of a sacred, pure, chaste woman.

Mahasweta Devi's short story titled "Draupadi" preserves many of the original characters and much of the orientation and conflict, with slight variations aimed at verisimilitude rather than strict agreement between the texts. But Devi's variations hold up the patriarchal ideology of the epic to a radical interrogation of Draupadi's purported helplessness. We may reframe the question generated by patriarchal narratives about saving women's honor thusly: Are women always an object in the war between good men and evil men? Who tells this story? For whose benefit? Do women tell the same story about their experiences? Or do they have another narrative in which they do not need to be saved from evil men by good men? Is the conflict always between good men and bad men "over a woman"? Or is the conflict between men and women? The goddess mythology offers women this alternate paradigm of empowerment. Devi's Draupadi is an exemplary development of this paradigm, which has always existed in the Hindu ethos in the mythology of the goddess but which has been subsumed under more prolific patriarchal myths about male deities as saviors of the world and of women.

Devi's titular character Draupadi is a Santal tribal woman hunted by the Indian military police in the forests of northeastern India. Devi transposed the setting of the disrobing of Draupadi to the interior of a forest and a community of India's aboriginal people—the tribals. The Indian police assume the identity of a rival group. Writing for *India Together News Services* in 2002, Devi observed that the Indian tribes are under a "death sentence"[11] in contemporary India. In this story, as well as in everyday Indian society, activists, whether of tribal ethnicity or not, who work on behalf of India's millions of impoverished tribal castes are deemed "criminals"; many of them are victims of standing government orders to "shoot on sight."

Much of Devi's work, both fictional and nonfictional, has been in the area of tribal land rights. Mahasweta Devi was born in West Bengal and has spent nearly sixty years working as an advocate for tribal rights in India's northeastern states, primarily Bengal, Bihar and Orissa. These are poor states even by Indian postindependence development standards. They house a significant number of India's indigenous tribal population, a demographic which has not benefited from India's economic and political prosperity in the postindependence years. In an interview with Gayatri Chakravorty Spivak, who has translated many of Devi's stories from their original Bengali into English, Devi described the nation's betrayal of the Indian tribal:

> Have you ever seen them, very carefully going very respectfully in file? If a thousand Indian tribals, men, women, and children sit, how quiet they are? How quietly they listen to people? Mainstream people cannot believe it. They shove and nudge, they hum and sing, they whisper. It is not in us. In their blood there is so much patience, it is like nature. Patience of the hills, of the rivers, the tribal contains everything. Each tribe is like a continent.

> But we never tried to know them. Never tried to respect
> them. This is true of every tribal. We destroyed them. . .
> . As far as the tribal is concerned, the road, the big road,
> is the enemy. It will take away whatever crop he grows,
> whatever vegetable he grows, and in times of famine and
> natural disasters like rain failure or flood they will come
> in lorries and trucks and take away their children to be
> sold in other places as bonded labour. . . . In the capitalist
> market there is great demand for children, especially tribal
> children. You pay them little; you can starve them; you can
> kill them; no one will come for them.[12]

The Indian government, as well as the elite Brahmins and other upper-caste Hindus, consider the tribals dispensable. Devi's story, "Draupadi," is set in the late 1970s among the Santal tribe in the state of Bihar, which saw a sudden surge in Naxalite uprisings by a united front of peasants and tribals against upper-caste Hindu landlords who controlled the feudal agrarian economy of the state. In Devi's story, the figure of the tribal and the figure of the woman are imprinted on each other, engendering, as it were, the tribal as woman and woman as tribal. This imprinting is a double coup insofar as it seeks to expose not merely the workings of patriarchy but also the workings of India's hegemonic forces that have disenfranchised scores of its "citizens" from basic human rights. This hegemonic narrative of the disenfranchisement of the tribal as woman surfaces in Devi's story in the character of Dopti who, in turn, afflicts her epic and mythical counterpart, the princess Draupadi of the *Mahabharata*, with the discomfort of disenfranchisement. Devi's retelling updates the myth to be a story about citizens' human rights, while the femaleness of its undefeated, autonomous protagonist engenders this fight with the Shakti of the goddess. Devi radically interrogates the multilayered, mythical layers upon which the narratives of both the Indian nation and Indian women are inscribed, by invoking the emergence of an alternate paradigm—the goddess myth—which ruptures the hegemonic fabric on which the Draupadi's story is told in the national epic. The imprinting of the goddess myth upon this story about Lord Krishna's power to save a woman's honor destabilizes the sacred space of the epic narrative, debunks its deity and re-energizes it with the power of the goddess.

In Devi's story, Dopti (who corresponds to Draupadi in the *Mahabharata*), as she is known among the Santals, is a chaste tribal woman in a loving, monogamous marriage. Along with her husband and other tribal men and women, she is hunted down by the Indian military. She is captured, raped and tortured by the Senanayak and the Indian army for participating in the beheading of a landlord who refused to give water to the indigenous people living in the forests of Bihar. Devi's treatment of the Draupadi story reveals the powerful potential of myths to project and anticipate symbolic structures and meanings not yet articulated. The character of the epic polyandrous Draupadi may be perceived as an anomaly in mainstream Indian sensibility, but her story is also a seed myth that belongs to a distinct paradigm of gender relations within the Hindu ethos. We have seen how, simultaneously married to five brothers and revered in the Hindu populist imagination as a *pativrata*, Draupadi is one of the imminent causes of the war between cousins Pandavas and Kauravas. As discussed in the earlier section of this article, Draupadi's participation in the patriarchal paradigm is most visible in her role as one of the "possessions" lost in a game of dice between the leaders of the warring cousins, Yudhishtira and Duryodhana. In an iconic scene that has become part and parcel of the monotheistic lore about the Hindu god Krishna, the Kaurava prince drags Draupadi, who is undergoing ritual seclusion during her monthly menses, by her hair into court, where an attempt is made to publicly disrobe her. In the standard version of the story, Draupadi prays to Krishna, her cousin, friend and god. In response to her supplications, Krishna prevents the disrobing of the menstruating Draupadi before the collective male gaze. The more the Kaurava prince pulls at Draupadi's sari, the more limitless the sari becomes, until he gives up in defeat. In one of the stated goals of the Kurukshetra war, Draupadi's husbands vow to avenge her violated honor by killing the cousins. However, this is not Draupadi's story. The epic tells the story of two sets of men—good men and evil men—and the gods intervene to help the good men. In the *Mahabharata*, Draupadi is a proxy for patriarchy.

The rape of Draupadi in the *Mahabharata* and the entire patriarchal discourse about female sexual purity and male honor is interrogated closely in Devi's story, which is titled for the epic's linchpin heroine. Myth is a language that communicates not merely at the level of a narrative or a story; it also interrogates the conscious and unconscious cultural underpinnings of the social matrix that gave birth to the story. Devi's debt to the *Mahabharata*, India's national epic, goes beyond intertextual play. Her story interrogates patriarchal myths about nation building and offers a counter-narrative from a distinctly woman-centered tradition that was always and already present in India in the form of goddess myths. Devi rearranged the essential building blocks of the Draupadi story in order to reveal its repressed feminist, goddess core. Devi's tribal heroine, Dopti, in turn re-energizes the epic heroine Draupadi. In Devi's narrative, no god comes to help a raped tribal woman. The battle is not between good men and evil men. It is between men and women. It is between the nation and the oppressed tribals.

Devi's updated Draupadi story shows how mythic narratives provide a semiotic, symbolic continuity to a group of people in which myth markers such as names—Draupadi, for instance—and structural requirements—the disrobing and rape—provide cultural resonance. Just as the synonyms of the goddess signify aspects or *gunas* of the goddess, the linguistic relation between the two names Draupadi and Dopti is significant. The morpheme *Draupadi* contains within itself its patronymic cognate *Drupada*. *Draupadi* means "of Drupada," or "Drupada's daughter." It is a morphemic derivation of Drupada, following regular word-formation rules in Sanskrit, the classical language of the epic.

Draupadi's patriarchal origin is part of her birth myth as described in the *Mahabharata*. She is fully divine and gifted to King Drupada, coming to him from Agni, the sacrificial fire. Draupadi has divine power, but this divinity is domesticated in the epic. Draupadi is not acknowledged as an aspect of the goddess; she is revered as a chaste wife. In Devi's retelling of Draupadi's story, the tribal Dopti, the epic heroine's namesake, gives the divine power of the epic's Draupadi back to her. The imprinting of the goddess myth on to the patriarchal framework of the epic is done through tendentious, critical use of proper names and common names in Devi's story. In Devi's story, for the most part, the tribal heroine is addressed by her tribal name, *Dopti*, a simplified form of *Draupadi*. The phonetic components of the patronymic *Drupada* are not present in the tribalization and simplification of the Sanskrit name. *Draupadi* and *Dopti* have phonological verisimilitude but are morphemically distinct, with *Dopti* containing zero patronymic valence of the Sanskrit name. The elimination of the father's name marker from her name while retaining just the barest verisimilitude with the discarded patronymic makes Dopti an unstable sign oscillating between the Draupadi of the hegemonic myth and an entity—an avatar of the kind described by Spivak—that signifies a specific kind of supernatural doubt. Is Dopti Draupadi? If so, who is Draupadi? Is she the helpless victim? Or is she a divine entity? Devi headlined this doubt by titling the story "Draupadi" yet calling its heroine Dopti. Thus, the title of the story becomes a tendentious marker of the retelling's intertextual bind with the epic narrative. The epic story is evoked through the ritual disrobing and rape tropes borrowed from the original Draupadi story of the *Mahabharata* and the verisimilitude of the names of the character. Devi's Dopti, like her epic counterpart, moves within a contested political world—India's purported democracy, in which the aboriginal tribal castes are hunted down by the government—similar to the contested kingdom and war in the *Mahabharata*.

Devi introduced the male protagonist of the story by his title and pro-fession—Senanayak, chief of the army—rather than by a proper name. Again, the *Senanayak* is an interesting nominalization for this character. It is an archaic term rarely used in contemporary Indian discourse or registers of the military, which has a preference for English, the language of India's colonial ruler, and the regional vernaculars of India's multiple languages. Like the story's title, "Draupadi," Senanayak is a classical term meant to evoke the ethos of the Indian epic. Its only purpose in Devi's retelling is to conjure an almost ahistorical, mythic allusion to the character's archetype within this story. Thus, Devi's Dopti is cast in a scene of verisimilitude with that of the epic (difference, not identity.) The scene is a war among tribal insurgents, the state police and the Indian government. Dopti and her fellow Santals are being hunted down by order of the government of India.

Devi put the Senanayak character to mythic service in her story. The transformation of Devi's tribal heroine Dopti from a rape victim to a figure that induces fear and incomprehension among the soldiers who violate her is communicated chiefly through the Senanayak's disbelief and doubt about the provenance of Dopti's strength and power. The birth of the goddess within the victim needs a witness; Senanayak is this witness. The Senanayak only gives orders; he does not participate in the rape and torture of Dopti. Like a disinterested scholar, perhaps, Senanayak is keen to "figure out" the tribal psychology and to "learn Dopti's song."[13] Gayatri Chakravorty Spivak astutely noted how the Senanayak's goals outside the violence of this story are similar to the goals of first-world scholars seeking to study the third and the fourth worlds from our transnational locations.[14] Thus, in his final complete noncomprehension of Dopti's actions, the Senanayak offers a radical theorizing of not only the rupture of patriarchy engendered by the goddess figure Draupadi but also the probable doubt or unknowability of the emergence of such a counter-hegemonic form within a particular culture. The hegemonic counter-narrative is a goddess narrative; it is a narrative about the myth of the goddess. The Senanayak is filled with doubt and fear—not knowledge—about this counter-narrative. His final fear of the woman he had ordered to be raped constitutes a mythical uncertainty. Devi seems to suggest that the potential for change in the social status quo of the tribals and women resides in the gap opened up by this incomprehension of their essential identities from the perspective of the master class and master narratives.

According to the patriarchal myth, Lord Krishna rescues the mythical Draupadi from being disrobed in front of the male audience. Devi's woman-centered retelling asks a different question: When there are no gods to save disenfranchised tribal women who are hunted down, raped and tortured, what is such a woman to do? Where does she go? Devi goes one step further. She turns Krishna into a ridiculous figure. She updates the epic intervention of Krishna for modern times: While waiting for the tribal insurgents to show up in the battalion's watchpost area, the soldiers pass time listening to Vividh Bharati radio and watching "Sanjeev Kumar and the Lord Krishna face-to-face in the movie This Is Life."[15] As with the proper names Dopti and Draupadi and the title Senanayak, the names—Sanjeev Kumar, a popular, sophisticated Indian actor, and Krishna, the archetypal god of erotic love with hundreds of thousands of lovers in Indian classical and popular imagination—are meant to cast the myth of the heroic exploits of Krishna in a ridiculous light. Krishna, the Hindu god most closely associated with erotic frolicking and whose escapades actually involve absconding with the clothes of bathing women, appears to be patriarchy's answer to saving a woman's honor. No god comes to rescue Dopti from being repeatedly raped by the soldiers of the Indian militia. The violation of tribal women by Indian government forces, which is reported frequently in Indian media,[16] is a crime without punitive consequences. In India's troubled record on women's rights, tribal women occupy the lowest rung of priority. Transgressions against tribal women are unpunished; they are unredeemed. Devi's tribal heroine, Dopti, cannot look toward any Indian epic hero, such as Krishna, to magically save her honor. She will have to avenge her dishonor herself.

The public rape of Dopti in Devi's story retells the public disrobing and dishonoring of Draupadi in the epic. In the epic, a patriarchal god, Krishna, comes to the rescue of Draupadi. However, Devi's Dopti is saved not by a male god but by her radical transformation from a victim of violence to a free, autonomous woman who instills fear and doubt in the hearts of the men who have violated her. Dopti's transformation is a reassessment of how the epic *Mahabharata* suppresses the footprints of the goddess; the suppression is most evident in the act of making the divinely born Draupadi—a goddess—wait to be rescued by a patriarchal god, Krishna. Devi makes evident this tendentious patriarchal constitution of the myth by superimposing another myth of the birth of the goddess Kali as a counter-narrative to the rescue of a violated woman by Krishna. The epic's Draupadi is a peripheral character in the myths of the exploits of Krishna. However, Devi's Dopti is a character in the myths of the goddess, an exemplum of what Spivak termed the "future anteriority of every being as potentially, unanticipatably *avatar* in the general sense." The *avatarana*, or descent, of the goddess invoked by Dopti is the myth of the birth of the goddess Kali. The goddess Kali is believed to have burst forth from the forehead of the goddess Durga in order to defeat the *asura*, Raktabija, in the mythology of the goddess in the Indian subcontinent. The goddess is literally born of woman. In Dopti's final transformation from rape victim to fearless woman who walks away from her violators through sheer willpower, Devi exposed the patriarchal foundations of the Indian epic and an alternate paradigm. The tribal Dopti forces us to read the epic Draupadi as a terrorized figure unaware of her own divine strength—the power of the goddess caught within a patriarchal matrix. The tribal woman releases the hidden goddess of the epic in an example of Spivak's *avatarana*. Dopti re-engenders Draupadi as the goddess Shakti. The goddess, in other words, is literally born of woman in Devi's woman-centered mythopoeia.

In Devi's story, Dopti wakes up after having been repeatedly raped by the Indian army: "Trying to move, she feels her arms and legs still tied to the four bedposts. . . . She senses that her vagina is bleeding. . . . Her breasts are bitten raw, the nipples torn. . . . Then Draupadi Mehjen is brought to the tent and thrown on the straw. Her piece of cloth is thrown over her body."[17] Roused from the floor where she is thrown and commanded to go to the Senanayak's tent, Dopti stands up, kicks the water pot away from her and tears her single cloth to pieces. "Senanayak walks out surprised and sees Draupadi, naked, walking toward him in the bright sunlight with her head high. . . . Draupadi stands before him, naked. Thigh and pubic hair matted with dry blood. Two breasts, two wounds. What is this? He is about to bark."[18]

Once again, the menstruating Draupadi from the epic narrative, in the form of Dopti, stands before the Senanayak and the collective male gaze. She stands with bloody genitals but with a critical difference: It is Draupadi who initiates this public exhibition of her exposed, raped and mutilated body, and she is not asking to be saved. It is noteworthy that, in the scene of her rape, Devi's tribal heroine, who is referred to as Dopti for most of the narrative, is unequivocally addressed by her epic name and that of her namesake: Draupadi. The helpless, violated Draupadi, waiting on Krishna to save her honor, being imprinted on Dopti, the tribal woman who does not wait for any man to save her, effectively exposes the patriarchal ideology of India's sacred national epic. There is only one alternate paradigm to challenge the entrenched myth of the powerlessness of women in the Hindu ethos: the myth of the goddess. Dopti/Draupadi embodies the goddess.

Although male nudity, such as those of ascetics and *sanyasis*, is either unremarked or revered, female nudity within the Indian ethos is erotically charged. In fact, the default value of the nude female body, from temple sculptures and frescoes to billboards, cinema and television, and tribal women and children, is as an erotic object. The only exceptions to this default of the erotically charged female are the accounts of female ascetics, such as Akka Mahadevi, a Veerashaivite poet-saint from 12th century Karnataka. Akka, who used to walk naked through the streets as a wandering poet-saint, conformed to the erotic-ascetic binary often identified with Siva in myths.

The Hindu ethos thus valorizes nudity differently across gender, caste and class. However, the Shakta tradition that worships the goddess Kali in the Indian subcontinent is an indigenous religious tradition in which female nudity in its bodily form is associated with the power of the goddess. Iconic representations of Kali show the goddess with an appearance that evokes fear rather than sexual desire in the eyes of the beholder. The *Devi Mahatmyam*, a collection of hymns for the goddess, describes the goddess as follows: "Armed with a sword and noose, and a skull-topped staff; she was wearing a garland of skulls, and was clad in a tiger's skin; her emaciated flesh dripped from her skeletal frame; her long tongue protruded from her gaping mouth; her deep-sunk blood-shot eyes glared out at the world as she filled the regions of the sky with her roars."[19] Devi's tribal Dopti/Draupadi embodies aspects of this fearsome goddess. In her final encounter with the Senanayak, Draupadi "wipes the blood on her palm and says in a voice that is as terrifying, sky splitting, and sharp as her ululation, 'What's the use of clothes? You can strip me, but how can you clothe me again?'"[20]

Why does Devi's tribal heroine Dopti tear the only piece of cloth covering her and walk out nude to the men who raped her body? Why is the Senanayak "afraid to stand before an unarmed *target*, terribly afraid?"[21] Rape achieves two simultaneous acts of annihilation with one stroke. It removes power from the subject of the rape, and it "marks" the body as devoid of spirit. In most cases, the true "object" of rape is not the body at all; it is the spirit or the ego, the essence of who we are. Devi's Draupadi obversely discovers her "spirit" and "power," her Shakti, as a result of the rape.

The brutalized body of a woman should not fill anyone with fear unless it is seen as a site of power. The Senanayak calls Dopti's body a "target," and yet it fills him with fear. When Dopti is raped in Devi's story, her body ceases to become a stable signifier for rape; a rape victim typically does not confront her attacker fearlessly immediately after the rape. Such an act takes away the assumption of male power inherent in the act of rape. Devi makes the Senanayak "afraid" as he watches Draupadi/Dopti walk toward him naked and bloody, because it destabilizes his understanding of a raped woman. The Senanayak is afraid, because he knows he is looking at a tribal woman whom his men raped under his orders. He also knows that he is looking at someone else in the body of a woman who has been raped. She is no longer his "target." Here we see the interruption of male power by Shakti, in a manifestation of the *dvaita* feeling that Spivak described as critical to Hindu religious thought. The Senanayak is the site of this intimation of the power of women, of the goddess. Devi effectively eliminated the myth of the patriarchal god rescuing a violated woman and replaced it with a story of a woman discovering the power to confront her attackers. Speaking this power and acting on it is an encounter with the goddess, Devi made evident the wiping out of the patriarchal myth and the rising of the goddess myth in the narrative by having her heroine addressed after the rape as Draupadi—her epic name—rather than her tribal name, Dopti.

During Dopti's rape by the Indian military police and in the final encounter between the Senanayak and Dopti, Devi categorically referred to her protagonist as Draupadi rather than by her tribal character name, Dopti. Particularly in the encounter between Dopti and the Senanayak, the narrator stops referring to the character by her tribal name, Dopti; instead she is textually referred to as Draupadi. Devi exposed the patriarchal circumscription of the original Draupadi story by making evident the presence of Shakti, which Princess Draupadi the epic of *Mahabharata* did not or could not access because she was a character in a story told by men to other men. Her tribal sister, Dopti, returns Shakti to Princess Draupadi. The Senanayak's inability to comprehend Draupadi's actions—why would a woman willfully want to be naked in front of anonymous men?—is consciously predicated on Devi's intent to present Draupadi's transformation from the "object of your search," a "target," into a "subject" who makes a definite choice to embrace her naked, tortured body without shame. In power, Draupadi no longer speaks as a subject waiting to be saved by the very patriarchal forces that violated her. Her intentional nudity is outside patriarchal prescriptions for Hindu women.

Devi consigned to the realm of the myth this transformation of a "target" of patriarchy into an autonomous subject, by making the source of this transformation remain *unknown* and *unknowable* to the men looking at her. It is crucial to the mythical structure of Devi's story that the men not fully understand the Shakti. The Senanayak does not understand the purpose and meaning of this public exhibition of Dopti's/Draupadi's body. We are told that the Senanayak thinks he has "almost deciphered" Dopti's tribal song but that it remains unknown to him as she "pushes Senanayak with her two mangled breasts."

> Draupadi's black body comes even closer. Draupadi shakes with an indomitable laughter that Senanayak simply cannot understand. Her ravaged lips bleed as she begins laughing. Draupadi wipes the blood on her palm and says in a voice that is as terrifying, sky splitting, and sharp as her ululation, 'What's the use of clothes? You can strip me, but how

can you clothe me again? Are you a man? . . . There isn't
a man here that I should be ashamed.'[22]

Devi's "Draupadi" not only updates the mythic character for modern
times but also humanizes and feminizes the epic in a radical manner. Myths
are important stories that human societies tell themselves about what matters to them. Devi's "Draupadi" puts women at the center of their own lives
and makes them the agents of change in their own lives. This is not a radical
idea in the Hindu ethos, which worships the goddess as both creatrix and
destroyer. When Devi's Dopti/Draupadi tears her single cloth into pieces,
she is tearing the fabric of patriarchy itself. The nude "skyclad" woman,
Kazi Nazrul Islam's "skyclad mother," emerges and stands in her place as
the sacred outcome of this rupture, because the goddess shares the female
body with all women of the world.

References

Bose, Tapan Kumar. "Rape of Adivasi Women." *International South
Asia Forum*. Accessed January 21, 2016. www.insafbulletin.net/
archives/264

_____. "Draupadi," *Breast Stories*. Translated by Gayatri Chakravorty
Spivak. Calcutta: Seagull, 2002.

_____. *Imaginary Maps*. Translated by Gayatri Chakravorty Spivak .
Calcutta: Thema, 2001.

Devi, Mahasweta. "Year of Birth: 1871: *Mahasweta Devi on India's
Denotified Tribes.*" *India Together News Service*, March 2002.
Accessed January 20, 2016. indiatogether.org/bhasha/budhan/birth1871.
htm

Saxena, Neela. *In the Beginning Is Desire: Tracing Kali's Footprints
in Indian Literature*. New Delhi: Indialog Publications, 2004.

Shimkhada, Deepak, and Phyllis K. Herman. *The Constant and
Changing Faces of the Goddess: Goddess Traditions of Asia*,
Newcastle, UK: Cambridge Scholars Publishing, 2009.

Spivak, Gayatri Chakravorty. "Moving Devi," *Cultural Critique* 47 (2001): 120–163.

Endnotes

1 Qtd. in Neela Saxena, *In the Beginning Is Desire: Tracing Kali's Footprints in Indian Literature* (New Delhi: Indialog Publications, 2004), 55.

2 The three *gunas* are primal qualities existing both in nature, Prakriti, and human nature. The Samkhya school of Hindu philosophy attributes all three *gunas* to Prakriti or nature itself; indeed the three *gunas* permeate all of Nature and all of life. *Sattwa* or *satwik guna* is pure and detached where it is present; *rajasic guna* is connected to self and pleasure and outcomes and *tamasik guna* manifests itself in chaos, delusion, ignorance and darkness. Chapters 17 and 18 of the *Bhagavad Gita* offer a clear explication of the three *gunas* in Krishna's exchanges with Arjuna.

3 *Ganas* are Siva's attendants. We might imagine them as ghosts, goblins or a generally spooky category of beings. *Ganas* are variously believed to be emanations of Siva himself, or creatures created by him. *Ganas* stay with Siva in both Mount Kailasa and in the cremation grounds.

4 Gayatri Chakravorty Spivak, "Moving Devi," *Cultural Critique* 47 (2001) 123.

5 Ibid.

6 Spivak, 124.

7 Spivak, 123.

8 Spivak, 122.

9 Saxena, 28.

10 Saxena, 42.

11 Mahasweta Devi, "Year of Birth: 1871: Mahasweta Devi on India's Denotified Tribes," *India Together News Service*, March 2002. Accessed January 21, 2016. www.indiatogether.org/bhasha/budhan/birth1871.htm/.

12 Mahasweta Devi, *Imaginary Maps*, trans. Gayatri Chakravorty Spivak (Calcutta: Thema, 2001), xv.

13 Mahasweta Devi, "Draupadi," *Breast Stories*, trans. Gayatri Chakravorty Spivak (Calcutta: Seagull, 2002), 24.

14 Devi, 2.

15 Devi, 26.

16 Tapan Kumar Bose, "Rape of Adivasi Women," *International South Asia Forum*. Accessed January 21, 2016. www.insafbulletin.net/archives/264

17 Devi, 34–35.

18 Devi, 36.

19 Deepak Shimkhada and Phyllis K. Herman, eds. *The Constant and Changing Faces of the Goddess: Goddess Traditions of Asia* (Newcastle, UK: Cambridge Scholars Publishing, 2009), 151.

20 Devi, 36.

21 Devi, 37.

22 Devi, 36.

DEMETER AND THE ELEUSINIAN MYSTERIES: ANCIENT ORIGINS AND MODERN IMPACT

Joan Cichon

Introduction

This article will explore two aspects of the Eleusinian Mysteries: their origins and how they have affected me as a woman. The first section, employing the tools of archaeomythology, will look at the reasons that Bronze Age Crete is one of the possible origin spots for Demeter and her Mysteries and why the Eleusinian Mysteries reflect an "amalgamation of cult" between the goddess civilization of ancient Crete and the patriarchal religion of the Mycenaeans and the Greek mainland. In the second section, I will survey the work of two scholars of the Eleusinian Mysteries—Mara Lynn Keller and Kathie Carlson—and discuss how their writings helped me to understand that, far from being merely a quaint story to explain the seasons of the year, the myth of Demeter and Persephone holds multiple levels of meaning relevant to modern women and men.

The Myth

We know the story of Demeter and Persephone principally and officially from the famous *Homeric Hymn to Demeter* written around 650 BCE. According to this hymn, the Goddess Persephone is abducted to the underworld by the god Hades while she is picking flowers with her girlfriends. Her mother, the Goddess Demeter, hears her frantic screams and wanders the earth, grief-stricken, in search of her for nine days. Demeter finally learns, with the help of the Goddess Hecate and the sun god Helios, that her daughter has been kidnapped by Hades and taken to the underworld to be his bride. She also learns that the god Zeus has colluded in her daughter's kidnapping.

Depressed, outraged and exhausted by her search, Demeter goes to Eleusis where, disguised as an old woman, she is befriended by the family of King Keleos and goes to his home to be nursemaid to the king's son Demophoon. Foiled in her attempt to make Demophoon immortal, Demeter drops her disguise and orders King Keleos to build her a temple. When the temple is completed, Demeter withdraws there "only to sink again into grief over her own lost child."[1] The goddess now decides to take away her gift of grain from both humans and the gods. Everything ceases to grow. Desperate, because famine threatens the lives of plants, animals and humans and nothing is being sacrificed to the gods, Zeus orders Persephone to be returned to her mother. Mother and daughter are reunited but only after Persephone has eaten pomegranate seeds in the underworld. Because she has eaten the seeds, Persephone must return there for a part of each year. Nevertheless, "the goddesses spent the day embracing and cheering each other's hearts. . . . Demeter restored the grain and the fields grew fat with crops."[2] Finally, Demeter taught the people of Eleusis her Mysteries.

The Mysteries

The religious rites that Demeter taught at Eleusis were celebrated there for over a thousand years, from approximately 1,450 BCE to 395 CE. The rites, at least the public aspect of them, were well known in antiquity and have come down to us from a variety of sources. They took place each year, beginning around the middle of September (some experts think they began several weeks later). Thealogian and philosopher Mara Lynn Keller believes that the middle of September was chosen to coincide with the full moon or so that the eighth day of the ritual would coincide with the Fall Equinox.[3] Prospective initiates were required first to have taken part in the Lesser Mysteries at the nearby village of Agra, essentially purification rites, before they presented themselves at Eleusis.[4]

The Mysteries festival began with a procession of the sacred objects (*hiera*) of the goddess, carried by the priestesses of Demeter, from Eleusis to Athens. (The *hiera* were probably relics from the Mycenaean Age.)

Those seeking initiation went first to the Painted Stoa in Athens, where all who understood the Greek language and who had atoned for any murder could present themselves as initiates. On the second day, the *mystai* (initiates) proceeded to the sea to bathe and purify themselves. The third day found the *mystai* participating in ceremonies and praying for the Boule (the Athenian Council) and Demos (the personification of the populace) of Athens and for the women and children of the commonwealth.[5] Day four was called the Asklepieia, in honor of Asklepios. For the initiates, it was probably a day of reflection about what had taken place and what was to take place. "It was also a day for more prayers and for healing dreams."[6] On the fifth day, led by the boy child Iacchos, the initiates journeyed to Eleusis via the Sacred Way, stopping at shrines, praying, giving offerings and finally crossing the bridge of jests, where they were insulted and teased so that "they would be humbled."[7] The long day ended at the outer court of the Sanctuary of Eleusis with a joyful celebration, including night-long dances in honor of Demeter. The remainder of day six was a day of rest. The initiates fasted and purified themselves. The next two days of the Mysteries comprised the secret rather than the "public" part of the rites, and thus we know almost nothing about what occurred on those seventh and eighth days. We know only that there were "things said, things enacted and things seen." Keller provided the following description of what might have happened:

> [*The Homeric Hymn to Demeter*] or some other version of the *mythos* of the Two Goddesses was recited, sung or performed. Probably initiates re-enacted portions of the sacred mythos of the Two Goddesses. There was a great fire inside the temple. A brass cymbal or gong was rung. Probably a communion drink called '*kykeon*' was shared inside Demeter's Hall of Initiation, the *Telesterion*. The highest stage of initiation was the *epopteia*, a vision, a special state of seeing. After the mysterious nighttime, daytime and second nighttime within Demeter's Temple, celebrants probably emerged from the Temple at dawn to walk to Demeter's fertile fields where, circumambulating them, they invoked the fertility of Earth and Sky.[8]

On the ninth and final day, the initiates returned home and transitioned back to everyday existence.

Because initiates left few records of their thoughts and feelings and almost nothing is known of the core rituals of the Eleusinian Mysteries, I have found it difficult to comprehend the Mysteries' meaning and to imagine their effect. Ancient writers left some clues, however. For example, Sophocles, the classical Greek tragic playwright and an initiate himself, wrote that "thrice blessed are those mortals who have seen these rites and enter into Hades."[9] Despite the comments of ancient authors and despite reading and re-reading the *Homeric Hymn to Demeter* and many other books about the Mysteries, it was still impossible for me to feel that I had any grasp of the effect of having participated in them. The veil shrouding the Eleusinian Mysteries was finally lifted for me by two feminist writers: Mara Lynn Keller and Kathie Carlson. In one of her insightful essays, Keller wrote that "their main purpose was to bring an experience of love to the most important life passages: birth, sexuality and death/rebirth."[10] Keller's work was seminal for me, enabling me to embrace the Mysteries. I will discuss her work and that of Jungian analyst Kathie Carlson, whose work about the Mysteries also affected me profoundly, in some detail. But before dealing with the end result of the Mysteries, let us consider their origins.

The Cretan Origins of Demeter
and the Eleusinian Mysteries

In looking for the origins of the goddess Demeter and her Mysteries in Bronze Age Crete, I will be using the lens of archaeomythology, a discipline which originated with archaeologist Marija Gimbutas and which employs archaeological, mythological, historical, literary, folkloric and linguistic evidence to understand ancient societies, especially their religions. As an archaeomythologist, I will be working within a worldview upon which Gimbutas elaborated in her books *The Goddesses and Gods of Old Europe*, *The Language of the Goddess*, *The Civilization of the Goddess and The Living Goddesses*. That worldview is composed of four parts:

- An understanding of the goddess as one with nature and as manifesting in three aspects: Life Giver, Life Taker and Regeneratrix.

- The deciphering of a complex symbolic system formulated around the worship of the goddess in her various aspects.

- A reinterpretation of Neolithic Europe, or Old Europe, as a "true civilization in the best meaning of the word,"[11] an egalitarian, matrilineal, peaceful and artistic one.

- An explanation of how and why the civilization of the goddess was overthrown and how the contact between the cultures of Old Europe and the cultures of the Indo-European invaders resulted in an amalgamation of cultures, with Old European religion and customs remaining a strong undercurrent and influencing the development of Western civilization.

For Gimbutas and other archaeomythologists, Bronze Age Crete is one of the prime examples of Old European-Anatolian civilization: artistic, refined, peaceful, egalitarian and matrilineal. It was a society in which women were highly visible and important and in which the supreme deity was a female who was worshipped in her triple aspect in temple complexes and household shrines, on mountain peaks and in cave sanctuaries.

The following pages will present literary, archaeological, linguistic and historical evidence in support of a Cretan origin for Demeter and her Mysteries. Underlying all of the evidence is this given: In Minoan Crete, a feminine divine was the supreme deity. Although, as the iconography and artifacts show us, she was "called" by many different names—Great Mother, Goddess of Nature, Mistress of the Animals, Britomartis, Dicktynna and Eileithyia, to name a few—she was one manifesting in three aspects: life giver, death wielder and regeneratrix. In Minoan Crete, the aspect most emphasized (as we know from Gimbutas's work in the *The Language of the Goddess*), was the regenerative: "Minoan art abundantly reflects regenerative symbols: double axes, butterflies, *bucrania* (bull skulls), and trees (or columns) of life."[12] It is the regenerative aspect of the Minoan goddess that comes down through the ages in Demeter and the Eleusinian Mysteries. It is she who provides her initiates with the ultimate understanding of life, death, rebirth and regeneration.

Mythological and Archaeological Evidence

There are four ancient literary textws that link Crete and Eleusis: the *Homeric Hymn to Demeter*, Homer's *Odyssey*, Hesiod's *Theogony*, and Diodorus's *Bibliotheca Historica*. Of all the evidence in support of Crete as the origin place of Demeter and her Mysteries, the literary is perhaps the strongest. Connections between Demeter and Crete are drawn in at least four ancient sources beginning with the *Homeric Hymn to Demeter*, "the most complete and well-known source of the story of Demeter and Persephone."[13] In the *Homeric Hymn to Demeter*, Demeter, in the guise of an old woman, declares that she comes from Crete: "Doso's my name, which my honored mother gave me. On the broad back of the sea I have come now from Crete, by no wish of my own. By force and necessity pirate men led me off against my desire."[14]

Gimbutas, on the basis of the *Homeric Hymn to Demeter,* concluded that "both the Minoan and Greek Demeter were the same goddess."[15] Elaborating further, she linked Demeter to the Neolithic vegetation goddess of Old Europe:

> The pregnant vegetation goddess, whose figurines inundate European Neolithic sites, is absent in Cretan archaeological remains. But her memory is preserved in legends and written sources, which record two Cretan goddesses of vegetation: Ariadne and Demeter. According to the *Homeric Hymn to Demeter*, this goddess came to Greece from Crete.[16]

Keller also believes that Demeter's declaration in the *Homeric Hymn to Demeter* ("I come to Crete over the sea's wide back not willingly; but pirates brought me thence by force of strength") also indicates that Demeter came to Greece from Crete. In addition, she remarked that it "may well point to the takeover of the female-preeminent culture of Crete by the Mycenaeans, occurring approximately at the same time as the first shrine to Demeter was built at Eleusis."[17] Carlson agreed: "Crete was the last place to succumb to the patriarchal invaders and preserved the Goddess-centered Old Religion long after the rest of southern Europe went under."[18]

Classicist Jane Ellen Harrison, writing in the early 20th century, also used the *Homeric Hymn to Demeter* to support her contention that the

Mysteries originated in Crete: "Demeter . . . probably came from Crete and brought her name with her."[19] "This may be a mere chance pirate legend, but such legends often echo ethnographic fact."[20] Harrison also cited other pieces of literary evidence to make her point: Homer's *Odyssey* and Hesiod's *Theogony*. In the *Odyssey*, "we learn that in Crete she [Demeter] had a sacred marriage."[21] Harrison believed that a "sacred marriage" was one of the acts performed or revealed on the seventh or eighth days of the Mysteries. As for the *Theogony*, Harrison noted that "Hesiod, if later in date, is almost always earlier in thought than Homer. He knows of the Marriage and knows it was in Crete."[22] And she quotes Hesiod:

Demeter brought forth Ploutos; a glorious goddess she,

and yet she loved Iasion, a mortal hero he.

In Crete's rich furrows lay they; glad and kindly was the birth

of him whose way is on the sea and over all the Earth

happy, happy is the mortal who doth meet him as he goes,

for his hands are full of blessings and his treasure overflows.[23]

Ronald F. Willetts, author of *Cretan Cults and Festivals*, wrote the following in reference to the *Homeric Hymn to Demeter*: "For Demeter is said to have reached Greece from Crete, where she was an emanation of the Minoan Mother Goddess."[24] Willetts also pointed out that the *Odyssey* places Demeter's sacred marriage to Iason in Crete.[25]

Scholar Károly Kerényi also cited the *Homeric Hymn to Demeter*, the *Odyssey* and the *Theogony* as evidence that Demeter and her Mysteries originated in Crete, "the great island whose advanced civilization had been shared by the Greeks since the fifteenth century. . . . The Homeric hymn tells us she came from Crete."[26] "The Cretan myth of Demeter is pre-Homeric. The Odyssey refers to it."[27]

Kerényi mentioned yet a fourth literary source in support of his argument: Diodorus of Sicily, a 1st century BCE Greek historian: "Ancient literature contains a single explicit mention of Crete in connection with the Eleusinian Mysteries."[28] Diodorus revealed more than just the origins of the Mysteries; he revealed some of their practices as well. Kerényi wrote the following:

> Diodorus does not name his authority. It was probably a historian from Crete. His proof of the Cretan origin of the Mysteries . . . is of interest: elsewhere—these are the exact words—such rites are communicated in secret, but in Crete, in Knossos, it had been the custom since time immemorial to speak of these ceremonies quite openly to all and, if anyone wished to learn of them, to conceal none of the things which elsewhere were imparted to the initiate under a vow of silence. Whoever wrote this may have generalized and drawn overhasty comparisons: but he may perfectly well have been referring to elements of the cult which in his day still survived in Knossos and which are unknown to us.[29]

Professor of Classical Literature Axel W. Persson also cited Diodorus's work as one of the pieces of evidence linking Demeter to Crete: "A double ancient tradition traces the mysteries to Crete: on the one hand the Homeric Hymn to Demeter . . . on the other Diodorus."[30]

> Mysticism, according to ancient tradition, had its chief stronghold in Crete. I shall only refer to what Diodoros has to say regarding this matter, V,77,3ff (his source is undoubtedly Epimenides of Knossos): "The inhabitants of Crete have left the following evidence that divine cults, sacrifices, and mystery rites were carried from Crete to other peoples; the dedication rites which were performed by the Athenians in Eleusis, perhaps the most famous of all, . . . these were all secret, but in Knossos it was an old custom to perform these rites openly, and that which among others is done in secret is not hidden by them from anyone who desires to know about it. They say that most of the gods have gone out from Crete to various parts of the world as benefactors of mankind, giving to each and all a share in their useful discoveries. It was thus that Demeter went to Attica and from there to Sicily, and later also to Egypt.[31]

Diodorus's recounting of the Mysteries' origins and their openness in Crete is often discounted by scholars. Keller believes that Diodorus is, in fact, accurate about the connection between Crete and Eleusis and that his work reflects the fact that in the prepatriarchal era the Eleusinian Mysteries were simple farming-community festivals. This had significantly changed by the time of Classical Athens, the time period of the Mysteries about which we know the most. "It seems to me quite possible that the celebration of Demeter's rites (which for several thousand years were probably celebrated in open fields) first moved into temples, and developed an official ritual form, priesthood, restricted access, and secrecy, only when class rule became the dominant social norm in Greece."[32]

Archaeological artifacts provide further evidence for Demeter's and the Mysteries' prepatriarchal Cretan origins. We will examine the following: two cups from the Minoan temple-palace of Phaistos; the remains of a building known as Mycenaean Megaron B at Eleusis; *kernoi*, a type of offering table; libation tables, golden double axes and other artifacts found at peak sanctuaries and other sacred sites in Crete and which contain inscriptions; several Minoan artifacts, including a pendant, several seals and a gold ring, which contain bee iconography; and, finally, Minoan and Eleusinian artifacts displaying the sacral knot.

One of the most intriguing of the artifacts, although least mentioned in the literature, is that offered by Kerényi—a famous cup found in the temple-palace of Phaistos (located in central Crete) and dated by its excavator, Doro Levi, to 2,000 BCE (the Old Palace Period). Kerényi called it "the earliest extant representation of Persephone."[33] Levi described the cup thusly:

> A low cup, the inner surface of which shows a religious scene. Two women are seen dancing in most lively attitudes around the Snake Goddess. The head of the Goddess rests on the top of an elongated triangular body with no arms but with a series of arcs running along each of the sides. The body of the goddess and the snakes immediately remind us of the very similar tubular clay idols, or sacrificial tubes, found at Prinias and in other early-Hellenic sites of more than 1,000 years later.[34]

What Levi did not say in this description is that at the foot of the "Snake Goddess" is a flower growing up from the earth. Kerényi called the cup "Persephone with two companions,"[35] and wrote that "we recognize the same scene preceding the abduction of the goddess in the hymn [*Homeric Hymn to Demeter*] and in the Phaistos cup: Persephone admiring the flower."[36]

Analysts Anne Baring and Jules Cashford, in their book *The Myth of the Goddess: Evolution of an Image*, also discussed the cup from Phaistos. They came to the same conclusion as Kerényi: "Two female figures appear, from the drooping gesture of their arms, to be mourning a third figure between them apparently about to pick a narcissus . . . and the direction of the picture is downwards into the earth."[37] On a companion piece to the above cup are also found three figures. However, on this cup "the same three figures are gesturing upwards together as in a celebration, the central one holding up a flower in each hand, and the scene has the feeling of rising movement, such as a return from below the earth."[38] Baring and Cashford called the first cup "Descent of the Goddess" and the second cup "Return of the Goddess."

A second, stronger piece of archaeological evidence supporting the theory of Cretan origins of Demeter and her Mysteries is Mycenaean Megaron B, the remains of one of the buildings excavated at the Sanctuary of Eleusis. Megaron B is considered by many experts to be the first temple to Demeter at Eleusis. Sometimes it is also referred to as the "proto-Telesterion." Megaron B is dated to the 15th century BCE and thus is Mycenaean. It is important to realize that, in linking the Mysteries to a Mycenaean temple, in all probability one is linking them to Crete as well. As Kerényi wrote about the construction of Megaron B, "This was a period of mutual influence, religious and otherwise, between Crete and continental Greece, then ruled over by Mycenaean kings."[39] It was a period of "mutual influence," because by the 15th century BCE the Mycenaeans had conquered and were ruling Crete. Although they had conquered the Minoans (ca. 1,450 BCE), they had not obliterated their civilization. Rather, as Kerényi made clear, the Mycenaeans had incorporated many elements of Minoan culture, including religious elements. Indeed they had incorporated so much that the great historian and classical archaeologist Martin P. Nilsson believed that there was virtually no difference between the Minoan and Mycenaean religions. In contrast, as an archaeomythologist instructed by the work of Gimbutas, I understand Mycenaean religion to be an amalgamation of Mycenae's own religion, Indo-European religion, and the religion of the civilization that the

Mycenaean's conquered, Old Europe/Minoan Crete. Gimbutas explained this in *The Living Goddesses*:

> The Mycenaeans adopted many elements from Minoan culture. Clay tablets written in Mycenaean Linear B occur both on Crete and in Mycenaean cities on the mainland. The tablets . . . include names of deities worshiped in later classical Greece, such as Zeus, Hera, Athena, Artemis Eileithyia, Poseidon, Dionysus, Ares, and possibly . . . Apollo.

> The Minoans also endowed the Mycenaeans with a style of arts and crafts. The highly skilled Cretan artists apparently moved to the mainland where, under their Mycenaean masters, they produced pottery and frescoes in the Minoan style. Many of the same symbols appear on the mainland as on Crete, and, in fact, the art of this time in the Aegean and on the mainland is often referred to as Mycenaean-Minoan art.

> The art, architecture, and written records of the Mycenaeans reveal a fascinating mixture of Old European and Indo-European elements. There is no doubt about the Indo-European ancestry of the Mycenaeans. They glorified war, and male warriors held prominence in society. Carrying on the Kurgan burial tradition, Mycenaean graves feature a prominent male warrior buried with his weapons. . . . At the same time, the archaeological evidence shows that the Mycenaeans retained strong Old European-Minoan beliefs. Much of the artwork—frescoes, signet rings and seals, pottery, and figurines—is quite similar to the Minoan. The same goddesses and symbols—the mistress of animals and mountains, the snake and bird goddesses, the horns of consecration, and the double ax—all occur in mainland Mycenaean art. . . . The Mycenaeans produced thousands of goddess figurines, which descend directly from Old European motifs.

> The Mycenaean civilization demonstrates that significant
> worship of the goddess persisted in Bronze Age Europe,
> even within heavily Indo-Europeanized cultures. The
> Mycenaeans represent an important transitional phase
> between Old European gynocentric culture and the clas-
> sical Greek culture, where the male element came to
> dominate almost completely.[40]

Although many scholars may agree that Mycenaean religion incorporated elements of Minoan religion and that both Minoan and Mycenaean
religions influenced classical Greek religion, not all agree that Megaron B
was involved in the worship of Demeter from the Mycenaean period. In
his 1981 study of the Mycenaean remains at Eleusis, archaeologist Pascal
Darque concluded that there is "no evidence for a Mycenaean proto-Telesterion."[41] Archaeologist Kevin Clinton believes that Megaron B probably
served some religious purpose but pointed out that "we have no evidence
that the Mysteries went back to the Mycenaean period."[42] Aegean archaeologist Oliver Dickinson concurred that there was "no reliable evidence of
prehistoric cult at all"[43] and added that "no evidence for any activity on the
site between the late thirteenth and late eighth centuries BC has ever been
published."[44] However, in response to Dickinson and others, I would note
that more recent excavations at Eleusis by Michael Cosmopolous uncovered
some shards of Kamares ware, exquisite Minoan thin-walled polychrome
pottery dating to 1,900–1,700 BCE, on the southwest slope.[45] Thus, a connection between Crete and Eleusis has been established as regards pottery,
and one may well think that the religious influence of Crete reached Eleusis
as it did the other Mycenaean centers at Mycenae, Argos and Tiryns.

If we cannot, at this point, resolve the controversy over Megaron B,
another piece of archaeological evidence to link Bronze Age Crete to
Demeter and the Eleusinian Mysteries can be offered: the *kernos*. The *kernos* was a sacred vessel of the Eleusinian cult.[46] A more detailed definition
is offered by archaeologist Stephanos Xanthoudides in his article "Cretan
Kernoi." He wrote that "a kernos is a clay vessel, to which were attached a
number of small cups containing various grains and liquids, offered as first
fruits of the harvest, especially in the Eleusinian worship, to the divinity."[47]
The official guide book to the archaeological site of Eleusis defines *kernos*
thusly: "Clay kernos; this cult vessel is made up of many small receptacles

suitable for receiving offerings such as wheat, lentils, honey, wine and oil for the goddesses."[48]

Why is the *kernos* important to my argument? There is no doubt that the *kernos* figured prominently in the Eleusinian Mysteries. According to archaeologist George Mylonas, one of the early excavators of Eleusis, the lower half of the Niinnion Tablet, "the only work of art that can be definitively linked with the Mysteries and which can give us some information regarding the preliminary rites of the cult of the Eleusinian Demeter,"[49] "represents the *kernophoria*, the bearing of the sacred kernos."[50] The tablet illustrates day five of the Mysteries. By then the pomp has ended. The celebrants or prospective initiates have reached Eleusis and are now in the outer court of the sanctuary. Iacchos is presenting the participants to Demeter.[51] Before proceeding, the *kernos*, with its first fruits, is offered to the Goddess: "Perhaps women bearing on their heads the mystic kernos performed a special dance in honor of the Goddess. . . . It seems to us . . . that it was the appropriate ending of the pompe, the moment of the arrival at the Sanctuary where the Goddess would receive her worshippers and acknowledge their presentation."[52] In addition, Mylonas informed us, numerous remains of *kernoi* have been found at Eleusis:

> In the excavations of Eleusis were found a number of vessels corresponding to the description of Athenaios [2nd century CE author]-Polemon [fl.c.190 BCE]. Some of these were surrounded by a good number of small cups stuck together. Others have but tiny symbolic cups, and from others the cups are missing; but the similar nature of the vessels is unmistakable. Their similarity also to the vessel borne by the woman on the Niinnion tablet is evident. . . . Apparently the vessels were used to hold a variety of cereals, representing a panspermia, that were being offered to the Goddess by the initiates in a service known as *kernophoria*; the worshipers could later partake of these cereals in remembrance of her benevolence to humanity and with the belief that they shared with the Goddess her bounty. In later years kernoi of a votive character were apparently made to be dedicated to the Goddess

and often these were made of marble or with symbolic little cups attached to the body of the vessel.[53]

Because *kernoi* are so intimately associated with Demeter at Eleusis, one would expect that *kernoi* should date from the same time and originate from the same place as Demeter. Therefore, if Crete is the origin place of the Mysteries and Demeter, we should look for the earliest *kernoi* there.

Archaeologist Xanthoudides provided substantial evidence to show that Crete is indeed the place where the *kernos* originated: "This sacred vessel occurs in Crete in all periods from the earliest Cretan or Cycladic to the latest historical times."[54] The *kernos* is "one more witness to the unbroken continuity of cult and custom, inherited by the historic Greeks from the prehistoric inhabitants of Greece and the islands."[55]

Xanthoudides argued that the *kernoi*, which are associated with Eleusis, evolved from libation- tables or tables-of-offering that originated in Crete in the Early Minoan period: "I believe . . . that altars, tables-of-offering and libation-tables, and *kernoi* were originally all alike, and that these different forms arose simply from the various places and manner of making offerings, and their material, composition and quantity."[56]

Xanthoudides described the early *kernoi* as receptacles (flat stone vessels) dating from the Early Minoan Period to the Late Minoan Period, with one to eight hollows or shallow depressions in them. They come from Palaikastro and Chamezi in eastern Crete; Koumasa, Hagia Triada, Phaistos, Knossos and the Diktean Cave in central Crete; and from the island of Melos, an island "colonized" by the Minoans. Their ritual use is established by the fact that they were found with other sacred objects in tombs and shrines and/or with inscriptions on them.

> Considering all these objects from the kernoi of Koumasa to those of Palaikastro, we see that although they are of various forms, yet in use they do not essentially differ, all being sacred objects from shrines or tombs used to hold the offerings of the faithful to the gods, or of the living to the divinely honoured dead. . . . In all these cases there is only variation in the form, size, and material according to the place of use and the objects offered. For fruit . . . a flat surface was enough; for cereals, and especially for

liquids, a receptacle was necessary, and so the hollows and *kotuliskoi* were added. If a single substance or a mixed libation was offered, one receptacle was enough, whilst if several substances were to be offered separately at the same time, several were needed and tables-of-offering with many hollows and kernoi with many little cups would be made. I believe therefore that altars, tables-of-offering and libation-tables and *kernoi* were originally all alike, and that these different forms arose simple from the various places and manner of making offerings, and their material, composition and quality. Of all these, the table with vases fastened to it and the *kernos* with *kotuliskoi* are the most complicated developments of the sacred table or altar. This latter type in Hellenic times gained a special sanctity and took a foremost place in certain centres of worship, especially in the mysteries of Eleusis, and was given the special name *kernos*.[57]

From these early, "simple" *kernoi*, Xanthoudides followed the development of the Cretan kernos to the Kourtes *kernos* found in a tomb in the Kourtes cemetery. Dating from Late Minoan (LM) III or the early Mycenaean period, this *kernos* is made of red clay and consists of a hollow ring in the upper part to which six little vases or cups are attached. Three human figures are set alternately between the cups or vases. Xanthoudides noted that human figures have never been observed on any other *kernos*. He believed that they represented "in an archaic way women taking part in the sacred Kernophoria."[58] Xanthoudides concluded, "There is no doubt that this object also served the same sacred purpose as the kernoi of Koumasa, the Melian kernoi . . . and the kernoi of the Greek period."[59]

Moving from the Mycenaean period to the late Greek/early Roman period, Xanthoudides offered yet another example of a Cretan kernos: the kernos now in the Archaeological Museum of Agios Nikolaos. This vessel, which comes from the ancient city of Latos, consists of "a large deep bowl, into which opens a low foot. Two thick handles are placed below the broad, level and projecting rim, upon the outside edge of which are symmetrically arranged nine small handless bell-shaped cups."[60] Interestingly he noted that Latos was the place of worship of the "Cretan goddess of agriculture

Diktynna." (Recently, linguist Gareth A. Owens has proposed that the name Diktynna is derived from the Linear A term JA-DI-KI-TU and that it is "the mountain epithet of the goddess who appears in the epiphany, i.e. the Great Mother Goddess.)[61] Xanthoudides concluded about this kernos in the museum that "its use was without doubt the same as that of the *kernoi* described by Athenaeus, and found at Eleusis and Athens."[62]

Xanthoudides's final example of a Cretan *kernos* took him to 1905, the year in which his article was written. Discussing the offering of first fruits in Greek Orthodox Churches in Crete, he related that it is the custom on many occasions during the year for congregation members to bring loaves of bread as well as oil, wine and corn to be blessed:

> On the loaves are placed seven lights, by means of a metal object with small sockets for holding seven lighted candles. In some old monasteries and churches this sevenfold candle stick is furnished with special receptacles or little cups to hold the corn and wine and oil, and thus the whole arrangement with the candles and offerings bears an extraordinary resemblance to the kernos of ancient Greek religion.[63]

He ended his article by noting that the ancient custom, known to us from the Niinnion Tablet, of the priestess of Demeter carrying on her head the *kernos* filled with its offerings is replicated in the Greek Church during the Eucharist, for at that point the priests come out "bearing on their heads the chalice and paten with the holy Bread."[64]

Is Xanthoudides's thesis correct? Most scholars of the *kernos* agree with his assessment of its development. His early 20th century contemporary, Jane Ellen Harrison, certainly concurred. In *Prolegomena to the Study of Greek Religion*, she quoted the late 2nd century CE Greek author Athenaeus's definition of *kernos* in his work *The Deipnosophists*: "a vessel made of earthenware having in it many little cups fastened to it in which are white poppies, wheat, barley, pulse, vetch, ochroi, lentils."[65] She added that "vessels exactly corresponding to that description given by Athenaeus have been found in considerable numbers in Melos and Crete, and, of later date, in the precinct at Eleusis.[66]

Martin P. Nilsson, in his famous work *The Minoan-Mycenaean Religion and Its Survival in Greek Religion*, also traced the origins of the *kernos* to Minoan Crete. Nilsson dated the first *kernoi* even earlier than Xanthoudides did. Noting that Sir Arthur Evans found the prototype of the *kernos* "in a vessel round or oval and of dark burnished clay, which makes its appearance in Early Minoan II,"[67] Nilsson argued that the "true prototypes" of the *kernoi* are to be discovered in vessels found in "the great cemetery of Pyrgos near Knossos dating from the earlier periods of the Early Minoan age. Among the different forms of composite vessels found there one is very characteristic. It consists of a stem spreading downwards into a base; at the top of the stem two cups are fastened by the rim or a little below the top, so that the stem projects above the cups."[68]

Although Nilsson did not agree with Xanthoudides that the flat stones with the shallow impressions are *kernoi*, he did agree that the vessels from Koumasa, Melia and Palaikastro are. Nilsson added to Xanthoudides's repertoire of Cretan *kernoi* by including a number of Mycenaean *kernoi* in his discussion. One consists of a ring "upon which three vessels, two with narrow mouths and one a cup with a handle, and a bull's head are fastened."[69] Nilsson also agreed with Xanthoudides's conclusion that the *kernos* has survived into modern times in the Greek Orthodox Church.

Indeed, the *kernos* is one of the examples that Nilsson uses to support the thesis of his work: that Minoan-Mycenaean religion "merged into the Greek religion." Although Nilsson spoke most of the time as though the Minoan and Mycenaean religions were one, unlike Gimbutas who believed that Minoan religion was amalgamated with Mycenaean religion with the coming of the Mycenaean invaders to Crete, both Nilsson and archaeo-mythologists posited that the *kernos*'s origins and evolution in Crete are important evidence supporting the argument for the origins of Demeter and her cult in Crete:

> The general assumption that the Minoan religion survived in the Greek religion will acquire much greater strength and actuality if traces of the Minoan cult can be detected in a later age and if it can be proved that in certain places a cult survived from the Minoan-Mycenaean age down to the Greek age. Such facts would establish valuable starting points for an attempt to distinguish those elements of Greek religion which may be due to a Minoan influence.[70]

Nilsson saw the *kernos* as one of those "traces of the Minoan cult detectable at a later age." He called the *kernos* "a Minoan cult vessel whose use seems to have continued in the Greek age and even down to modern times."

> As already noted, however, the chief point is the similarity of this vessel to those occurring in the Minoan Age, and this similarity is so striking that nobody denies the connection, although about a thousand years intervene between the Minoan specimens and the Greek specimens. It is not to be believed that such a curiously shaped vessel can have been created independently a second and even a third time in the same country. But the continuity of this cult implement, which was used in the Greek Mysteries, is very important evidence for the Minoan affinities of this mystic cult.[71]

The *kernos* is one of several pieces of evidence that Nilsson offered to prove continuity of cult from the Minoan time to Classical Greek times. So too, Eleusis is one of the places Nilsson cited where "a cult survived from the Minoan-Mycenaean age down to the Greek age."

> It was a Mycenaean town, its acropolis is strewn with Mycenaean and pre-Mycenaean sherds, and it contains a Mycenaean necropolis and a small beehive tomb. . . . Professor Persson called attention to the fact . . . that the polygonal walls of Eleusinian limestone of the oldest hall of mysteries and of the sacred precinct date from the Mycenaean age and has justly taken this as a starting point for demonstrating the Mycenaean origin of the Eleusinian mysteries.[72]

Nilsson went on to describe Megaron B:

> It is tempting to recognize this building as a Mycenaean cult-house . . . but it is far from certain. Remains of a cult are scarce . . . but the continuity of the settlement justifies an assumption of the continuity of the cult. It is possible

that it originated in the Mycenaean age. I have already
pointed out that the kernos was used in the Eleusinian
cult. . . . The far-reaching conclusion is that the famous
Eleusinian cult is of Mycenaean origin.[73]

And at another point, he wrote, "A conspicuous Mycenaean building
was found beneath the assembly hall, and it must be a well-founded sup-
position that Minoan elements may have survived in the cult."[74]

In the preceding pages, I have touched upon the fact that not all scholars agree with the theory of a Cretan origin to the Eleusinian Mysteries,
whether on the basis of literary sources or archaeological evidence. One of
the best-known critics of the Cretan origin theory, mentioned briefly earlier in this article, is archaeologist George Mylonas. Although he believed
that Megaron B dates from the Mycenaean period and that the worship
of Demeter there began at that time, in his 1961 book *Eleusis and the
Eleusinian Mysteries*, Mylonas countered most of the rest of the arguments I have set forth here.

I shall begin with the *kernos*. Obviously aware of Xanthoudides's article and Nilsson's book, Mylonas wrote the following:

> The sanctuaries of Demeter have yielded a special type of
> vase known as the Kernos. It is very characteristic of our
> site and of the Eleusinian cult, and it was taken as evidence
> of Kretan or Minoan influence. In spite of differences, the
> Kernoi can be compared to Minoan multiple pots and as
> Nilsson remarks, "nobody denies the connexion, although
> about a thousand years intervene between the Minoan and
> the Greek (Eleusinian) specimens." This chronological
> difference, we believe, excludes Minoan influence; if it
> existed we would expect to find such vessels in the early
> strata of the Sanctuary. To date not a single fragment has
> been found in the prehistoric strata of the site, and we
> can conclude that, in later years, this peculiar vessel was
> developed at Eleusis independently to fill a need that arose
> from the evolution and crystallization of the ritual of the
> Eleusinian cult. In exactly the same manner, the Kernos of
> the Christian worship was developed independently to fill

a need of the ritual, long after the secret pagan cults and
their utensils were forgotten.[75]

Mylonas also discounted theories of a Cretan origin of the Mysteries based
on literary evidence. What of Hesiod's *Theogony*, which places Demeter
and Iasion in Crete? Mylonas thought that Hesiod's myth was of a "later
date" and that it "reflects an allegorical and poetic interpretation of the
rewards of successful soil cultivation that has nothing to do with the cult of
Demeter at Eleusis . . . and that it had nothing to do with the cult is indicated
by the fact that it is not mentioned in the Hymn which gives us the official
version of the story of the introduction of the rites."[76]

Of the argument that the *Homeric Hymn to Demeter* itself proclaims
that Demeter came from Crete, kidnapped by pirates, Mylonas wrote, "We
must remember that in the *Hymn* the Goddess is telling a story to conceal
her identity and explain her presence. The use of Krete to hide the real
provenance of a traveler or a guest is not unusual in epic poetry."[77] When
it suited his purpose, Mylonas argued for the veracity and reliability of the
"official" version of the myth in the *Homeric Hymn to Demeter*. When it
did not suit his purpose, we find no such insistence.

Finally, Mylonas argued on the basis of linguistic evidence that there
is no Crete-Eleusis connection. He wrote that "Demeter is a Greek name
and has no relation to Kretan pre-Hellenic names."[78] It is on this last point
that Mylonas is perhaps the most mistaken. In 1995–1996, 35 years after
the publication of Mylonas's book, linguist Gareth A. Owens published two
articles proposing translations for Linear A inscriptions that link Demeter
to Bronze Age Crete. I turn now to considering linguistic evidence that
connects Crete and Eleusis.

Owens presented his theories in "Evidence for the Minoan Language
(1): The Minoan Libation Formula" and "New Evidence for Minoan
Demeter." For these articles, Owens studied and translated (according to
Linear B sound values and spelling rules) 100 Linear A religious and personal inscriptions. These inscriptions appear on stone libation tables and
other artifacts found in peak sanctuaries and other sacred sites. Of the 100
inscriptions, 66 contain what scholars have called the Minoan Libation
Formula: "the repetition of sign groups on stone libation tables and other
objects."[79] Experts agree that the Minoan Libation Formula is clearly a
series of religious or sacred words.

Two inscriptions that Owens has translated are of particular relevance to this study. The first is A/JA-DI-KI-TU. This word occurs eight times in the inscriptions. Owens labeled this word an oronym (place name), because he believed it referred to a specific place—Mount Juktas in Crete. Other scholars agree with his identification of the word as an oronym. Owens traced the word to the Indo-European root *deik-/dik*, which means "to show or declare or make known, especially to point out something with the finger" (*daktalos*, meaning "digit"). Owens wrote that JA-DI-KI-TU could be interpreted as "the mountain where something was made clear."[80] Because Owens believed that iconographical evidence must be taken into account when deciphering Linear A, he concluded that what was most often pointed out, revealed or made clear on the mountain tops of Minoan Crete was the epiphany of the goddess.

A second important term that Owens looked at, "I DA," occurs eleven times in the Minoan Libation Formula. Like A/JA-DI-KI-TU, "it too should be seen as an oronym." Ida was the name in Classical and probably Minoan times for the Psiloriti massif, the highest peak on Crete. "Psiloriti/ Ida is visible from the towns of Nerokourou, Iouktas, Kophinas, Syme, and Archalochori, in fact from all of the places where this term has been found with the exception of Petsophas in East Crete."[81] Owens hypothesized that Ida may come from the Indo-European word *wid* (to see): "This would explain Ida as from Indo-European wid—meaning the mountain where the vision was seen/where the epiphany took place. The most common scene in Minoan religious iconography is the epiphany of the goddess who appears on the mountain."[82] He asked, "Is it a coincidence that both holy mountains—Dikte and Ida—can be explained by Indo-European roots meaning to make clear, reveal, say?"[83]

Owens believes that identifying the root Ida from Indo-European *wid* "would have important consequences for a number of other words including I-D-A-MA-TE."[84] I-D-A-MA-TE was first found on two metal double axes from the cave of Archalochori in central Crete. In 1954, after the translation of Linear B by Michael Ventris, scholar Nikolaos Boufides claimed that in the repeated word I-DA-MA-TE he could identify the Minoan goddess Demeter.[85] In 1993–1994 the term was also found on a vessel from the peak sanctuary of Agios Georgios above the Minoan site of Kastri on the neighboring island of Kythera. That discovery plus the fact that "in the last decade more information has come to light concerning the sign group I-D-A- etc." led Owens to conclude that "a re-appraisal of the evidence for the Minoan origin of Demeter can now be undertaken."[86] "From the cave of Archalochori in the Pediadah, the mountains of Psiloriti/Ida and Lasithi/Dikte, with their holy caves, are visible, as are the peak sanctuaries of Kopinas and Iouktas. This term could be interpreted as Ida Mater, Mother of Ida, where the epiphany took place. This is a direct textual reference to the Great Mother Goddess.[87] Ida Mater, "the best known iconographically of Minoan deities,"[88] brought to Owens's mind Demeter/Damater, "the goddess of fertility."

> In Minoan iconography fertility is one of the main attributes of the Mother Goddess of the Mountain. It was known in Classical times that Demeter had a Pre-Hellenic character and it is now proposed that she came from Minoan Crete. It is of note that Classical Grammarians always had problems to explain satisfactorily the etymology of Demeter. It has been variously suggested that Demeter = da meter where da = ga = ge earth, thus explaining her roots in the land. Also it has been suggested that Demeter = Deai Meter where deai = krithai, a Cretan word for grain. Both of these are unlikely and are the result of false popular etymology because of her connection with the earth. . . . The hypothesized root ghd = earth could be rendered as d/h/gh, thus explaining the confusion with Ida and Ge. In Phrygian Damater is known as Semele while in Thrakian, Hesychios states that Mother Earth, i.e., Demeter, was Gdan Ma. None of these correspondences is convincing on its own but taken together they are indicative of a connection on Minoan Crete between Damater/Demeter and I-DA-MA-TE. The origin of Demeter lies in I-DA-MA-TE, the Mother (MA-TE) who appeared on Ida (I-DA), the sacred mountain of the epiphany.[89]

Owens concludes the article "New Evidence for Minoan Demeter" by noting that "The earliest reference to Demeter is still the sign group I-DA-MA-TE found on the two Linear A inscribed axes at Archalochori and dated to c 1600 BC."[90]

If Owens is correct, we have compelling linguistic evidence to link Demeter to Crete. In attempting to assess Owens's hypothesis, several factors must be kept in mind. First is the fact that scholars are not in agreement with the use of Linear B spelling and sound values to translate Linear A. Owens's translation remains a hypothesis, because as far as the scholarly world is concerned, Linear A remains undeciphered. Secondly, Owens referred to Linear A as an Indo-European language. Again, this is a hypothesis that other scholars do not unanimously support. However, I think that one can make a case for Owens's I-D-A-MA-TE if one keeps in mind that in the language of Linear A we may be observing an amalgamation of Indo-European and Old European language elements, just as in the religions of the Mycenaeans and the classical Greeks we see an amalgamation of Indo-European and Old European religious elements.

Some scholars have argued that as early as 1,600 BCE, Mycenaean influence began to be felt in Crete. Archaeologist Nanno Marinatos hypothesized that the Mycenaeans went to Crete peacefully at first, perhaps invited. She wondered if there were interdynastic marriages.[91] It is not too difficult to imagine the Mycenaeans arriving peacefully and gradually, at least in the beginning. I think of Mary Mackey's novels about Old Europe and the Indo-European takeover and speculate that a peaceful, egalitarian society like the Minoan would be open and welcoming to the first Mycenaean strangers. I also think of Susan Evasdaughter's work and remember that the priestesses of Crete probably possessed great oracular powers. If they could indeed foresee the future, they knew it was merely a matter of time before the Indo-European Mycenaeans overran their civilization. Did the Minoans decide that it would be more advantageous for them to allow the Mycenaeans to enter in peace? If that was the case, an amalgamation of the two languages, Indo-European and Old European, becomes a distinct possibility.

There is another piece of evidence in favor of a Cretan origin for Demeter and the Eleusinian Mysteries that could also be classified as a linguistic one: *melissai*, meaning "honeybees." From Mylonas, we learn that among the functionaries of the cult of Demeter were "*priestesses panageis* . . . all holy ones."[92] Mylonas wrote that their role remains uncertain. "They seemed to have had the right of 'touching the Hiera' and they lived together in special dwellings situated perhaps in the auxiliary area of the Sanctuary; apparently they were called melissae or bees."[93]

234

The fact that the priestesses of Demeter who carried the *hiera* were called *melissae* (honeybees) is yet another astonishing and at the same time obvious link to Minoan Crete. The bee as the epiphany of the goddess is a common symbol in Minoan Crete. We learn from Gimbutas in *The Living Goddesses* that "the bee is . . . [an] important regenerative symbol inherited from Neolithic and then Minoan times."[94] Why bees as a symbol of regeneration? Gimbutas began a lengthy discussion of the bee and butterfly as epiphany of the Great Goddess by noting the ancient belief that bees were begotten by bulls. She quoted Antigonos of Karystos (250 BCE), one of the earliest writers to observe that the bull putrefies and "is resolved into bees."[95] "The idea of a 'life in death' . . . is expressed by the belief that the life of the bull passed into that of the bees."[96]

Yet another reason that bees were associated with regeneration, according to Gimbutas, is that the bee has "antennae like bull horns and wings in the form of a lunar crescent." Finally, "the periodic swarming and activity associated with the production of honey"[97] also must have contributed to the use of the bee as a symbol of regeneration.

Gimbutas detailed the many instances of the bee in Minoan iconography. Among the most well known are the following:

- The famous Mallia pendant, gold, on which two bees hold what appears to be a large drop of honey.

- The onyx gem from Knossos that portrays the Bee Goddess flanked by winged dogs with bull's horns and a double axe above the goddess's head (1,500 BCE).

- The Early Minoan three-sided bead seal of yellow steatite that portrays the goddess in the shape of a bee.

- The gold ring of Isopata (found in a tomb near Knossos, dated 1,500 BCE) that portrays a goddess and three worshippers, "usually assumed to be melissae, or bees."[98]

In religious iconography, the bee did not end with the Minoans. According to Gimbutas, when the Indo-European invaders learned the art of beekeeping from the Minoans "they . . . inherited the mythical image of the Goddess as a bee, the Goddess of Regeneration, the image of her virgin priestesses or nymphs as bees and many other myths and beliefs connected with the bee and honey."[99] Thus, the symbol of the bee is found in both Mycenaean and classical Greek art. Gimbutas pointed out a Mycenaean gem of Minoan workmanship in which two genii clad in bee skins hold jugs over horns from which new life springs in the shape of a plant.[100] She then traced the bee symbolism to Greek jewelry of the 7th through 5th centuries, to a Boetian amphora dating from 700 BCE and to Artemis of Ephesus: "At Ephesus, Artemis was associated with the bee as her cult animal. In fact, the whole organization of the sanctuary in classical times seems to have rested on the symbolic analogy of a beehive, with swarms of priestesses called bees, melissai, and numerous eunuch priests called drones, essenes."[101]

Not only was the social organization of the temple of Artemis at Ephesus modeled on the "symbolic analogy of a beehive," but the social organization of Minoan civilization was as well. Author Susan Evasdaughter has called attention to the fact that, in addition to being a symbol for regeneration, the bee was an important symbol in Minoan religion, "because its social organisation mirrored that of the Bronze Age Cretans. In both instances the success of the whole population was dependent on the cooperation of all its elements. Each individual worked for the good of the whole group."[102] Evasdaughter also noted other ways in which the sacred associations of the bee continued from Minoan Crete into classical times: "The omphalos at Delphi is shaped like a beehive and Pythia, the chief oracular priestess there, was called the Delphic bee."[103] How appropriate, then, that the women who carried the sacred relics at Eleusis were linked to the goddess in her aspect of regeneratrix by their names—*melissae*! How appropriate, also, that they were referred to as *panageis* (all holy ones), for that is the current appellation given by the Greek Orthodox Church to the Virgin Mary— Panagia, the one manifestation of the goddess who has managed to stay in our consciousness when all the others have been driven underground.

One final piece of evidence linking Eleusis and Crete remains to be discussed, and that is the iconographic link of the sacred knot. Keller made the important discovery that "the Sacred Knot that appears on the *Dadouchos* [Torchbearer] is similar to that worn by priestesses and priests in Krete."[104] Mylonas described the dadouchos (torchbearer) in the Eleusinian Mysteries as follows:

> . . . among the male celebrants, second in importance to
> the Hierophant . . . he participated in the celebration of the

Mysteries and in the initiation of the worshipers, took part in the purificatory sacrifices, and as a special privilege, he alone could use the "Fleece of Zeus" for the purification of those tainted with blood. . . . He wore elaborate vestments like the Hierophant, a knot of hair (krobylos) on the nape of his neck, and a stophion, a head band.[105]

It was Sir Arthur Evans who first identified the knots as seen in Crete and gave them the term sacral. The most famous sacred knot of Minoan Crete is the one that appears on the nape of the neck of the priestess in the fresco known as the *La Parisienne*. (Is she appearing as the epiphany of the Goddess?) There are many other examples. Nilsson, who was cautious about interpreting the knot, described some of the various representations that had been found:

> . . . one of ivory in the S.E. house at Knossos, and three pairs made of faience in the IVth shaft grave at Mycenae. The upper part of such a knot is preserved on a wall painting in the main corridor of the palace of Nirou Khani. . . . Gems from Crete and Mycenea show a lion and the object in question [sacral knot]. A gold ring from the Vaphio tomb with a tree cult scene shows a great Mycenaean shield lying to the right and above this the same object [sacral knot].[106]

What did the sacred knot symbolize for the Minoans? Author Rodney Castleden theorized that it may suggest a bond between the wearer and the deity.[107] Professor Persson concurred: "The sacred knot indicates that the object to which it is appended is connected with the divinity."[108]

> When female votaries wear the knot—the goddess is never shown wearing it—at the nape of their necks . . . their relation and office to the divinity is made plain. Just so, whenever we see the knot represented at the bull games or under certain other circumstances, a religious relationship is established in the scene or object. The occult significance of knots is still widespread. And let me remind you that when Alexander the Great cut the Gordian knot he

thereby severed the connection that existed between the temple and its protective deity.[109]

Susan Evasdaughter believes that the sacral knot symbolized "concentrated sacredness" and was an insignia of "theocratic office."[110] Baring and Cashford agreed: "High priestesses . . . would . . . have worn the sacred knot of the goddess as a sign of their role. It is not inconceivable that what the Greeks called 'Ariadne's thread' referred to the priestess's knot, which was unraveled at various ceremonies with a particular ritual meaning."[111] Discussing the various Minoan artifacts exhibiting sacred knots, Baring and Cashford made the following observation:

> In the various Minoan signet rings and images . . . the ritual status of the sacred knot is unmistakable. When the knot is drawn on its own, it can often look very like the butterfly [a symbol for rebirth and regeneration like the bee] whose wings are stylized to represent the double axe. It may have then been understood as a composite symbol, holding as one idea the images of the knot, the double axe and the butterfly, and evoking as well the figure of the goddess herself, where the wing-axes become arms and the vertical knot the body.[112]

Sir Arthur Evans noted the similarity of some of the double axe and sacral knot representations found on Minoan pottery to the Egyptian ankh. Baring and Cashford wrote that "in Egypt the symbol of eternal life—called the ankh—which was held by the goddesses . . . as a sign of their divinity, bears a similar shape to the knot."[113] Baring and Cashford made two further connections: "The resemblance to the curved reed bundle that was the image of the goddess Inanna in Sumeria is remarkable; so also is the resemblance to the knotted headband or necklace of the Egyptian goddesses Hathor and Isis, called the menat.[114]

The importance of the sacral knot in Crete is undeniable. That it appears in the ritual costume of the Torchbearer at Eleusis, the second most important priest of Demeter's Mysteries in Greece, provides us with another connection between the religious beliefs and rites of Crete and the Eleusinian Mysteries.

Conclusion to Part I

I believe that, when one combines all of the evidence offered in the preceding pages, one can construct a firm foundation upon which to argue for links between Bronze Age Crete and Demeter and for Crete as the origin of the Eleusinian Mysteries. The linguistic evidence ("I-DA-MA-TE" = Demeter) is probably the most compelling. If that translation is correct, if Linear A is an amalgamation of Old European and Indo-European languages, we have a very convincing piece of evidence from which to argue the Crete/Eleusis connection. The combination of the linguistic with the symbolic, the fact that I-DA-MA-TE appears on double axes, symbols of regeneration and rebirth themselves found in a sacred cave, the symbol par excellence of rebirth and regeneration, makes the argument even more tantalizing. Equally persuasive is the linguistic and symbolic evidence of the *melissae*. Since the Neolithic Era, the bee has been a symbol of the goddess in her aspect of rebirth and regeneration. At Eleusis the favored priestesses of Demeter, those who carried the *hiera* (perhaps symbols of rebirth and regeneration themselves), were called bees. They were also called *panageis*. I see these priestesses as links—between the goddess as regeneratrix, who in Old Europe appeared as a bee, and the goddess who survived the onslaughts of patriarchy and now appears as the Virgin Mary, the Panagia, in the Greek Orthodox Church.

Of the archaeological material, the evidence tracing the origins and evolution of the *kernos* to Minoan Crete, offered by Nilsson and especially Xanthoudides, further builds the case for the Crete/ Eleusis connection. Also significant is the sacral knot's appearance in both places.

Finally, there is the literary evidence of Homer, Hesiod, the poet of the *Homeric Hymn to Demeter*, and Diodorus. Highlighting all of this is Gimbutas's brilliant analysis and conclusion, essentially confirmed, in my opinion, by current archaeological literature about Mycenaean religion, that elements of both Old European religion and Indo-European religion gave form to Mycenaean religion and the religion of the Classical Greeks that followed.

The use of linguistic, archaeological, literary, historical and mythological evidence to build a case for the Cretan origins of Demeter and her Mysteries is an example of how scholars can use the tool of archaeomythology to reconstruct what has been denied of our heritage. Only by using the tools of archaeomythology can we unearth that denied/suppressed/forgotten/lost history at all. If we rely only on traditionally empiricist studies, disciplines such as archaeology, we may conclude, as archaeologist Michael Cosmopoulos did, that "a Cretan origin for the Eleusinian Mysteries is not supported by any archaeological evidence."[115] If one does not know about or acknowledge the archaeological evidence I have discussed here, relatively few connections can be made. In my view, the artifact of the *kernos* itself provides us, as Xanthoudides and Nilsson were able to show, a strong case for links among Crete, Demeter and Eleusis. And if one is willing to use linguistics, mythology, literary sources, history, folklore and art in addition to archaeology, one can follow numerous threads and find that they all link Demeter from Bronze Age Crete to Eleusis.

Part II: Modern Effect

Although it gives me great satisfaction to find evidence linking Demeter back to ancient Crete, just as satisfying for my soul is finding that the Eleusinian Mysteries resonate with me. As I indicated at the beginning of this article, that was not always the case. It has only been with my reading of the works of Keller and Carlson that I have finally understood the myth as more than a quaint story to explain the agricultural cycles. I was especially happy when, recently, as I did my morning meditation, I was filled with love and reminded, thanks to Keller, that all of the great spiritual teachings of the world, including the Eleusinian Mysteries, emphasize love as the central component.

That the Eleusinian Mysteries revolve around love is explained in three works by -Keller. Her reading of the archaeological and literary evidence, framed by her understanding of the prepatriarchal epoch and her feminist point of view, has led her to interpret the Mysteries as focused on three interrelated dimensions of life: fertility and birth, sexuality and marriage, and death and rebirth. Love is central to all of these.

I would like to focus here on what Keller has said about the Eleusinian Mysteries' relation to death and rebirth. For me, these are the most challenging and difficult of life's mysteries to fathom and certainly the ones that I have spent the most time trying to understand and come to terms with. What do the Mysteries have to say about death and rebirth?

> The belief of ancient peoples in the resurrection of life was closely related to their experience of nature, their experience of love. The reunion of the daughter with the mother/Goddess in the Demeter/Persephone myth must have been seen as a symbol of the human soul's return, after the death of the body, to its universal origin or loving source. In Athens, those who had died were called Demetrioi, the people of Demeter.[116]

In another work Keller added that "the daughter's separation from, and eventual reunion with the Mother, ultimately symbolizes the human soul's journey through suffering and death toward reunion with the primal source of love in the universe. The purpose of the Eleusinian ritual, then, was to generate, to transmit the *experience* of this soul journey."[117]

I believe that what we all really long for in this life is to know, not just intellectually but with our hearts, that we are or will be one with the primal source of love in the universe. I am certain it was because the core of the Mysteries imparted that sense to initiates—and the hope that at death they would be reunited with all-embracing love—that an ancient author could say "The Mysteries were Athens' greatest gift to humanity" or Pindar could write "Blessed is he who has seen this and thus goes beneath the earth, he knows the end of life, he knows the beginning given by Zeus."[118]

Reading about what Keller, quoting Diotima in Plato's *Symposium*, referred to as the "vast sea of love" that enveloped the *mystai* (initiates) at Eleusis, I thought about Carol P. Christ and what she wrote in *Odyssey to the Goddess* at the time of her mother's death:

> As my mother was dying, I had an absolutely clear sense that she was going "to love." . . . When my mother passed from this life she was surrounded by a great matrix of love. As she died, I began to understand that I too am surrounded by love and always have been. That knowledge is a great mystery.[119]

Two close friends of mine who were also present at their mothers' deaths described their experiences in the same way Christ did. Both related to me that a sea of love surrounded them and their mothers.

Elaborating further, Keller called the love between Demeter and Persephone "divinely transformative."

> The love of the Mother and Daughter symbolizes the divine
> bond between the individual soul and the whole realm of
> nature, that is, of each human to the Great Mystery of the
> cosmos and universal life. By identifying with the suffering
> and love of the Mother and Daughter, the initiate during
> the nine days of the rites at Athens and Eleusis is guided
> through an experience of spiritual death and rebirth.[120]

"By identifying with the suffering and love of the Mother and Daughter, the initiate during the nine days of the rites at Athens and Eleusis is guided through an experience of spiritual death and rebirth."[121] This last sentence contains a key point for me as a woman. I find the myth profoundly healing, because I am being asked to identify with the experiences of other women. I can identify with the suffering and love of a mother or daughter much more easily than I can identify with a father or son.

I do not wish, by diverting the discussion to identification with the mother and daughter, to lose track of the fact that the story of Demeter and Persephone is a universal human story "of a lost and wounded spirit returning to the depths of love from which it sprang." Because the story is universal, Keller believes that the Eleusinian rites restored (and, if practiced today, could now restore?) the sacred bonds among all humans. Is that why the ancients believed that if the Mysteries ended the world also would come to an end? Moreover, Keller believes that the Mysteries kept in balance (and, if practiced today, could now rebalance?) the human sphere with the rest of the earth's biosphere![122] This is a truly profound thought. If we would only come back into balance with divine love, not only would we as human beings be well but the ailing earth would be healed as well!

Yet another scholar whose analysis of the myth has had a profound effect on me is Kathie Carlson. Her work, *Life's Daughter / Death's Bride: Inner Transformation through the Goddess Demeter/Persephone*, contains six points that are key. First, like Keller, she believes that the myth's origins are in the prepatriarchal civilization of Old Europe. She maintains that her "favored" analysis of the myth, from a "matriarchal perspective," "accounts for more of the myth's original meaning and is more in tune with the tenor of early Greek belief."[113] What is a "matriarchal perspective" of the myth of Demeter and Persephone? For Carlson, it is one that emphasizes the feminine, its powers of transformation and the positive bond between mother and daughter; acknowledges that the goddess has prevailed, bringing back her daughter and preserving the matriarchal unit; restores the Triple Goddess; and reconnects life and death.

Looking at the myth from the prospective of a Jungian analyst, Carlson is convinced of the following:

> [It] marked and reflected a transition point in the collective unconscious (and possibly literal history as well) that held in tension two opposing accents and perspectives: a "matriarchal accent" that represented the psychological predominance of the transpersonal Feminine in the Old Religion of the Goddess and a "patriarchal accent" that reflected the psychological predominance of the transpersonal Masculine in the religion of the northern (Indo-European) invaders.[124]

As we know, the Indo-European invaders and the transpersonal masculine eventually won out and have dominated for the last 3,000 to 5,000 years. Thus, Carlson offered her book as a "balancing factor vis-à-vis a collective unconsciousness still deeply permeated by the legacy of patriarchal thinking."[125]

Like Keller, Carlson maintains that "the myth is about the triumph of life over death" and reunion with the Mother.[126] Although Carlson's understanding of the myth and Mysteries certainly acknowledges a universal source of love at the center, it does not place quite the same emphasis on it as Keller's interpretation does. The difference is subtle, but it is there. She called the myth and the Mysteries "a revisioning of death." "The destruction of life by its rapist was transformed by a vision of death as reunion with the Mother who could protest stultification effectively and gestate it back into her endless recycling of death into new birth."[127]

> The woman with the torch, Demeter, Persephone, Hecate, the Triple Goddess of old, affords a kindly face to death, brings to its dark embrace a maternal promise: that death is a return to the Origin for man and woman alike, a return

243

> to the Source, both human and divine, a dying into her
> transformative womb, only to sprout again in her holy,
> never-ending cycle. Every one of our deaths on every level
> becomes thus a regression to the Source and even the most
> destructive and traumatic experience becomes her fruit,
> carrying within it her seeds not of eternity, not of unending
> life or fixated death, but of vibrant, perpetual renewal.[128]

Demeter brings her daughter back from the realm of the dead and is reunited with her. But before that occurs, Demeter, like human beings, vacillates between despair and hope. This brings us to the fourth of Carlson's points: The Mysteries were, first and foremost, Demeter's initiation into the transformative power of death, something that, in her grief, she forgot. The Mysteries are Demeter's gift to humanity so that we will never forget the transformative power of death.

> The vacillation is profoundly meaningful and is itself a
> gift from the Goddess. Clearly possessing the power to
> transform life out of death . . . she nevertheless bends low
> to us, takes on the human perspective on death—the grief
> and terror and rage and depression we humans feel when
> faced with what seems like the certain and final end of the
> life that we love. It is as if she goes before us, takes on our
> dumbness and our pain, becomes initiated herself, setting
> forth the model and the pattern that human beings would
> follow for the next fifteen hundred years.[129]

One of the things I like most about Carlson's analysis is that she emphasized that the myth teaches us a way to resist the destructive aspects of patriarchy and even patriarchy itself. Demeter does not sit by silently and allow her daughter to be taken from her. Yes, she grieves and rages, but finally she acts, ultimately taking away from humanity the gift she is most associated with: fertility. "She never buys into the patriarchal perspective, refuses to go on serving the system that has brought this about, and effectively protests and subverts it on both a human and transpersonal level. Never will she reconcile herself or her daughter to such a brutal and unrelational display of power."[130] Carlson reminded us that we all must resist and subvert, with whatever means are available to us, the excesses of the patriarchal system and ultimately reconfigure the system, if we are to survive.

> There is another meaning as well, one that mirrors a historical, psychological reality that is still extreme in its influence and still profoundly relevant to our lives today. For this myth also mirrors the need for the death-dealing forces in patriarchy to be resisted and transformed. . . . It remains for us to this day to recognize and repeat the path that Demeter laid out for us before the Hades forces have swallowed not only the Greeks and ourselves, but the entire planet.[131]

One of the many negative aspects of patriarchy is that it has destroyed feminine wholeness by denigrating an important aspect of women—the crone. Carlson and Keller both pointed out that the myth restores the Triple Goddess to the fore. Discussing the part of the myth in which the goddesses are reunited, Carlson observed that at this point Hecate also reappears and "from then on preceded and followed Persephone."[132]

> The ancient Death goddess, the Crone and her darkness, are restored to their proper place; like winter, which both precedes and follows the seasons of spring and of harvest, the Crone is relinked with the Maiden. The cycle is restored: the Maiden who germinates from the Crone's fertile death grows into the fruitfulness of the Mother and dies back into the Dark One, only to rise from her anew.[133]

A final key point in Carlson's work is that many women "unlike Kore . . . begin their lives in the realm of Hades and must live the myth backward, discovering their connections with the Mother and separating from a more familiar realm dominated by the patriarchal shadow of Hades."[134] When I read that sentence I was thunderstruck! That is exactly how I had lived my life: in the realm of Hades until midlife! It took me until the age of 35 to begin to loosen myself from the grip of Hades. Indeed, reading that sentence and the chapter elaborating on it, "Relational Dynamics—Women Who Live the Myth Backwards," helped me to put my own struggles into perspective. Sometimes I chide myself. It took me many years to realize that the goddess, the transpersonal feminine, was the key ingredient missing from my life. It took "a deep initiatory process, a symbolic death and rebirth" for me to transform into a "Demeterian Kore, a mother-nourished, one-in-herself person . . . able to survive and creatively gestate the on-slaughts of patriarchal shadow from within [and] without."[135] For those still living the myth backward, Carlson's work offers hope, gives courage and makes us realize that most of us are or were in this predicament together. It gives us a mythological, archetypal framework within which to understand our experiences and transform ourselves.

Conclusion

Writing this article has been a great blessing for me. I was able to uncover evidence linking Demeter to Bronze Age Crete, which was very satisfying to the archaeomythologist part of me, and I finally was able to deeply relate to the myth. I believe that these two events are connected. I was able to trace the myth and the Mysteries back to their prepatriarchal origins in order to find out for myself that there is indeed a solid foundation upon which to build the Crete/Eleusis connection. This provided me with a basis from which to understand and tackle Keller's and Carlson's work.

Confirming through my own research the myth's ancient roots was immediately healing. Also healing was Carlson's terminology: "living the myth backwards." Having words to describe that period of my life somehow helped me to feel more compassion for myself. True, I was in the grip of Hades for many years, but with hard work and help, I finally freed myself.

What has been most healing for me is the understanding that came from reading Mara Lynn Keller's works and discovering that the reunion of Demeter and Persephone is a symbol for the all-embracing love that the soul experiences at death. Perhaps that is immediately obvious to others when they read the myth, but it certainly was not to me. The day I finally felt that truth in my heart, as I was re-reading one of Keller's articles, I felt a tremendous feeling of release and of being surrounded by love. It was as though the goddess had given me a sign. It was as though she had said, "Here is a taste, a preview, of what is in store for you."

The goddess also gave me another sign in the form of a dream. In my dream, I am doing a yoga pose called a headstand. Although I have practiced

246

yoga for many years, I still have not mastered the headstand. One yoga teacher said that the headstand is symbolic of change—it turns your world upside down. I have often thought that my difficulty with the pose is that I have not yet learned to flow with change. In the dream, I am doing a headstand and my mother is gently steadying my feet. In other words, with my mother's help, I am integrating change, preparing myself for the ultimate change—death itself. We are doing it together. The dream is a beautiful vision of the reunion with the universal loving source.

It is so perfect that I have finally understood the myth of Demeter and Persephone, for it comes at a time in my life when I struggle to come to terms with my mother's impending death. In our case, it shall be the mother who is taken from the daughter. My newfound understanding of the Eleusinian Mysteries gives me hope that when that time comes, though I may be stood on my head, I can look forward to us both being embraced by and enveloped in a sea of love. With that love to steady me, I will endure.

References

Athenaeus, *Deipnosophists*, xi 52, p763.

Baring, Anne, and Jules Cashford. *The Myth of the Goddess: Evolution of An Image*. London: Arkana, 1991.

Carlson, Kathie. *Life's Daughter, Death's Bride: Inner Transformation Through the Goddess Demeter/Persephone*. Boston: Shambhala, 1997.

Christ, Carol P. *Odyssey with the Goddess*. New York: Continuum, 1995.

Cosmopoulos, Michael B, e-mail message to author, March 6, 2002.

———. "Recherches sur la Stratigraphie Prehistorique D'Eleusis: Travaux 1995." *Echos du Monde Classique/Classical Views* 40 (1996): 17.

Darque, P. "Les Vestiges Mycéniens découverts sous le Télestérion d'Eleusis." *Bulletin de Correspondance Héllenique* 105 (1981): 593–605.

Dickinson, O. T. P. K. "Comments on a Popular Model of Minoan Religion." *Oxford Journal of Archaeology* 13 (1994): 174.

Evasdaughter, Susan. *Crete Reclaimed: A Feminist Exploration of Bronze Age Crete*. Loughborough, UK: Heart of Albion Press, 1996.

Foley, Helene P. , ed. *The Homeric Hymn to Demeter: Translation, Commentary and Interpretive Essays*. Princeton: Princeton University Press, 1994.

Gimbutas, Marija. *The Civilization of the Goddess*. San Francisco: HarperSanFrancisco, 1991.

―――. *Goddesses and Gods of Old Europe*. Berkeley, CA: University of California Press, 1982.

―――. *The Living Goddesses*. Edited and supplemented by Miriam Robbins Dexter. Berkeley, CA: University of California Press, 1999.

Harrison, Jane Ellen. *Prolegomena to the Study of Greek Religion*. 3rd ed. Princeton: Princeton University Press, 1922.

Keller, Mara Lynn. "The Eleusinian Mysteries: Ancient Nature Religion of Demeter and Persephone." In *Reweaving the World: The Emergence of Ecofeminism*. Edited by Irene Diamond and Gloria Feman Orenstein. San Francisco: Sierra Club Books, 1990.

―――. "The Greater Mysteries of Demeter and Persephone" Unpublished manuscript, 2001.

Kerenyi, Carl. *Eleusis: Archetypal Image of Mother and Daughter*. Bollingen Series LXV. Translated by Ralph Manheim. Princeton: Princeton University Press, 1967.

Levi, Doro. "A Magnificent Crater and Rich Pottery from the Crete of 4,000 Years Ago." *Illustrated London News*, October 6, 1956.

Marinatos, Nanno. *Minoan Religion: Ritual, Image and Symbol*. Columbia, SC: University of South Carolina Press, 1993.

Mylonas, George E. *Eleusis and the Eleusinian Mysteries*. Princeton: Princeton University Press, 1961.

Nilssen, Martin R. *Minoan-Mycenaean Religion and its Survival in Greek Religion*. New York: Biblio and Tannen, 1971.

Owens, Gareth Alun. "Evidence for the Minoan Language (1): The Minoan Libation Formula." *Cretan Studies* 5 (1996): 169.

―――. "New Evidence for Minoan Demeter," *Kadmos* 35 (1996): 173.

Persson, Axel W. *The Religion of Greece in Prehistoric Times.* Berkeley: University of California Press, 1942.

Preka-Alexandri, Kalliope. *Eleusis.* 3rd ed. Athens: Ministry of Culture, 2000.

Willetts, R. F. *Cretan Cults and Festivals.* New York: Barnes & Noble, 1962.

Xanthoudides, Stephan. "Cretan Kernoi." *Annual of the British School at Athens*, 12 (1905–06): 9.

Endnotes

1 Kathie Carlson, *Life's Daughter, Death's Bride: Inner Transformation Through the Goddess Demeter/Persephone* (Boston: Shambhala, 1997), 31.

2 Ibid., 37.

3 Mara Lynn Keller, "The Greater Mysteries of Demeter and Persephone" (unpublished manuscript, 2001), xv.

4 Carlson, 40.

5 George E. Mylonas, *Eleusis and the Eleusinian Mysteries* (Princeton: Princeton University Press, 1961), 250.

6 Mara Lynn Keller, "The Eleusinian Mysteries: Ancient Nature Religion of Demeter and Persephone," in *Reweaving the World: The Emergence of Ecofeminism*, eds. I. Diamond and G. Feman Orenstein (San Francisco: Sierra Club Books, 1990), 49.

7 Mylonas, 256.

8 Keller, "The Greater Mysteries of Demeter and Persephone," xiii–xiv.

9 Sophocles, frag. 837, quoted in *The Homeric Hymn to Demeter: Translation, Commentary and Interpretive Essays*. ed. Helene Foley (Princeton: Princeton University Press, 1994), 70.

10 Keller, "The Eleusinian Mysteries of Demeter and Persephone," 28.

11 Marija Gimbutas, *The Civilization of the Goddess* (San Francisco: Harper San Francisco, 1991), viii.

12 Marija Gimbutas, *The Living Goddesses*, ed. M. Robbins Dexter (Berkeley: University of California Press, 1999), 142.

13 Carlson, 19.

14 Helene P. Foley, ed., *The Homeric Hymn to Demeter: Translation, Commentary and Interpretive Essays* (Princeton: Princeton University Press, 1994), 8.

15 Gimbutas, *The Living Goddesses*, 160.

16 Ibid., 144–145.

17 Keller, "The Eleusinian Mysteries of Demeter and Persephone," 44.

18 Carlson, 26.

19 Jane Ellen Harrison, *Prolegomena to the Study of Greek Religion*, 3rd ed. (Princeton, NJ: Princeton University Press, 1922), 272.

20 Ibid., 564.

21 Ibid.

22 Ibid., 565.

23 Ibid.

24 R. F. Willetts, *Cretan Cults and Festivals* (New York: Barnes & Noble, 1962), 20.

25 Ibid., 148.

26 Carl Kerenyi, *Eleusis: Archetypal Image of Mother and Daughter*, trans. R. Manheim, Bollingen Series LXV (Princeton: Princeton University Press, 1967), 24.

27 Ibid., 30.

28 Ibid., 24.

29 Ibid.

30 Axel W. Persson, *The Religion of Greece in Prehistoric Times* (Berkeley, CA: University of California Press, 1942), 149–150.

31 Ibid., 149.

32 Keller, "The Eleusinian Mysteries of Demeter and Persephone," 51.

33 Kerenyi, xix.

34 Doro Levi, "A Magnificent Crater and Rich Pottery from the Crete of 4,000 Years Ago," *Illustrated London News*, October 6, 1956.

35 Ibid.

36 Ibid., xx.

37 Anne Baring and Jules Cashford, *The Myth of the Goddess: Evolution of An Image* (London: Arkana, 1991), 116.

38 Ibid., 116–117.

39 Kerenyi, 21.

40 Gimbutas, *The Living Goddesses*, 151–152.

41 P. Darque, "Les Vestiges Mycéniens découverts sous le Télestérion d'Eleusis," *Bulletin de Correspondance Héllenique* 105 (1981), 593–605, quoted in Kevin Clinton, "The Sanctuary of Demeter and Kore at Eleusis," in *Greek Sanctuaries: New Approaches*, eds. N. Marinatos and R. Hagg (London: Routledge, 1993), 114.

42 Clinton, 114.

43 O. T. P. K. Dickinson, "Comments on a Popular Model of Minoan Religion," *Oxford Journal of Archaeology* 13 (1994): 174.

44 Ibid., 182.

45 Michael B. Cosmopoulos, "Recherches sur la Stratigraphie Prehistorique D'Eleusis: Travaux 1995," *Echos du Monde Classique/Classical Views* 40 (1996): 17.

46 Mylonas, 319.

47 Stephan Xanthoudides, "Cretan Kernoi," *Annual of the British School at Athens*, 12 (1905–06): 9.

48 Kalliope Preka-Alexandri, *Eleusis*, 3rd ed. (Athens: Ministry of Culture, 2000), 20.

49 Mylonas, 221.

50 Ibid., 214.

51 Ibid., 219.

52 Ibid., 257.

53 Ibid., 222.

54 Xanthoudides, 10.

55 Ibid.

56 Ibid., 15.

57 Ibid., 14–15.

58 Ibid., 18.

59 Ibid., 17–18.

60 Ibid., 19.

61 Gareth Alun Owens, "Evidence for the Minoan Language (1): The Minoan Libation Formula," *Cretan Studies* 5 (1996): 169.

62 Xanthoudides, 19.

63 Ibid., 22.

64 Ibid., 23.

65 Athenaeus, *Deipnosophists*, xi 52, 763.

66 Harrison, 159.

67 Martin R. Nilssen, *Minoan-Mycenaean Religion and Its Survival in Greek Religion* (New York: Biblio and Tannen, 1971), 135.

68 Ibid., 137.

69 Ibid., 140.

70 Ibid., 448

71 Ibid., 452–453.

72 Ibid., 470.

73 Ibid.

74 Ibid., 558.

75 Mylonas, 17.

76 Ibid., 18.

77 Ibid.

78 Ibid., 19.

79 Owens, "Evidence for the Minoan Language (1)," 163.

80 Ibid., 168.

81 Gareth Alun Owens, "New Evidence for Minoan Demeter," *Kadmos* 35 (1996), 173.

82 Owens, "Evidence for the Minoan Language (1)," 176.

8. Ibid., 168.

84 Owens, "New Evidence for Minoan Demeter," 174.

85 Ibid., 172.

86 Ibid., 172–173.

87 Ibid., 174.

88 Owens, "Evidence for the Minoan Language (1)," 177.

89 Ibid.

90 Gareth Alun Owens, "New Evidence for Minoan Demeter," 175.

91 Nanno Marinatos, *Minoan Religion: Ritual, Image and Symbol* (Columbia, SC: University of South Carolina Press, 1993), 221.

92 Mylonas, 231.

93 Ibid., 231–232.

94 Gimbutas, *The Living Goddesses*, 157.

95 Marija Gimbutas, *Goddesses and Gods of Old Europe* (Berkeley, CA: University of California Press, 1982), 181.

96 Ibid.

97 Ibid., 183.

98 Ibid., 183–185.

99 Ibid., 184–185.

100 Ibid., 184.

101 Ibid., 183.

102 Susan Evasdaughter, *Crete Reclaimed: A Feminist Exploration of Bronze Age Crete* (Loughborough, UK: Heart of Albion Press, 1996), 143.

103 Ibid., 145.

104 Keller, "The Greater Mysteries of Demeter and Persephone,", 93n.

105 Mylonas, 232.

106 Nilssen, 162.

107 Evasdaughter, 154.

108 Persson, 92.

109 Ibid., 93.

110 Evasdaughter, 152.

111 Baring and Cashford, 121.

112 Ibid., 122.

113 Ibid.

114 Ibid., 120–121.

115 Michael Cosmopoulos, e-mail message to author, March 6, 2002.

116 Keller, "The Eleusinian Mysteries," 48.

117 Keller, "The Greater Mysteries of Demeter and Persephone," x.

118 Cicero, *De Legibus* 2.14.36; Pindar, *Dirges*, frag. 137a, quoted in Helene P. Foley, ed., *The Homeric Hymn to Demeter: Translation, Commentary and Interpretive Essays* (Princeton Princeton University Press, 1994), 70–71.

119 Carol P. Christ, *Odyssey with the Goddess* (New York: Continuum, 1995), 22–23.

120 Keller, "The Greater Mysteries of Demeter and Persephone," ii.

121 Ibid.

122 Ibid., x.

123 Carlson, 14.

124 Ibid., 10.

125 Ibid., 16.

126 Ibid., 3.

127 Ibid., 221.

128 Ibid., 223.

129 Ibid., 32.

130 Ibid., 24.

131 Ibid., 32.

132 Ibid., 37.

133 Ibid.

134 Ibid., 16.

135 Ibid., 161.

THE THREE FACES OF PERSEPHONE: CUP, DEMOTED SPROUTLING AND DISEMBODIED PSYCHOSIS

Alexis Martin Faaberg

The Persephone Puzzle: An Analysis of the Phaistos Cup

The Western understanding of the goddess Persephone evolved from a representation of life-affirming womanhood in the Neolithic era to a rapeable maid in the Late Greek period. The aged myth of the female community and female agency is part of the West's cultural literacy. Persephone, and the women who worship her are understood through the symbols attributed to her. A large, shallow cup, discovered under the stairs at the Minoan palace of Phaistos and dated from 1,900 BCE, contains the first known images of the myth.[1] In addition to the cup, there is Homer's Hymn to Demeter, which has dominated our Western psyche since time was broken into seasons. His interpretation of the myth showcases the great shift from matriarchal sisterhood to married maid. Lastly, modern psychologists are reinterpreting the myth to showcase how woman can embody the Persephone archetype.

Archaeomythology, developed by archaeologist Marija Gimbutas, is a methodology for deconstructing historical objects by the admission and correlation of multiple disciplines, focusing on interpreting painted and other symbols and the evolution of the imagery by using literature, archaeology and mythology. Gimbutas believed that it was not possible to ascertain the meaning of symbols simply by examining an artifact itself, and through her exploration of context a new methodology was born that combined archaeology, mythology, ethnology, folklore, historical linguistics, comparative relation and previous historical research.[2] This multidisciplinary approach has enabled scholars to renew their explorations of ancient texts and art.

I have added a second layer to this approach by incorporating my viewpoint as a women's spirituality scholar. Women's spirituality is the lens by which women *experience* religion. Most often, these experiences are rooted in the daily rituals in which family relationships, maternal bonds, food, dance and song coalesce into a spiritual life. The impetus of my research is to bring women's place in history to the center of the conversation. By incorporating the idea that women's bodies are as inherently divine and powerful as are traditional male deities, we can begin to see our origin story in a more balanced, albeit complicated, chronicle of the human experience. Our goddesses and heroines have spent too long as ornaments to male domination.

Ancient Crete is the historical birthplace of the goddess Persephone. At the time of the Phaistos Cup's construction, there were a multitude of images featuring men and women. The most well-known images are the frescoes of Knossos and beautiful Kamares pottery from the same time period. They often featured women in ritualistic dance or as objects of praise in relationship to some form of agriculture. The image below is of the inner bowl area of the Phaistos Cup. This is the image that the drinker would see when the beverage had been drunk or poured out of the cup.[3,4]

Phiastos Cup, by Sid Reger

My interest in Persephone began when I first saw the above image. I was moved by the simplicity and beauty of the image and felt called to it in a way that I had not experienced before with Grecian artwork. I was struck by how few descriptions of the goddess matched the female figure in the cup. In the fall of 2012, I traveled to Crete with prominent women's spirituality scholar Carol P. Christ to immerse myself in Persephone's universe.[5] I visited three of the main ritual palaces on Crete and was privileged to see the workshop in Phaistos Palace, where the cup was discovered and likely was created. The palace abounded with images of spirals, flowers, labrys and celebration. Based on my own observations and research, it is clear that the original personification of the goddess Persephone is a woman who has been hidden from us.

Dynamics of the Myth

Myths are stories that contain the creation stories of deities but also speak about important ethics and social priorities of cultures. By dissecting myths, researchers can understand what was valued by that culture at the time the myth was created or changed. A great place to start is with the etymology of names. Persephone is known by the name "Kore, which means 'maiden,' which is also the feminine form of koros, meaning 'sprout.'"[6] Persephone, rather than a name, is a title for her as queen of the underworld.[7] In the 7th century, Persephone was linked with her mother, Demeter, and together they form the complete agriculture calendar.

An upcoming leader in the field of archaeomythology, Adrian Poruciuc traced the linguistic meaning of Demeter's name. He stated that *Da* is an old name for earth and that *Daeira* is an ancient name for a Persephone-type of goddess.[8] The etymology of their names clearly emphasizes that each goddess should be viewed as a separate being. Names are vital in understanding identities. Poruciuc explained that "Pythagoras was said to have viewed 'men's wives' as bearers of divine names," showing that each woman was a virgin (Persephone), a bride and a mother (Demeter), making her the property of a man at each stage.[9] In this way mortal men were able to see their ownership of women as approved by the male gods that they were emulating. It is interesting to note that the virgin and death aspects were conjoined outside the realm of the mother. It is likely that this is due to virginity and death being unassailable stages for the sexual

258

desires of men, whereas a mother, by the example of her offspring, has proven herself as accepting a male presence via cocreation. The later patriarchally constructed Persephone is not only a derivative of the great goddess but also represents male fear of the uncontainable female. She is both an alluring goddess and a monster.[10] This makes her a prize for the male who conquers her.

Feminist mythologists Anne Baring and Jules Cashford stated that Persephone and Demeter are linked by lineage and that their characteristics showcase one great goddess split into two aspects of the same realm: "The one goddess is divided into the two aspects of above and below, living and dead; though since these generally opposed states of being are imagined as mother and daughter, they are here not polarized, but joined at the root."[11] This description explains the cooperative relationship.

Neolithic Persephone: Interpreting Art

The Phaistos Cup is one of the earliest representations of a female goddess figure believed to be the goddess Persephone. The cup is circular in shape and has 105 round circles surrounding the center image. Inside the cup are three female figures with four curled lines swooping back from the forehead and a lily in full bloom. The body of the central figure has a smooth cone shape with half circles. There are no feet or another appendages visible. Excavators described this central goddess figure on the cup as the "goddess of lilies.[12] There are two floating female figures in the image, one on either side of the central goddess figure. They have the same plumage as does the central figure, but each of them possesses a bee-like body, splayed fingers, small feet, a diamond-shaped chest, one arm pointing up and one arm pointing down. The lower halves of their bodies are filled with full, round circles. The background of the cup is littered with white specks that resemble oblong seeds. These images all relate to the core elements of the identification and worship of the goddess Persephone.

Marija Gimbutas referred to the two floating female figures as "Lady Birds" and said that they are anthropomorphic images representing the goddess.[13] As "Lady Birds" these female figures possessed the powers of flight, and their bee-shaped bodies are indicative of the industriousness of the bee. The snake-like plumage sprouting from their heads alludes to their regenerative powers. However, these women are still secondary to the primary and larger central goddess figure. It is possible that these women represent the Minoan priestesses who would have been in charge of communicating with Persephone to ensure plentiful harvests, the nourishment of the dead and the fertility of women. Gimbutas stated that the "Lady Bird" goddess likely was created during the pre-Indo-European period and that her image continued into the Greek period as Athena, evidence of further fragmentation.[14] The separation of the female figures from the symbols of vegetation portrayed in the cup show the further fragmentation of the great goddess into multiple smaller forms after the advent of patriarchy. Archaeologist Ann Suter, whose work is centered on the male saturated era of Classical Greece, sees these women as dangerous. Suter described the floating figures as possible "spirits or demons" and explained that her assumption was based on Persephone's later association, in the Homeric *Hymn to Demeter*, with the underworld.[15]

Conversely, Suter discussed the *Homeric Hymn to Demeter*'s focus on Persephone as powerless:

[Hades] snatched the unwilling maid into his golden chariot

and led her off lamenting. She screamed with a shrill voice,

calling on her father, the son of Kronos highest and best.

Not one of the immortals or of humankind

heard her voice, nor the olives bright with fruit,

except the daughter of Persaios; tender of heart

she heard it from her cave, Hekate of the delicate veil.[16]

Gaia has betrayed the female community by siding with Zeus. Without a net of womanly protection, Persephone is powerless to defend herself. Her abduction makes her property of Hades and, therefore, her realms are now in his possession. Hekate is the only one who can hear her, because as a virgin goddess Persephone's strongest connection is to the earth and women—she is not a man's possession. Homer alluded to this when he stated that she was kept "tender of heart."[17]

Archaeologist Diane Bolger stated that "religious rituals were used to legitimate the social hierarchy and figurines were symbols manipulated for particular purposes," meaning that the images on the Phaistos Cup can be read to extrapolate the role of women or goddess in society.[18] The imagery of the cup showcases a singular goddess with attendant priestesses. Therefore, it is important to question the addition of Demeter to Persephone's storyline. Demeter's presence serves to civilize Persephone. In Greek mythology, Demeter corrals her daughter's gifts by partitioning her to one season—spring. Persephone also is monitored at each turn of the wheel. In the myth, Demeter observes Persephone in the spring and summer and Hades controls her in the dark season.

Currently, humanity views creation of life as a dualistic act that requires both a male and female; however, in the myth two women create life. Thus, the Phaistos cup is an example of parthenogenesis. The design and functional uses of the cup are essential to understanding the religious significance of the imagery. The design is a womb shape and can be likened to a human female's womb, which both fills and empties. The round body of the cup can be viewed as a container for life and a representation of fertility. The choice of the artistry on the cup heightens this understanding. By jutting from the exterior, the central goddess figure assumes a phallic position in the artist's design. The white half circles surrounding the phallic image resemble seeds or flecks of semen. In this way, the cup can be seen as a vessel for life.

The myth of Demeter and Persephone may be called the greatest female love story of all time. The devotion that this mother and daughter show one another is unparalleled. I believe that the focus on the mother/daughter relationship is exaggerated and that it is the community of women that is central to the myth. In the Phaistos Cup and other early depictions of Persephone, her "Lady Birds" or other female companions surround her. In the *Homeric Hymn to Demeter*, the daughters of Ocean surround Persephone, and other goddesses and a mortal woman's female household help Demeter by consoling her and looking for her daughter. It is only the popular and overly simplistic myth that is taught to children in one-dimensional language that dissolves the original web. The question that scholars should be asking is why is this redacted travesty being perpetuated?

The love between Demeter and Persephone is a microcosm of this greater pool of supportive female community. Helene P. Foley, a classical scholar and expert on the myth, described their relationship as a romance.[19] Foley's research focuses on the Homeric hymn and the sociopolitical climate of classical Greece. Her book about the *Homeric Hymn to Demeter* showcases the need, at the time, to package the world into ordered spaces all under the control of men. Siblings Hades and Zeus ruled the supernatural realms and male mortals ruled the earth. Interestingly, Foley used the text of the *Homeric Hymn to Demeter* to subvert this patriarchal way of thinking by focusing on the intelligent agency of the female characters, the constellation of women who bond together over the love of their children. Within this view, the Homeric Hymn to Demeter can be seen as a treatise on the magnificence of motherhood. Foley wrote, "the structure of the Hymn suggests strongly that the rites originate above all from the divine relation between mother and daughter, and it is presumably the bliss encountered in Demeter's and Persephone's reunion that the mystery initiates shared at climactic moments of the rite."[20] In the context of the *Homeric Hymn to Demeter*, this moment is celebrated in front of a variety of other goddesses. Hera, Demeter's mother, is present, and it is through her that a deal is negotiated with Zeus that will solidify their maternal bond and share their skills and way of being with the mortal world. The witnessing of the event is a moralizing reminder that nurturing relationships are the cornerstone of a healthy society.

Rape and Male Inheritance

In the *Homeric Hymn to Demeter*, Homer described Persephone as "slim ankled."[21] This description matches the images of the two female figures surrounding the central goddess figure on the Phaistos Cup. This is the one of the many breaks with the artistic historical representation of Persephone. It is assumed that these women are dressed to re-enact the deeds of the goddess and provide an example to their mortal followers. The word *delicate* alludes to a fragile state, making the reader believe that Persephone requires protection from either her mother or Hades, her part-time husband.

The Getty Villa, in Los Angeles, California, recently showcased an exhibit titled *The Sanctuaries of Demeter and Persephone at Morgantina*, which contained pieces from the Neolithic to Classical Greece.[22] In this arena, it was easy to discern the diametrically different imaginings of the myth. The later works are predominately two-dimensional, and the detailed artwork appears to be reserved for Hades. Below is a mass-produced bust of Persephone with the *polos* (divine crown) upon her head. The figure is not smiling, and she is a single bust. The image lacks the constellation of supportive women, which is present in both the Phaistos Cup and the *Homeric Hymn to Demeter.*[23]

Spring Fresco from complex D at Akrotiri, Thera, 16th century BCE, National Archaeological Museum of Athens, Greece

The Symbols of the Myth

Erich Neumann described symbols as what "sets consciousness in motion" and considered them "energy transformers" because of their power to recall the mind into a web of knowledge otherwise hidden from the individual.[24] The symbols of the Persephone myth have remained, but the ideas behind them have not hung in stasis. The main symbols of the myth are soil, womb, seeds, fertility, spring and time. Each is an aspect of Persephone as a rebirthing goddess. These symbols represent a story centered on the transfer of life between women.

Soil

Soil is the deathbed of the deceased and the birthing room of infants. The Phaistos Cup valorizes earth, utilizing a mound of soil as both a throne space and the body of the goddess. This imagery links Persephone to her chthonian attributes. Homer also legitimized the importance of soil in describing the identifying factors of Persephone in his *Hymn to Demeter*:

She played with the deep-breasted daughters of Ocean,

plucking flowers in the lush meadow. . .

which Earth grew as a snare for the flower-faced maiden

in order to gratify by Zeus's design the Host-to-Many,

a flower wondrous and bright, awesome for all to see,

. . .

The girl marveled and stretched out both hands at once

to take the lovely toy. The earth with its wide ways yawned.[25]

This passage is full of symbols that also exist on the Phaistos Cup. First, the daughters of Ocean assist Persephone; in the cup, the central goddess figure is surrounded by two female figures. Second, flowers are abundant in Homer's account of Persephone; there is a large flower next to the central goddess figure in the cup. Third, the narcissus flower is described as having in a similar fashion as "Lady Birds." Fourth, the two assistant women pictured in the cup are floating in the sky area and perhaps spreading the fragrance of the flowers. This shows that earth, sea and sky are each involved in some way with the scene of Persephone, making this act a part of a relational existence in which she is at the center. Thus, the similarity of the imagery of the cup and the description within the Homeric *Hymn to Demeter* make clear that the goddess shown in the cup is Persephone.

Time

The images on the cup are a snapshot in time, idolizing the moment of spring. The earth is bursting forth with life, and women are dancing with joy at the earth's regeneration. The full circles surrounding the rim of the cup are symbolic of the sun, which provides light and sustenance for the earth. Lawyer-turned-mythologist Craig Barnes, in his book *In Search of the Lost Feminine*, stated that the Minoans understood time to be circular rather than linear.[26] Within a circular understanding of time, everything is connected: birth, death and regeneration.

Barnes referenced another piece of Minoan artwork, the *Spring Fresco*, to frame his argument. In this painting, there are "central mysterious shapes rising out of the ground [and] several of them look uncannily like the bodies of women."[27] In the *Spring Fresco*, there are three life stages: a tight bud, a lily in full bloom and a wilting lily. The lily on the cup has four stamens, representing the four seasons. The representation in the *Spring Fresco* of the entire life cycle of a flower indicates that the Minoans understood time to be cyclical. The Phaistos Cup shows only one aspect of the life cycle, meaning that the focus of the artist was on representing the spring season; however, within the context of the culture, the viewer understands that the other life stages are present as well. Barnes stated that circular time was how Minoans unified their experiences as "limitless and timeless" and had a "boundless identification with the cycles of life and death."[28] Barnes stated that this goddess was described not by her attributes or realms but as an extension of other beings. In this way, he reiterated that she is part of a continuous world where everything is connected and ever-changing.[29] She exists within a liminal space where time is cyclical—both the heralded advent of spring and the nurturing of the dead.

Seeds

Feminist artist Winifred Milius Lubell wrote that the pomegranate seed was a symbol of sisterhood for Greek women: "Women's ritualized eating of pomegranate seeds may have been . . . a gesture symbolic of sisterhood with Persephone . . . and it may be that the succulent fruit was allowed to drip onto the earth instead of, or alongside of, the magic 'moon blood.'"[30] The giving of women's own menstrual blood may have been a way for women to participate in passing their own fertility to the earth. Consequently, the seeds present in both the *Phaistos Cup* and the Homeric *Hymn to Demeter*, represent a way for women to continue to bring life and regeneration to their bodies and the soil.[31]

The small, white, oblong shapes scattered throughout the image on the cup can be seen as seeds, which possess the possibility of life. Within the understanding that the Phaistos Cup represents a womb, the seed would be nourished by both Persephone and her "Lady Birds." The cup is a representation of a ritual celebration in which the seeds of the season's harvest are celebrated for their realized potential and can be seen as the dead plants being reborn to life and, by extension, human life as well. Thus, the seed imagery represented on the Phaistos Cup also alludes to the ability of the culture's ancestors to continue to exist with the living—ancestor reverence. Gimbutas stated that Persephone is "the spirit of the grain," that she "dies and is born again. Seeds were ritualized as a symbol of the divine. Seeds from harvest time were kept in underground pits so that they could be fertilized by contact with the dead."[32] Gimbutas further explained that the Cretan temple places functioned as holy places of regeneration, focusing on the transition from death to life and back again. She stated that the populace "joyously celebrated birth and the flowering of life. Furthermore, the presence of the goddess radiated the west to east" and, consequently, the central goddess figure in the cup is facing east, toward the open lily.[33] This positioning may allude to the combined celebration of sprouting plant life and the regeneration of the spirits of the dead. The eastern direction is symbolic, because Neolithic sites were often situated toward the east to accept the powers of the sun.

Sexuality

The Phaistos Cup shows its viewers that fertility is an entirely female power. The imagery is artistic in its presentation of sexuality, portraying the fertilization of the earth with seeds belonging to the realm of woman. Iambe, the ribald goddess who awakens Demeter from her grief so that she can rescue her abducted daughter, continues this sexual imagery in the *Homeric Hymn to Demeter*:

[Demeter] Sat wasting with desire for her deep-girt daughter,

until knowing Iambe jested with her and

mocking with many a joke moved the holy goddess

to smile and laugh and keep a gracious heart—

Iambe, jested with her and mocking with many a joke moved
the holy goddess

to smile and laugh, and keep a gracious heart[34]

Iambe does not physically show her sexual organs, but her sexuality is inherent. She is in control of her sexuality and how her sexuality will affect the world around her. In *Sacred Display: Divine and Magical Female Figures of Eurasia*, Miriam Robbins Dexter and Victor H. Mair referenced George Devereux, who believed that Iambe's role is to remind Demeter that she can reproduce again, making the loss of Persephone unimportant because she is replaceable.[35] Robbins Dexter and Mair discounted this theory as being based on outdated psychoanalytical theory; however, Devereux's argument does point to the inherent issue of birth and regeneration around which the myth of Persephone and the imagery of the Phaistos Cup are centered. For example, men were excluded from the annual, three-day ritual of Thesmophoria in which women gathered together to eat sacred pomegranates and make ribald jokes.[36] This short respite was a rare treat for the women of Athens. They lived in a phallocracy and were ruled in total by the men in their lives. Women were valued only for what their bodies could provide men—sex and children. The scene with Iambe humanizes the abduction, but more importantly it is the only point in the *Homeric Hymn to Demeter* that female sexuality is appreciated and is shown as a unifying experience for women. In the poem, female sexuality is not sexualized in the pornographic way we visualize sex and gender today but rather by the greatest joy being seen as a reunion between mother and daughter rather than sexual satisfaction.

The rape of Persephone shows the audience that Hades and Zeus, by planning and executing the rape, deny Persephone her full self by minimizing her existence to her sexual union with Hades. Marriage becomes her defining identity. After her abduction, Persephone is split between being identified with Demeter and being identified with Hades, but she is no longer identified with herself. Her abduction is a stark example of what was lost from Neolithic Crete to Classical Greece. And by looking beyond Persephone as an individual, we see that women themselves have been denied their rights as whole citizens of their communities. Art historian Eva C. Keuls wonderfully articulated this in *The Reign of the Phallus: Sexual Politics in Ancient Athens*. She stated that in Athens, near the myth's ritual pilgrimage site Eleusis, "the female was indoctrinated by means of cultic ritual. Whether necessary or not, this 'moral' upbringing was confined in art and stern social rules, most particularly child marriage." Keul quoted prominent thinkers of the time, including the philosopher Democritus, who left us this pearl of wisdom: "He who teaches letters to his wife is ill-advised: He's giving additional poison to a horrible snake.'"[37] What is interesting about this misogynistic advice is that it references two powerful symbols: education and the snake. The latter is a commonly known symbol for transformation and prepatriarchal female deities. It is therefore likely that Democritus's advice is meant to stunt a female's growth so as to prevent her from maturing to her ancestors' level of power. Persephone would have received all of her education from her sole active parent—her mother. Mortal societal structure mirrored that of divine families by removing girls from their mother's care and teaching them through marriage. Admittedly, this approach could not be fully realized because of the high regard for the goddesses and that their role was now to educate humanity about how to maintain their crops.

In addition to child marriages, the *Homeric Hymn to Demeter* normalizes other gender-constrictive behaviors. One of the most interesting is upper-class men's habit of locking up their wives in the *gynaeceum* (female quarters). One such aristocrat named Iscomachus said he had to lock up his wife to protect himself against theft by being cuckolded.[38] Men had to control the wombs of their wives and daughters to ensure that their lines were protected. Women, including goddesses, had become property. Persephone is the daughter of Zeus through his adulterous relationship with her mother. Zeus could legally give his daughter, his property, to his brother Hades. In this light, the rape of Persephone is seen as a contract between two wealthy men. Keul accurately pointed out that this is apparent in the iconography of the time, in which wives were usually pictured alone and behind closed doors, signifying their status as property. Persephone is locked away in Hades and completely shut off from everyone's view, including that of her mother.

Keul identified how the rape of Persephone acutely epitomizes the experience of the sacrificial bride. Much like the experiences of wives portrayed in Athenian art, the proceedings of rituals at Eleusis primarily occurred indoors, further showcasing the need to hide the mothers or, more accurately, the female property, from public access. Keul stated that the sovereignty of Demeter's and Persephone's knowledge was finally stripped from them in the 7th century BC, when the final defeminization act occurred by the introduction of Iakchos/Triptolemos, who would be the sole male heir to the realm of Demeter and Persephone.[39] This new male god, intended be the messenger of his mothers, was placed as the focal point of the ritual; however, his worship was never truly accepted by the people, and the goddesses continued to hold sway over their flock.

Down into the Psyche of the Persephones

Our modern interpretation of Persephone is to make her experience that of the "everywoman." Her descent into the underworld and her desire to reconnect with her mother are considered, by some psychologists, to be the common experience of every Western woman. Is this interpretation helpful? My concern is that this is a further dilution of the great goddess who we met originally in the Phaistos Cup.

Great Goddess

Erich Neumann was one of the first to analyze the great goddess archetype and try to understand its effect on the modern female psyche. He stated, "The term Great Mother, as a partial aspect of the Archetypal Feminine, is a late abstraction, presupposing a highly developed speculative consciousness. And indeed, it is only relatively late in the history of mankind that we find the Archetypal Feminine designated as Magna Mater."[40] Unlike women's spirituality scholars, Neumann believed that Great Mother is a subset of the overall feminine experience or archetype. Although I respect Neumann's perspective, I disagree. I subscribe to the women's spirituality belief that the mother as the rebirther of all life is the epitome of the feminine, because all life stems from her. Neumann asserted that all people have access to the great goddess archetype through their collective unconsciousness but that man's concern is focused on the womb. He wrote, "At the beginning stands the primeval goddess, resting in the materiality of her elemental character, knowing nothing but the secret of her womb," meaning that it is procreation and the continuance of the male line that is of primary interest to the male being.[41]

There is a connection between the modern understanding of the myth, by scholars like Neumann, and the perpetuation of modern rape culture. In "The Woman's Experience of Herself and the Eleusinian Mysteries," when he wrote about the reunion of the goddesses, Neumann discussed the incursion of the female womb space:

> Psychologically, this "finding again" signifies the annulment of the male rape and incursion, the restoration after marriage of the matriarchal unity of mother and daughter. In other words, the nuclear situation of the matriarchal group, the primordial relation of daughter to mother, which has been endangered by the incursion of the male into the female world, is renewed and secured in the mystery.[42]

Essentially, Neumann stated that Persephone is introduced to sexuality through the rape and even alluded to her being "fascinated" by the experience. He also described the sexual violence as not having a lasting effect, because when she is returned to her matriarchal group she is "renewed and secured." Neumann, like the classical Greek men, seems focused on controlling or violating the female body.

Neumann took his argument even further and described the rape as beneficial for Persephone. He wrote that Persephone willingly gave herself in sacrifice to the experience. He described the abduction as a *heruesis* (process of discovery): "Only then has the Feminine undergone a central transformation . . . as by achieving union on a higher plane with the spiritual aspect of the Feminine, the Sophia aspect of the Great Mother."[43] Unless I am mistaken, it seems that Neumann is suggesting that by surviving the experience Persephone has gained some sort of essential wisdom needed to become a goddess. Women, mortal or immortal, should not have foundation myths that profess the need for violent sexual experience to attain a higher plane of consciousness.

A feminist re-examination of the myth focuses on the women's community. Some psychologists have suggested that an unbreakable bond between mother and daughter is unhealthy. They may suggest that forced separation is necessary for each to live an independent life. I concede that this may be partly true, because through her forced marriage Persephone is given a social status in the underworld that is anomalous to that in the ancient world.[44] Foley discussed this possibility at length, saying that by becoming independent both women reach a "mature dependence."[45]

270

Feminist psychologists have taken the reins from Neumann and have attempted to reclaim the myth as a way to help foster healthy mother/ daughter relationships in their practices. The most prolific of these is Kathie Carlson, who wrote a fascinating exposé on the myth, from a female psychological perspective, titled *Life's Daughter/Death's Bride: Inner Transformations through the Goddess Demeter/Persephone*.[46] Readers can see from the book's title that she has become part of the dialogue by equalizing the goddesses, making them interchangeable. The matristric cultural bonds, according to Carlson, are the heart of the myth:

> *The feminine bond is primary while the presences of the Masculine is peripheral or effaced. Matriarchal bonding between women . . . is characterized by an intensification and emphasis on the feminine connection between client and therapist and the relegation of the Masculine as an actual man (the impact of the father, husband, lover) or animus to the periphery.*[47]

Carlson was suggesting not that men are regulated to the margins of such a society but rather that the maternal bond is at the center. Within this new viewing, we see that Rhea defies her husband in order to protect her daughters' happiness and that mortal mother Metaneira defies a goddess to keep her child close. The scads of other women in the story—Iambe, Hekate and the four daughters of Metaneira—also share the same devotion to helping mothers; each acts as nursemaid to Persephone or Demeter, working to re-establish the rule of the mother.

In her practice, Carlson seeks to reunite mothers and daughters. She believes that the separation between mother and daughter, as shown in the myth, has become an archetype by which modern women navigate their female relationships:

> Women who have spent their lives in the underworld of Hades have no memory of being mothered; they may long for a mother but, at least in the beginning of therapy, are identified with their estrangement and attack themselves for wanting or needing care. They are separated not only from a mothering source-ground, but from the daughter who longs for its nurturance. The child is lost or, more

potently, hated and suppressed by the woman herself who
turns a cold Hades eye on her own need for nurturance.

In essence, Carlson sees the suffering of mother and daughter in the myth
as the same path traveled by her clients. Her female clients agonize about
wanting a mothering presence but at the same time wanting to be independent. Then, in an abusive cycle, the child becomes the cold mother
who she ran from in the first place. I can relate to the experiences of
Carlson's patients.

Conclusion

The symbols that were painted on the Phaistos cup in 1,900 BCE have
remained in the mythology of Persephone, ruler of the vegetation and
the underworld, but the meaning attributed to each object has changed.
Originally, the womb, seed, woman and underworld were all seen as parts
of one continuous cycle of nourishment. The advent of a male-dominator
model separated the aspects of the great goddess and put each attribute
under the ownership of men or minimized the goddess's powers. This
change reverberated throughout the ancient world, changing the realms of
women to be the property of men. This changed how time, food, women and
property were perceived, lessening respect for the natural world and giving
preference to dominance. However, the latent powers of Persephone remain,
giving women a glance into a world where they are free of subjugation.

By reviewing the evidence through an archaeomythogical lens, we
have been able to touch upon the abject symbolic annihilation of the great
goddesses Persephone and Demeter and on the forced dissolution of the
strong female community. I cannot help but ponder what Western society
would look like if we still held the Neolithic values of Persephone. Would
psychologists still imagine that women are broken from the start? Would
women still have trouble finding fulfilling female friendships? What would
the modern mother/daughter dyads look like? Unfortunately, we do not
know the answers to these questions. We need to reclaim this myth and
discover the answers to these questions in the upcoming generations of
women. May Persephone be with us on this journey and nurture us as we
sprout our new herstories.

_____

References

Baring, Ann, and Jules Cashford. *The Myth of the Goddess: Evolution of an Image*. London: Arkana/Penguin Books, 1991.

Barnes, Craig. *In Search of the Lost Feminine: Decoding the Myths That Radically Reshaped Civilization*. Golden, CO: Fulcrum Publishing, 2006.

Carlson, Kathie. *Life's Daughter/Death's Bride: Inner Transformations Through the Goddess Demeter/Persephone*, Boston: Shambhala, 1997.

Connelly, Jennifer. *Portrait of a Priestess: Women and Ritual in Ancient Greece*. Princeton: Princeton University Press, 2007.

Dean-Jones, Lesley, Edited by Elaine Fantham et al., "Medicine: The 'Proof' of Anatomy." In *Women in the Classical World*. Edited by Elaine Fantham, Helene Peet foley, Natalie Boymel Kampen, Sarah B. Pomeroy and H. A. Shapiro. New York: Oxford University Press, 1994.

Evasdaughter, Susan. *Crete Reclaimed: A Feminist Exploration of Bronze Age Crete*. Loughborough, UK: Heart of Albion Press, 1996.

Faraone, C. A. "The Rise of the Demon Womb in Greco-Roman Antiquity." In *Finding Persephone: Women's Rituals in the Ancient Mediterranean. Edited by M. Parca and A. Tzanctou*. Bloomington, IN: Indiana University Press, 2007.

Foley, Helene P. *The Homeric Hymn to Demeter: Translation, Commentary, and Interpretive Essays*, Princeton: Princeton University Press, 1994.

Getty Villa. *The Sanctuaries of Demeter and Persephone at Morgantina*. Personal viewing , January 2012. www.getty.edu/art/exhibitions/morgantina/.

_____. *The Goddesses and Gods of Old Europe: Myths and Cult Images*. Berkeley: University of California Press, 1982.

Gimbutas, Marija. *The Language of the Goddess*. San Francisco: HarperCollins, 1989.

_____. *The Living Goddesses*. Berkeley: University of California Press, 1999.

Keuls, Eva C. *Reign of the Phallus: Sexual Politics in Ancient Athens*. Berkeley: University of California Press, 1993.

Lubell, W. M. *The Metamorphosis of Baubo: Myths of Women's Sexuality*. Nashville, TN: Vanderbilt University Press, 1994.

Marler, Joan. "Introduction to Archaeomythology," *ReVision : A Journal of Consciousness and Transformation* 23, no. 1 (Summer 2000)

Nelson, S. M. *Gender in Archaeology: Analyzing Power and Prestige*. 2nd ed. Lanham, MD: AltaMira Press, 2004.

Neumann, Erich. *The Great Mother: An Analysis of the Archetype*. Princeton: Princeton University Press, 1972.

_____. "The Woman's Experience of Herself and the Eleusinian Mysteries." In *The Long Journey Home: Re-visioning the Myth of Demeter and Persephone for Our Time*. Edited by Christine Downing. Boston: Shambhala, 1994.

Poruciuc, Adrian. "Demeter as 'Earth Mother' and Dionysos as "Earth's Bridegroom." In *Prehistoric Roots of Romanian and Southeast European Traditions. Edited by Joan Marler and Miriam Robbins Dexter.* Santa Rosa, CA: Institute of Archaeomythology, 2010.

Robbins Dexter, Miriam, and V. H. Mair *Sacred Display: Divine and Magical Female Figures of Eurasia*. Amherst, NY: Cambria Press, 2010.

Sacred-Texts.com. *Homeric Hymn to Demeter.* Retrieved April 15, 2012, from Sacred-Texts.com: www.sacred-texts.com/cla/demeter.htm.

Spretnak, Charlene. "Demeter and Persephone." In *Lost Goddesses of Early Greece: A Collection of Pre-Hellenic Myths*. (Boston: Beacon Press, 1992).

Stein, Charles. *Persephone Unveiled: Seeing the Goddess & Freeing Your Soul*. Berkeley: North Atlantic Books, 2006.

Suter, Ann. "Outside the Hymn: The Archaeological and Historical Evidence." In *The Narcissus and the Pomegranate: The Archaeology of the Homeric Hymn to Demeter*. Ann Arbor, MI: University of Michigan Press, 2002.

Endnotes

1 Ann Suter, "Outside the Hymn: The Archaeological and Historical Evidence," in *The Narcissus and the Pomegranate: The Archaeology of the Homeric Hymn to Demeter* Ann Arbor, MI: University of Michigan Press, 2002), 174.

2 Joan Marler, "Introduction to Archaeomythology," *ReVision: A Journal of Consciousness and Transformation* 23, no. 1 (Summer 2000), 3.

3 This is an artistic representation of the Phaistos Cup. Unfortunately, the actual cup is not available to the public at this time due to austerity measures.

4 Early Women Masters "Homeric Hymn to Demeter Interlinear Translation," www.earlywomenmasters.net/demeter/myth_015.html.

5 Carol P. Christ leads the Goddess Pilgrimage to Crete.

6 Anne Baring and Jules Cashford, *The Myth of the Goddess: Evolution of an Image* (London: Arkana/Penguin Books, 1991), 368.

7 Throughout this article, I refer to Kore Persephone as Persephone.

8 Adrian Poruciuc, "Demeter as 'Earth Mother' and Dionysos as 'Earth's Bridegroom'," in *Prehistoric Roots of Romanian and Southeast European Traditions* eds. Joan Marler and Miriam Robbins Dexter. (Santa Rosa, CA: Institute of Archaeomythology, 2010), 51.

9 Poruciuc, 54.

10 Miriam Robbins Dexter, and V. H. Mair *Sacred Display: Divine and Magical Female Figures of Eurasia* (Amherst, NY: Cambria Press, 2010), 75.

11 Ibid, 369.

12 Suter, 176.

13 Marija Gimbutas, *The Goddesses and Gods of Old Europe: Myths and Cult Images*. (Berkeley: University of California Press, 1982), 145–146.

14 Ibid 147–150.

15 Suter, 18.

16 Helene P. Foley, *The Homeric Hymn to Demeter: Translation, Commentary, and Interpretive Essays* (Princeton: Princeton University Press, 1994), 2, lines 19–24.

17 Foley, 2, line 24.

18 S. Nelson, *Gender in Archaeology: Analyzing Power and Prestige,* 2nd ed. (Lanham, MD: AltaMira Press, 2004), 133.

19 Foley, 118.

20 Foley, 2, line 2.

21 Ibid

22 Getty Villa, *The Sanctuaries of Demeter and Persephone at Morgantina,* Personal viewing, January 2012 www.getty.edu/art/exhibitions/morgantina/.

23 Villa, www.getty.edu/art/exhibitions/morgantina/.

24 Erich Neumann, *The Great Mother: An Analysis of the Archetype,* (Princeton: Princeton University Press, 1972), 8.

25 Foley, lines 5–16.

26 Craig Barnes, *In Search of the Lost Feminine: Decoding the Myths That Radically Reshaped Civilization* (Golden, CO: Fulcrum Publishing, 2006), 40.

27 Barnes, 33.

28 Barnes, 40.

29 Ibid., lines 40–41.

30 Winifred Milius Lubell, *The Metamorphosis of Baubo: Myths of Women's Sexuality* (Nashville, TN: Vanderbilt University Press, 1994), 38.

31 Lubell, 38–39.

32 Gimbutas, 145.

33 Ibid., 138.

34 Foley, 12, lines 201–204.

35 Robbins Dexter and Mair, 33–41.

36 Lubell, 38.

37 Eva C. Keuls, *Reign of the Phallus*, Sexual Politics in Ancient Athens, (Berkeley, CA: University of California Press, 1993), 104.

38 Ibid., 109.

39 Ibid., 351.

40 Neumann, 11.

41 Ibid., 334.

42 Erich Neumann, "The Woman's Experience of Herself and the Eleusinian Mysteries," in *The Long Journey Home: Re-visioning the Myth of Demeter and Persephone for Our Time*, ed. Christine downing (Boston, MA: Shambhala, 1994), 73.

43 Ibid., 75.

44 Foley, 131.

45 Ibid

46 Kathie Carlson, *Life's Daughter/Death's Bride: Inner Transformations Through The Goddess Demeter/Persephone*, (Boston: Shambhala, 1997).

47 Kathie, 158.

DEITY IN SISTERHOOD:
THE COLLECTIVE SACRED FEMALE
IN GERMANIC EUROPE

Dawn E. Work-MaKinne

In the Rhine River valley, in the first centuries of the Common Era, Germans, Romans and Celts venerated a group of goddesses, the *Deae Matronae*. Votive artwork depicts these matrons as a group of adult women—two with the bonnet headdresses of married women and one with the loose, flowing hair of the unmarried woman. Almost a thousand years later, the Old Norse texts told of the complex fear and fascination of a group known as the *Norns*. The Norns are also a group of women. Sometimes they are named in the texts, as Urð, Verðandi and Skuld; other times they are unnamed and their numbers vary. Another group that is unnamed and unnumbered in the Old Norse texts is the *Dísir*, a word that means "goddesses." The Dísir are guardian goddesses, protectresses and guides. The Norns and Dísir are sisterhoods of goddesses, dispensing fate, guidance, protection and all manner of experience along the continuum from birth through life to death and beyond. Another group of females is also active during the Christian era in Germanic lands: the *Drei Heiligen Jungfrauen*, or the Three Holy Maidens of the Roman Catholic Church. Again, the group consists of three adult women; in this case, they are literally sisters.

The theme of the collective sacred female is carried like a musical motif through Germanic religious history. This theme is elaborated in the Roman Era worship of the Deae Matronae, the Scandinavian texts about the Norns and Dísir, and the Roman Catholic veneration of the *Drei*

Heiligen Jungfrauen, which is attested as far back as the 14th century and is still robust today. The collective sacred female—in essence, collective goddesses—plays an important role in Germanic religious history, is uncommonly widespread in Greece, and also is known in Baltic and Slavic lands, in India, in Persia, in Rome and among the Celts. In Germanic tradition, the collectives also appear in the folkloric material, hence collectives of witches, godmothers, wood wives, *Buschfrauen* (bush women) and the like. In the realm of the sacred, there are known collectives of Germanic male saints, but they are somewhat rare. Collectivity seems largely the province of the female.

There are five hallmarks of the collective sacred female, or of collective deity more broadly. First and most obviously, a collective deity consists of a group of sacred or supernatural beings; this "group-ness," or quality of being part of a group, is the defining characteristic. Second, the group is collected under one group name, although the members may carry individual names or descriptive epithets. The sacred Germanic collectives are collected under the group names of the Deae Matronae, the Norns, the Dísir and the Jungfrauen. The name *Matronae* generally is modified with a group epithet that further describes a group characteristic, and the Jungfrauen have individual first names of Aubet, Cubet and Guere. As already mentioned, the Norns sometimes carry the first names Urð, Verðandi and Skuld in addition to their group name, the Norns. Third, although each of these groups is known by a collective name, the members of each groups are not conflated into a single being. They are not mystically one or meant in any way to be a single individual. They are, instead, groups of individuals. Fourth, these individuals are worshipped collectively. Veneration is not singled out to one of the individuals, but rather applies to the group as a whole. Finally, these groups act and wield their powers collectively and, by extension, consensually. They do not act as individuals, separately. They do not work in disjunction with one another, except in one case of the Norns. They do not work by majority rule. The group as a whole answers prayers, fulfills vows and fates, protects the life continuum and guides and heals.

It is clear from the outset that collective deity is not the only form in which deity can be multiple or can contain multiplicity. In addition to collective deity, there are what I call plural deity or plurality; trinity, as evinced by the Christian Trinity; and triplicity, as in the Triple Goddess of the Goddess religion. In addition, there are divine pairings, such as divine couples or divine parent-child combinations. In many religions, there are complete pantheons, groups of gods and goddesses that represent or comprise entire religious structures.

In plural deity, the deity is repeated, most often tripled, to emphasize its power and attributes. An example is the Triple Brigid artifact, which shows the goddess three times, each instance holding a different artifact that symbolizes one of her powers. There are triple Junos, triples Ceres and a triple Coventina. There exists a triple Hecate of the crossroads, which is sometimes rendered as a plurality. Miranda J. Green wrote of several plural male deities or sacred figures.[1] In plural deity, the deity keeps her or his first name, which is generally rendered in the plural. The figures do not have separate or individual first names. Proinsias MacCana reported that these deities exist as a group but have only one identity, character and personality.[2] This single identity and personality marks the difference between the plural deities and the collective deities. The collectives are a group of several identities, often with their own first names, who work together and are worshipped together. They are not a single being.

The Christian Trinity is a unique form of multiple deity. In brief, the doctrine of the Trinity holds that God the Father, Jesus Christ the Son and the Holy Spirit are coequal within God, all three being divine, all three being God, yet there is still only one God.[3] The First Council of Nicaea (325 CE) cemented the current concept of the Trinity, as did Augustine of Hippo (354–430 CE), who declared that each member of the Trinity participates in one divine substance, which the three share. The insistence on one divine substance lets the Christian religion retain its status as a monotheistic religion, even with a multiple form of deity at its heart. Laurel C. Schneider went so far as to say that "monotheism remains a Christian doctrine by virtue of ecclesial fiat rather than internal coherence."[4] The triune God of the Christian religion has been one of the bastions of male monotheism despite the mystic triplicity. Like collective deities, the three carry first names and have distinct histories and personalities. However, unlike collective deities, they are mystically conflated into one being and, paradoxically, often venerated separately. Collective deities are not conflated into one being, but they are venerated as a group.

Roger E. Olson and Christopher A. Hall mentioned a group of heretical Christians, known as Modalists, who looked upon the Father, Son and Holy Spirit as modes or manifestations of one God but rejected an ontological distinctness among the three.[5] There was one God but with three modes, or faces. This bears some similarity to contemporary concepts of the Goddess, in which the Goddess is seen as a single being, perhaps comprising all of the multiverses, but with many faces. Perhaps most common is the Triple Goddess, with the three faces of Maiden, Mother and Crone. This description of the Triple Goddess occurs quite often but is by no means universal. Classicist Jane Ellen Harrison described it earliest (1903), when she theorized that prehistoric Europe worshipped a threefold goddess: the Maiden, ruling the living; the Mother, ruling the underworld; and a third, unnamed figure.[6] Interestingly, she developed her theory partly by noting the pagan Greek (triple) collectives, such as the Fates and the Graces. The equivocal magician Aleister Crowley added to the idea of the Triple Goddess by writing, in his 1929 work *Moonchild*, about Artemis, the Virgin Goddess; Isis of light and purity; and Hecate, barren, hideous and malicious.[7] In *The White Goddess: A Historical Grammar of Poetic Myth*, Robert Graves adopted Harrison's work into his poetic view of history. He believed that there had been a matriarchal period in prehistory and that people had worshipped the Triple Goddess: Maiden, Mother and Crone. Archaeologist Marija Gimbutas called the Triple Goddess an "astonishingly long-lived image" and documented it as early as the Magdalenian epoch, continuing through prehistory and history.[8]

Following these thinkers, many Goddess feminists, witches, Wiccans and other pagans affirm the Triple Goddess as Maiden, Mother and Crone. They may do so in a polytheistic setting, essentially tritheism. Or they may honor the Maiden, Mother and Crone as part of a triple deity known as the Goddess or the Triple Goddess. In this case, the goddess has three phases or faces yet remains one goddess. (This has some similarities to the practice of Christian Modalists.) There are no hard and fast rules, and different practitioners may follow different paths at different times. In either the tritheistic religion or the triple deity, the Triple Goddess is not quite the same as a collective deity. Generally, she is seen as cyclical, with various first names and various personalities, histories and attributes. "Triple Goddess" both is and is not a group name. The three or more goddesses may be mystically conflated into a single being, or they may not. The faces of the Triple Goddess are venerated both separately and together. In short, the Triple Goddess shapeshifts, crosses the boundaries between single deity and collective deity and remains unique. Melissa Raphael noted that some modern pagans believe that the Triple Goddess is the model for all triune deities that have followed, including the Christian Trinity.[9]

Divine couples and pantheons have significant differences from collective deities. Divine couples do not carry a group name. They keep their individual first names, personalities, attributes and epithets. They are not mystically conflated into a single being, although the fact of their marriage may have mystical connective overtones. They may be worshipped together, at least at some times or festivals, but they also are venerated separately. The divine couple may work together in some sense for the good of their worshippers; the fact of their marriage, for instance, may bring blessing or fertility to land and people. However, they do not necessarily work together collectively.

Larger groupings, such as pantheons or families of deities, also are significantly different from collectives. They do sometimes carry group names—note the families of the Æsir and Vanir deities of Norse religion. The individuals always have their own first names, personalities, attributes and epithets. The individuals are not mystically conflated into a single being. However, they are generally not worshipped as a collective, and they do not work together collectively or consensually for their worshippers.

Collective deities must evince all five hallmarks: an identifiable group, a group name, not conflated into one being, worshipped together, and working together collectively and consensually. In the Germanic examples, the collectives are overwhelmingly female, and this theme, of the collective sacred female, sounds again and again throughout history. It is my assertion that these particular traits of deity—sacredness, femaleness, collectivity and consensus—form a unique expression of deity that is important historically, thealogically and practically. I believe that the collective goddess form is one of the most important expressions of deity in Germanic religious history.

The form of deity that a person worships or venerates is an underappreciated factor in community, psychology and identity formation. Feminist theologian Elizabeth A. Johnson argues that the language and symbols used to express divinity act upon consciousness in complex ways.[10] Thealogian Carol P. Christ knew this in her early writings about the importance of the symbol of the Goddess for women: It affirms women's consciousness of their power, of the female body, of female will, and of women's bonds and heritage.[11]

Western culture has overemphasized the masculine, the individual, the single and the monolithic. Those people situated in cultures built around the male monotheism of the Abrahamic religious traditions surely have experienced its language and symbols acting upon consciousness in complex ways, possibly the depth of which the affected people can neither reach nor understand. People have been affected not only in their vision of deity but also in their sense of self and their sense of their lives in community with others.

I suggest that seeing both self and deity as a collective sisterhood may offer a vastly different view of identity, deity and community for those of us living in the pervasive monotheism of the dominant culture. It is not new to think of the self in terms of multiple identities rather than one monolithic self; indeed, much of the wisdom of postmodernism involves such multiplicities. James Hillman thought of monotheism versus polytheism in the human psyche,[12] and feminist scholars have put forth such concepts in Gloria Anzaldúa's *Borderlands / La Frontera: The New Mestiza* (1987), Donna Haraway's "Cyborgs and Symbionts: Living Together in the New World Order" (1995) and Rosi Braidotti's *Feminismo, Diferencia Sexual y Subjetividad Nómade* (2004). Self as sisterhood builds on these ideas and extends them with the optimistic element of consensus. With sisterhood manifest in deity as well as self, there are powerful religious elements of sisterhood and consensus to support and guide alternative ways of thinking, perceiving and community making. The presence of collective deity, especially collective goddesses, in religious history provides an extensive historical structure of myth and practice that describe collectivity at work in the realms of birth, life, death, rebirth, healing, protection, succor and the life of the land.

It is interesting that in the history of European collective deities there are so many female collectives but that male collectives remain something of a rarity. This is not necessarily the case with the other forms of multiple deity: the plural deities, the trinities, the divine pairings and the pantheons. But for some reason, collectivity seems to have connected with women in our ancestors' minds. The collectives also are found across Indo-European-speaking lands but chiefly in a broad north-south swath of Europe. Miriam Robbins Dexter has done pioneering linguistic work identifying the goddesses most probably brought with our proto-Indo-European ancestors when they left their homeland. They brought only four goddesses: a dawn goddess, a sun maiden, an earth goddess and *Danu*, a goddess of a watery place, river or stream.[13] None of these goddesses is a collective. This indicates that the female collective deities of Europe either were in place before the proto-Indo-European phenomenon or arose later, after the Indo-Europeans had settled in Europe. Several scholars—Enrico Campanile, Edgar C. Polomé and Michael York—think that a pre-Indo-European origin is possible but that the evidence remains suggestive rather than definitive.

Many feminist groups and other social justice groups value consensus decision making, as either a main or an ancillary system of judgment. Yet often the consensually working community and strong feelings of sisterhood remain in real-life communities an ideal rather than a reality. People leave their groups as the ideals of power sharing and consensus break down. Yet, as Kristy S. Coleman wrote in a recent ethnography of spiritual feminists, women cling to hopes for healing, renewed sisterhood, connection to Goddess, and another try at consensus and power sharing.[14] Given these deeply held hopes, the collective sacred female seems urgent as a vision. In the historical record and in current practice, the Germanic collective female goddesses are fulfilling vows and answering prayers, there are women worshipping in procession, rituals of food and drink, the Norns regenerating the World Tree, women acting as priestess for family and community and people carrying the saints through their fields in thanks and blessing. The collectives were and are venerated by people from all walks and ways of life: women and men, all social and economic classes, Roman and German, Tyrolean and Scandinavian, military and civilian, tradesman and slave, farmer's wife and king's daughter. The collective goddess form, besides being a widespread phenomenon socially and geographically, has had tremendous persistence over time. Records concerning the Germanic goddesses date from the Roman period in the 1st century CE. Germanic collective deities surface tantalizingly in the source material here and there during the first millennium and then appear consistently from the High Middle Ages to the present. Collective female deity has been a potent expression of deity for thousands of years and for unknown thousands of worshippers. The presence of the collective sacred female provides an alternate holy reality to the prevailing kyriarchal religions, structures, and worldviews that are built around domination, oppression and submission. The collectives perform a counter-hegemonic role, allowing room for ideas to flourish: of the sacred female, of community and consensus and of healing and regeneration. Kyriarchal power structures are not monolithic totalizing narratives but rather carry the seeds of a different vision within and alongside themselves. That vision, deity in sisterhood, belongs to us all.

References

Christ, Carol P. "Why Women Need the Goddess: Phenomenological, Psychological and Political Reflections." In *The Politics of Women's Spirituality: Essays on the Rise of Spiritual Power within the Feminist Movement.* Edited by Charlene Spretnak. Garden City, NY: Anchor Books, 1982.

Coleman, Kristy S. *Re-Riting Woman: Dianic Wicca and the Feminine Divine.* Lanham, MD: AltaMira Press, 2009.

Dexter, Miriam Robbins. *Whence the Goddesses: A Source Book.* New York: Teachers College Press, 1990.

Gimbutas, Marija. *The Language of the Goddess: Unearthing the Hidden Symbols of Western Civilization.* San Francisco, CA: Harper and Row, 1989.

Green, Miranda J. *The Gods of the Celts.* Gloucestershire, UK: Sutton, 1997.

Hillman, James. *The Essential James Hillman: A Blue Fire.* London, England: Routledge, 1990.

Hutton, Ronald. *The Triumph of the Moon: A History of Modern Pagan Witchcraft.* Oxford: Oxford University Press, 1999.

Johnson, Elizabeth A. *She Who Is: The Mystery of God in Feminist Theological Discourse.* New York: Crossroad, 1993.

MacCana, Proinsias. *Celtic Mythology.* New rev. ed. Library of the World's Myths and Legends. Worthing, UK: Littlehampton Book Services, 1983.

Olson, Roger E., and Christopher A. Hall. *The Trinity: Guides to Theology.* Grand Rapids, MI: W. B. Eerdmans, 2002.

Raphael, Melissa. *Introducing Thealogy: Discourse on the Goddess.* Cleveland, OH: Pilgrim Press, 2000.

Schneider, Laurel C. *Re-Imagining the Divine: Confronting the Backlash against Feminist Theology*. Cleveland, OH: Pilgrim Press, 1998.

Swinburne, Richard. *The Christian God*. Oxford: Clarendon Press, 1994.

Endnotes

1 Miranda J. Green, *The Gods of the Celts* (Gloucestershire, UK: Sutton, 1997), 208–09.

2 Proinsias MacCana, *Celtic Mythology*, New rev. ed., Library of the World's Myths and Legends. (Worthing, UK: Littlehampton Book Services, 1983), 86.

3 Richard Swinburne, *The Christian God* (Oxford, England: Clarendon Press, 1994), 180.

4 Laurel C. Schneider, *Re-Imagining the Divine: Confronting the Backlash against Feminist Theology* (Cleveland, OH: Pilgrim Press, 1998), 165.

5 Roger E. Olson and Christopher A. Hall, *The Trinity: Guides to Theology* (Grand Rapids, MI: W. B. Eerdmans, 2002), 2.

6 Ronald Hutton, *The Triumph of the Moon: A History of Modern Pagan Witchcraft* (Oxford: Oxford University Press, 1999), 36.

7 Ibid., 179.

8 Marija Gimbutas, *The Language of the Goddess: Unearthing the Hidden Symbols of Western Civilization* (San Francisco: Harper and Row, 1989), 97.

9 Melissa Raphael, *Introducing Thealogy: Discourse on the Goddess* (Cleveland, OH: Pilgrim Press, 2000), 67.

10 Elizabeth A. Johnson, *She Who Is: The Mystery of God in Feminist Theological Discourse* (New York: Crossroad, 1993), 36.

11 Carol P. Christ, "Why Women Need the Goddess: Phenomenological, Psychological and Political Reflections," in *The Politics of Women's Spirituality: Essays on the Rise of Spiritual Power within the*

Feminist Movement, ed. Charlene Spretnak (Garden City, NY: Anchor Books, 1982), 74.

12 James Hillman, *The Essential James Hillman: A Blue Fire* (London: Routledge, 1990), 44–45.

13 Miriam Robbins Dexter, *Whence the Goddesses: A Source Book* (New York: Teachers College Press, 1990), 36–46.

14 Kristy S. Coleman, *Re-Riting Woman: Dianic Wicca and the Feminine Divine* (Lanham, MD: AltaMira Press, 2009), 176.

AFTERWORD
Borderlands

I was the keynote speaker at the 2014 annual conference of the Association for the Study of Women and Mythology (ASWM), held in San Antonio, Texas, close to the United States' border with Mexico. It was there that Sid Reger, president of the ASWM, asked all who were there, "What should be the next step for the organization?" My immediate response was to urge the ASWM to publish proceedings. By this, I meant a publication of papers presented at ASWM conferences. I had been impressed by the quality of scholarship, thoughtful speculation and research that had been done by the presenters who had summed up their findings and conclusions. I also had learned that they had difficulty publishing in journals, which makes their theories and findings difficult or impossible for others to find, learn from and add to. Therefore, I saw the necessity for proceedings to be published.

"Borderlands" was both the theme of this particular conference and the title of my talk. It struck me that publication of the presenters' papers in established journals would be difficult, because the papers were in the "borderlands" among many fields of knowledge as well as the enormous range and diversity of subject matter that falls under the study of women and mythology. Mythology relates to culture, religion, symbols, gender and social stratification; women are affected by all of these elements that define their roles. As a result, the range of subjects presented at ASWM conferences are unlikely to fit into established academic publications.

Even if a particular paper fits the subject matter of an established journal, women who present papers at the ASWM may find that they do not fit the profile of accepted authors. "Who are you?" and "What is your academic lineage?" matter to journals, especially peer-reviewed ones, who want to know "Where did you get your degrees?" and "Have you been published

288

before?" A graduate student who helps a senior researcher becomes one of several co-authors (shortened to et al in footnotes). These are "border guard" questions. If you are a woman whose ASWM presentation is distilled from your thesis about women's spirituality or cross-cultural goddess rituals, or even archaeological findings, your subject and academic lineage may prevent your work from being published—until there are ASWM Proceedings that can become indexed and available through university libraries and the internet.

It seems to me that women in the second and third phases of life who do thesis research may begin with an original idea or approach rather than replicating or challenging someone else's research or theory. In contrast, academic research done at various leading and well-funded institutions takes on something of a team effort. Very few women who present at the ASWM are likely to get grants to do further research, but once published in ASWM Proceedings, ideas and findings presented at ASWM conferences become accessible knowledge.

Marija Gimbutas, a distinguished, influential archaeologist of Neolithic and Bronze Age cultures of Old Europe, was an original thinker: she drew on her knowledge of linguistics and customs and used her intuitive grasp of connections to make sense of archaeological findings. Her work and conclusions are still dismissed by mainstream archaeologists. Yet they have become known and have formed a foundation for further study, through the publication of her books: *The Goddesses and Gods of Old Europe* (1974), *The Language of the Goddess* (1989), *The Civilization of the Goddess* (1991) and *The Living Goddesses* (1999). The last two books are trade publications, written for the general public, which is another route for authors of papers in ASWM Proceedings. Trade publishers such as Harpers, my publisher (*Goddesses in Everywoman* and five other books), and Gimbutas's publisher are interested in leading-edge ideas from the "borderlands." I believe that women who are published for the first time in the ASWM Proceedings will be empowered by seeing their words in print. ASWM "has their back," tangibly supports them taking the next steps, whatever they may be (further research, journal publication or trade publication) and, in itself, may have a ripple effect of influencing someone else.

Change happens when a critical number of people accept a new premise that, in turn, changes the way things are done and valued. The use of gender-free references to divinity, addressing prayer in churches to "Mother-Father God" and the ordination of women as clergy are fundamental beginning changes and challenges to patriarchy that are supported by the writing and research presented at ASWM conferences. Patriarchy depends upon the worship of a male sky god who has power over creation and the assumptions that men are in the image of God and that wars are inevitable aspects of human nature. Consciousness raising about sexism is deepened by knowledge of suppression of the goddess and women, just as consciousness raising about racism can be deepened by the awareness of the colonization of indigenous people and their divinities. The ASWM inhabits the "borderlands," contributing to grassroots change from the bottom up. It may be that articles in the ASWM Proceedings will be like seeds carried by the winds to land on fertile minds, way beyond the "borderlands." Consciousness is where change and activism begin.

With love, hope, perseverance, trust and optimism,

Jean Shinoda Bolen, MD
www.jeanbolen.com

ACKNOWLEDGMENTS

"Many hands make light work," and there have been many hands that have lovingly held this project from beginning to end. We are thankful for the careful editing of Louann Pope (www.louannpope. com) and the cover-to-cover book design by Rebekkah Dreskin (www. blameitonrebekkah.com).

There have been many hands that have carefully held this project from idea to realization. Our thanks to Marna Hauk, Margaret Merisante, Sid Reger, and the Board of Directors of ASWM. Our deepest thanks to Jean Shinoda Bolen for sparking the creation of this volume.

The editors are grateful for the unfailing commitment, support and camaraderie of Dr. Anne Key and Paula Bauman. They are the true heroines who made the completion of this anthology possible. Lastly, we are grateful to each of the women whose noteworthy contributions to this anthology serve to restore the feminine to the study of mythology and, in turn, enable us to reclaim sacred spaces for everyday spiritual practice.

ABOUT THE CONTRIBUTORS

Alexandra Cichon, Ph.D. is a wounded healer, researcher, actor, and psychodramatist received her doctorate in clinical psychology, within the tradition of depth psychology, from Pacifica Graduate Institute in California. As an actor, she is the recipient of the Oxford University Dramatic Society's Best Actress Award, for a performance piece she conceived and directed for ensemble on the Sumerian myth of Inanna and Ereshkigal, and the Joseph Jefferson Award (non-Equity) for Performance. She directed (jointly with the playwright) and performed in the English premiere of Commedia at the Oxford University Playhouse (a work in the improvisatorial Commedia dell'Arte tradition). Her article "It's just fuckin' there! Lessons of the Theatrical Improviser's Art From the Legendary Del Close" appeared in the 2014 The Double Dealer, literary journal of the New Orleans' Pirates Alley Faulkner Society. She currently explores Goddess spirituality as a Sister of Avalon, member of the Priestess of Avalon training in Glastonbury, England.

Joan M. Cichon, a retired history professor and reference librarian, has her PhD in women's spirituality from the California Institute of Integral Studies. Her dissertation is titled "Matriarchy in Minoan Crete: A Perspective from Archaeomythology and Modern Matriarchal Studies." Joan's areas of interest are archaeomythology, matriarchal studies, and the role of women and Goddess in Bronze Age Crete. She is currently training to become a Priestess of Avalon.

Dr. Gayatri Devi is associate professor of English at Lock Haven University, Pennsylvania, where she teaches literature, linguistics and women's studies courses. Her book *Humor in Middle Eastern Cinema* (Wayne State University Press 2014) examines the sublime and aporetic modalities of humor in select films from the Middle East and the Middle Eastern diaspora. Her articles and book chapters on South Asian and Middle Eastern literature and film have been published in select scholarly anthologies and journals including *World Literature Today, North Dakota Quarterly, The Guardian, Ms. Magazine,* and *South Asian Review*. She serves on the Executive Board of the Association for the Study of Women and Mythology.

April Heaslip is a doctoral candidate in mythological studies at Pacifica Graduate Institute and holds a Master's in social ecology from Goddard College with undergraduate work in psychology and women's studies at West Chester University and Universidade Federal de Uberlândia, Brazil. Her dissertation, "Regenerating Magdalene," considers the resurgence of the lost archetypal bride in Western cultures as ecofeminist grail quest. Her teaching and research in gender & women's studies and sustainability focus on applied mythology as cultural animation, feminist studies, and the bricolage as creative problem solving. April is currently a visiting research assistant for the Native American & Indigenous Studies Initiative at Penn, University of Pennsylvania.

Mara Lynn Keller (PhD Philosophy, Yale University) is a professor of philosophy, religion and women's spirituality at the California Institute of Integral Studies. She served as director of the Women's Spirituality graduate program 1998-2008. Her articles include "Eleusinian Mysteries of Demeter and Persephone," "Ritual Path of Initiation into the Eleusinian Mysteries," "Ancient Crete of the Earth Mother Goddess," "Goddesses around the World," "Women's Spirituality and Higher Education" and "Marion Rosen: Finding a New Life Later in Life." She taught philosophy and women's studies at the University of California at Riverside and San Francisco State University, where she cofounded and coordinated the Global Peace Studies program.

Alexis Martin Faaberg holds an MA in women's spirituality at the California Institute of Integral Studies. She is passionate about reclaiming women's community, healing women's circles, and decolonizing minds.

Arieahn Matamonasa-Bennett, Ph.D. is a healer, teacher, artist and writer. She is an assistant professor at DePaul University in Chicago and a licensed psychologist with a small private practice specializing in equine (horse) assisted therapies and healing for healers. Her areas of scholarship and expertise are Native American cultural studies, feminist views on violence against women and animal human interaction. She has spoken internationally and nationally and published in these areas over the last decade. Her current work includes the book *All My Relations: Indigenous Perspectives on Human-Animal Relationships and Animal-Assisted Therapies*, 2015.

Mary Beth Moser, Ph.D. earned a doctorate in philosophy and religion with a specialty in women's spirituality at the California Institute of Integral Studies. Her dissertation, "The Everyday Spirituality of Women in the Italian Alps: A Trentino American Woman's Search for Spiritual Agency, Folk Wisdom, and Ancestral Values," received the 2014 Kore Award for best dissertation. Mary Beth lectures at colleges, at conferences and in her community. Her publications include *Honoring Darkness: Exploring the Power of Black Madonnas in Italy* (2008) and several articles. She is passionate about her ancestral culture and serves as president of the Seattle Trentino Club.

Natasha Redina is a psychotherapist and researcher with extensive experience of working with trauma. Having worked in the health-care profession since 1998, she has excellent clinical understanding of life-transition phases and archetypal symbology. She studied world religions at SOAS, University of London and went on to complete her Master's in psychotherapy, with her research focused on Peruvian Vegetalismo. She is passionate about research and including marginal voices in academic discourse, as well as exploring ways of disseminating narratives through arts-based media. She offers one-to-one and group psychotherapy and supervision in London and worldwide via Skype.

Natasha is of Greek and English heritage and has been an apprentice to the Mexihka medicine and to the curandera Miahuatzin (Ivonne M. Buendia Sanches) from Mexico since 2005.

Dr. Savithri Shanker de Tourreil retired from the faculty of religion at Concordia University in Montreal, Quebec. Dr. de Tourreil's research, publication and areas of specialization include Hindu women's rituals with special focus on Nayar female-centered rituals. "Nayars of Kerala and Matriliny Revisited" was published in *Societies of Peace: Matriarchies Past Present and Future* (Inanna Publications 2009).

Denise Saint Arnault, PhD, RN is an associate professor of nursing at the University of Michigan. She is an educator who began her Goddess studies in 1983. Her work has included anti-racism, cultural education, and scholarship focusing on interactions among women in communities. As a Priestess of Her Torch, her work involves bringing together disparate themes and illuminating patterns when clarity is elusive. She has carried out this work in counseling, anthropology, women's leadership and Goddess scholarship. She brings these to her community through teaching, mentorship, leadership, international scholarship, and research on the topics of culture, gender and mental health.

Dawn E. Work-MaKinne is an independent scholar of Germanic goddess traditions. She received her Ph.D. in women's studies in religion from The Union Institute in 2010. Her award-winning dissertation is titled "Deity in Sisterhood: The Collective Sacred Female in Germanic Europe." She continues to research, write and teach, and she is currently writing her dissertation into a book for Goddess Ink Press. Dawn is on the faculty of the Women's Thealogical Institute and the Board of Trustees of the Association for the Study of Women and Mythology. Dawn makes her home in Des Moines, Iowa.

CPSIA information can be obtained
at www.ICGtesting.com
Printed in the USA
FSOW02n0430051117
40638FS

9 780996 961721